NEW HORIZONS IN JOURNALISM
## Howard Rusk Long, *General Editor*

Also in the New Horizons in Journalism series

# GREAT WOMEN
# OF
# THE PRESS

BY
MADELON GOLDEN SCHILPP
AND
SHARON M. MURPHY

*Foreword by Howard Rusk Long*

SOUTHERN ILLINOIS UNIVERSITY PRESS
Carbondale and Edwardsville

Copyright © 1983 by the Board of Trustees,
Southern Illinois
University
All rights reserved
Printed in the United States of America
Edited by Dan Seiters
Designed by Quentin Fiore
Production supervised by John DeBacher

*Library of Congress Cataloging in Publication Data*
Schilpp, Madelon Golden.
    Great women of the press.
    (New horizons in journalism)
    Bibliography: p.
    1. Women journalists—United States—Biography.
I. Murphy, Sharon. II. Title. III. series.
PN4872.S34 1983   070'.92'2 [B]   82–19574
ISBN 0–8093–1098–8
86 85 84     6 5 4 3 2

*Madelon dedicates this book to her family:*

EDITH FITZGERALD GOLDEN
GEORGE ANDREW GOLDEN
PAUL ARTHUR SCHILPP
ERICH ANDREW SCHILPP
MARGOT MARLENE SCHILPP

*Sharon dedicates this book to her family:*
JIM, SHANNON, AND ERIN MURPHY

# Contents

Foreword

CONTENTS

# Foreword

The role of women in American journalism is established. Professionally the best women are every bit as good at their work as the best men. Neither brilliance and success nor mediocrity and failure are accidents of gender. Yet injustice persists because in any traditional society the cake of custom impedes the efforts of those rare individuals whose talents cause them to trespass into creative areas closed to them by stereotyped popular disapproval.

From the slow start generated by the Industrial Revolution, however, a little freedom bred a little more freedom until in our time this accretion has developed into a revolutionary force of the strength to sweep aside canons older than the written word. For one who equates the future with promise the prevailing winds of advocacy point to a new Age of Reason in which women of all societies will share equally with men. Meanwhile, one can but endure and long for the day when only the psychologically ill care a tootle whether supervisors and supervised and the observers and the observed are male or female.

Of all the machines that contributed to the progress toward emancipation of humanity, none is more important than the printing press, with its associated technology. Not only did the printed page break the monopoly of the mind exercised by church and state, but the related struggle to control the materials people were permitted to read created a circumstance that opened to women the world of journalism. Fredrick S. Seibert, in his 1952 account of continuing abortive attempts by the British Crown to control the content of the burgeoning volume of printed materials, tells how the Tudor monarchs hit upon a scheme that required the printers themselves to protect the public from exposure to blasphemy and sedition. The existing printers were licensed, organized as the Royal Company of Stationers, and charged with registering each imprint, after examination for "objectionable" content. In return for this self-censorship the printers were granted monopolistic privileges because under the provisions, stationers alone could grant new licenses.

Life expectancies were short; under the conditions of the times a man elderly by accepted standards was very apt to have a younger wife. Thus a growing number of widows became master printers by right of inheritance, and women in Britain made their first small escape from the slavery of kitchen or cloister. In this manner journalism became the first profession open to respectable females. Along with other English institutions and customs, this practice of women inheriting presses and working as journalists came to America with the colonists. Indeed, Isaiah Thomas tells us that technically the first printer in the North American colonies was the widow of Joseph Glover, the clergyman who died at sea while bringing a press owned by him to be installed at Harvard College. Altogether more than a dozen widows figure in the history of colonial printing, not the least of whom was Elizabeth Timothy, whose story is related in the first chapter of this volume.

The forces at work in the sprawling and brawling infant republic created issues, stimulated discussion, and broadened participation in public life; the turmoil and activity achieved a scale that virtually demanded a popular press capable of serving as a vehicle for debate from one end of the land to the other. No longer was the traditional printer, with shears, myopic observations of public affairs, and the casual scribblings of volunteer contributors, able to cope with the demands of a readership eager to take part in the decision-making process. The resulting division of labor was inevitable; gradually printers retreated to the back rooms and a new breed of editors and writers, who were to call themselves journalists, emerged.

By the fourth decade of the nineteenth century, when the penny press with its mass readership was entrenched in the larger cities, writing for pay had become an accepted way to make a living, or at least to gain supplementary income. Women with brains and education and with perhaps a little more spirit than their meeker sisters found it comparatively easy to disguise their handwriting, adopt a pseudonym, and make a place for themselves in the male world of public debate and controversy. Polite society at least ignored strictures of decorum that would deny women this right. By the time those who ruled over morals and manners were willing to accept the genteel poverty of pedagogy as suitable for women of refinement, the more venturesome of those so ridiculously described as the "weaker sex" were storming the sanctums, removing cuspidors, ash trays, and pipeholders, and confidently making themselves at home as editors and star reporters.

Parallel with the development of the daily newspaper and the large-circulation magazine of urban America was the prodigious growth of the country weekly in the hinterland. Until comparatively recent times women found their most pervasive role in the service of the little sheets that sprang up in county seats and country trading points just a little behind the westward movement of the frontier. A handful of subscribers who squared their accounts with products from farm or garden plus a modicum of commercial printing and retail advertising, with paid public notices, or with political patronage, offered the flimsy economic support of these marginal enterprises, alive only because the proprietor could borrow a few dollars for the down payment on a "shirttail full of type" and a secondhand press. If necessary, the venture could limp along for years without a payroll and with few operating costs beyond expenditures for paper and ink.

In the turbulent years after the War Between the States there might be competition from four or five organs in the same town, each encouraged, if not truly supported, by rival political parties or their scismatic sects. For reasons too complex to explain here, there is no reliable list of American newspaper titles for this period of expansion, which seems to have peaked in the ten years after the turn of the century, more or less coincidental with the final defeat of William Jennings Bryan and the end of a major period of agrarian revolt.

During these years the classified advertising columns of the *Publishers' Auxiliary*, trade publication of the country editor, carried a generous budget of newspapers listed for sale. Most of these announcements concluded with the statement, "Fine man and wife sit." Interpreted this means that until driven out of business by the small town's decline under the pressure of automobile transportation, plus the insurmountable expense of installing typesetting machinery, literally thousands of small weekly newspapers existed through the pooled labor of a man and wife team and their children. Usually both could set type, both could operate the simple presses, and both could write the items for the upcoming edition. When she was able, the wife worked the same long hours as her husband. Legends abound of infants cradled in the woodbox of the newspaper office and of small children, before starting to school, learning their letters at the type case. For two or three generations at the end of the horse and buggy era "mom and pop" weeklies in crossroads hamlets and backwoods county seats represented a large proportion of the newspaper titles entered with the United States Post Office Department. Yes, the wife certainly pulled her weight. Given these circumstances it is difficult to believe that the woman of dominant personality was denied the major role she always has enjoyed in the matrimonial partnership.

Now it may be true that some of the women presented in this volume are only supernumeraries on the broader stage of a general history of American journalism, (footnotes if you will); yet the fact remains, each in some way was unique in the sense that she played a role distinctive for her time and her place. Without exception each broke new ground in one area of journalism or another. So many of them are important because they did their work well while at the same time opening doors previously closed to persons of their gender. Some of these prototypes were household names in their day in fields other than journalism. Few will question *their* right to a place in this collection of essays. And it may be a virtue that the authors in sifting the records, beginning with those of the first English language press in North America, came forward with names relatively obscure to all except the specialist. This rehabilitation of names insufficiently preserved suggests further examination of primary sources may reveal additional women worthy of consideration.

By intent the final roster, as revealed by the names in the chapter headings, spans the greater part of three centuries; the materials are organized to parallel the growth and development of the printed page as a force in the United States from its roots in the primary groups of European colonists to modern times. The record shows that journalists always have moved freely from one medium to another; thus we find our heroines identified with newspapers, periodicals, and the golden age of photojournalism, many with credits in more than one area. But where are the women cartoonists? The decision to consider only those whose records are closed leaves for other workers the stories of the younger generation of women who have and are contributing so much to the broadcast media.

Any established professional, certainly one classified as an elder statesman, is capable of coming forward with one or more names "that might just as well have been included." With this view the authors have no quarrel, for they propose not to present THE greatest women in American journalism. They claim only to have examined the records of hundreds of individuals where and when they could find them in search of heroines who, because of active social restraints as well as neglect, remained in the shadows with the unsung heroes. Thus the familiar and the obscure appear together in these stories of eighteen women presented within the framework of family background and the socioeconomic environment of their times.

The contributions of women in the development of American journalism, as mined from primary sources by Frank Luther Mott, are presented in sympathetic perspective in his superb works, the Pulitzer Prize-winning series *A History of American Magazines*, and in the various editions of his comprehensive *American Journalism*. These remain the classics of a popular area of study worked by many competent scholars. All these materials by and about women journalists, as the authors have demonstrated in their bibliography, are substantial. Yet for the student and the casual reader there exists the need for a collection of short biographies offering an introduction to the journalistic contributions of women to various periods of American history. With the bibliography, the materials of this presentation offer interesting and substantial supplementary readings for a variety of disciplines.

Although the collaborators profess themselves dependent upon secondary materials, a careful examination of their sources reveals considerable original research, including voluminous reading of the writings of their subjects as found in newspapers, periodicals, and first or early editions of their books. There were visits to the archives of the University of Chicago, the University of South Carolina and Tulane University. There was a personal interview with Mrs. Alfreda M. Duster, daughter of Mrs. Ida Wells-Barnett. Newspapers and magazines edited by or carrying the works of women being studied were examined in microfilm. Again, the stories told here are not those of *the* eighteen greatest women in American journalism and there is no such claim. A fair representation of the women who helped to make history was the intent; the effectiveness of this effort is left to the judgment of the reader. It was intentional that no living journalist, however outstanding, was included.

*Carbondale, Illinois*                    Howard Rusk Long
1983

# Acknowledgments

Many persons have contributed in various ways to this book—reading, discussing, researching, and encouraging. We express our appreciation to:

Colleagues across the country whose research has preceded this work, and whose interest, encouragement and support, especially through their long-time active involvement in the Committee on the Status of Women in Journalism Education, have suggested directions, dimensions, resources, and possibilities. Though any listing runs the risk of neglecting someone, we must recognize Donna Allen, Maurine Beasley, Catherine Covert, Susan Henry, Marion Marzolf, Carol Oukrop, Ramona Rush, and Mary Ann Yodelis-Smith;

Our colleagues in the school of journalism at Southern Illinois University, Carbondale, including Vernon Stone, Harry W. Stonecipher, Erwin Atwood, and Florence Clark Riffe;

Graduate and undergraduate students, Linda Applegate, Donald Avery, Alayne Blickle, Kristen Dollase, Patrick Eagan, Deborah Goldstein, Linda Hildebrand, Tracy Howard, Margot Schilpp, Michael Sherer, Kathryn Urbaszewski, Chuck Wanager, Irene Weibel, Brenda Wilgenbusch, and Ralph Woodworth;

Staff members at Morris Library, Southern Illinois University, Carbondale, including Charlotte Clark, Annie Woodbridge, Kathleen Eads, Jean Ray, Alan Cohn, and most especially librarian Charles Holliday whose expert knowledge and dedication to this project over a decade contributed substantially;

Staff members at the libraries of Tulane University, New Orleans; the South Caroliniana Library, Columbia; the Golda Meier Library, University of Wisconsin, Milwaukee;

Southern Illinois University's Office of Research Development and Administration and its director, Michael Dingerson;

Our untiring research assistant, word processor, and proof-reader par excellence, J. D. Fairbanks;

Above all we thank Dr. Howard Rusk Long who bore with this project, faithfully encouraging through good days and bad over a period of more than ten years from inception.

And last but far from least we thank our families for their enduring support. Most especially we thank our husbands, Paul Arthur Schilpp and James E. Murphy, both of whom also read and critiqued the manuscript.

*Great Women of the Press*

# I

# ELIZABETH TIMOTHY
*First Woman Publisher*
[*c.* 1700–1757]

A small back-page notice in the January 4, 1739, issue of Charleston's *South-Carolina Gazette*[1] told readers that the paper was changing hands and that because "the late Printer of the Gazette hath been deprived of his Life, I shall contain the said Paper as usual and hope, by the Assistance of my Friends, to make it as entertaining and correct as may reasonably be expected."[2]

With this simple statement, Elizabeth Timothy accepted her pioneering role as America's first female newspaper publisher. She was among at least fourteen colonial women printers who worked at one time or other in seven colonies and ten towns to support themselves and their children after their husbands died.[3] Timothy, however, was the first woman to edit and publish a newspaper in the colonies. Indeed, one historian of colonial and southern history calls her "the first known woman in American journalism."[4]

But to understand just what the venture meant, one must follow colonial women through their daily routines and then superimpose the burdens of editorship in colonial times.

Charleston pioneer women in the 1730s were expected to keep their households stocked with soap, candles, wax, clothing, preserved foods, and daily meal necessities. They managed any household help available to them in the form of apprentices, bound-out children relatives, and slaves. Colonial women often oversaw and managed the lands granted to them and/or their husbands. The production, processing, preservation, and preparation of food was their responsibility, as was the training in homemaking tasks of daughters, women servants, slaves, and bound-out children in their households. They taught and performed upholstery, leather repair, spinning, and weaving. Often they provided the sole source of the elementary education of the females in their households. Though the pioneer communities saw the need of female labor, they did not see the need for these feminine laborers to have the same quality or regularity of schooling available to boys and young men.

In addition to homemaking, colonial women also played other roles, reflecting the fact that Charleston, like other towns in the young colonies, was rapidly being developed along the old-country models its inhabitants remembered. To meet the goals they set, colonial leaders enlisted, literally, every able man, woman, and child. Thus colonial women were tobacconists; real estate sellers; hardware, drug, and cosmetic store owners; and managers of book stores, binderies, bakeries, and dry goods stores. They were whalers, leather workers, rope and net makers, and owners of iron foundries and print and stationery shops.

Into this environment Lewis and Elizabeth Timothy entered with enthusiasm and no little relief in September, 1731.[5] They arrived at Philadelphia harbor from Rotterdam with their four children, ages one to six. Lewis took the requisite Oath of Allegiance to George II and began looking for work. A French Huguenot, he had fled his country for Holland following the revocation of the Edict of Nantes. He was well educated, as was his wife, and first sought employment as a teacher and tutor of French language. Eventually, his knowledge of printing, mastered in Holland, brought him and Benjamin Franklin together at a time when that innovative entrepreneur was developing what later became a journalistic empire. Very little is known of Mrs. Timothy's background, other than that she was described as well-educated by both Benjamin Franklin and historian Isaiah Thomas.

After a successful apprenticeship with Franklin, the

new colonist was named first librarian for the Library Company in Philadelphia. The untimely deaths in 1731 and 1733 of the first and second editors of the *South-Carolina Gazette* put the colony's first newspaper out of business. But Franklin, the paper's sponsor, was determined and selected Lewis Timothy as partner in the third attempt at a newspaper for Charleston.

It was to be a good choice and the beginning of a long-lived newspaper. On February 3, 1734, the *South-Carolina Gazette* reappeared, with Lewis Timothy as editor. The Franklin-Timothy partnership was a six-year journeyman's contract to carry on the interrupted printing/publishing business of the late *Gazette* publisher, Thomas Whitemarsh. Timothy was also named official printer and postmaster for the colony, a usual practice at the time, and rapidly expanded his operation to include a wide assortment of books, pamphlets, and supplies.[6]

The new editor did well and was rewarded in 1736 with a 600-acre tract of valuable land in Charleston. The family increased to eight with the birth of two more children. Elizabeth was busy with the nurturing and education of her household, and young Peter was beginning his apprenticeship in the family print shop. The agreement with Franklin made him successor to his father in the event of the latter's death.

But the successes were not long to be enjoyed. The Timothys' infant son died of smallpox in summer, 1738, and Elizabeth no doubt watched with interest and no little apprehension the smallpox inoculation controversy in the *Gazette* and in separately published pamphlets. In fact, her husband apologized in October for the delay in printing one smallpox tract: he was fighting his own bout with the disease. Then in December the editor himself was dead "of an unhappy accident."[7]

Elizabeth Timothy took over the business immediately in the name of her son Peter, then thirteen years old. She also assumed the vacant postmaster's chair. In her inaugural editorial on January 4, 1739, she showed the motivation for her industry and for shunning widow's weeds in favor of a printer's apron: "Wherefore I flatter myself, that all those Persons, who, by Subscription or otherwise, assisted my late Husband, on the prosecution of the Said Undertaking, will be kindly pleased to continue their Favors and good Offices to his poor afflicted Widow and six small Children and another hourly expected."

This arrangement was not without its drawbacks. The new editor was not as skilled a compositor as her late husband, although observers have noted a gradual improvement in the quality of the paper, possibly as young Peter was able to be of more assistance in the shop. Even so, the four-page *Gazette* appeared regularly each Saturday, served the important mercantile needs of growing Charleston, and had an enthusiastic following.

The positive financial aspect of Mrs. Timothy's proprietorship became immediately apparent, however, to the man most apt to notice. In his *Autobiography*, Benjamin Franklin contrasted the management styles of husband and wife and very decidedly preferred her as a business partner. He called Lewis Timothy "a man of learning, and honest but ignorant in matters of account." The widow, on the other hand, "not only sent me as clear a statement as she could find of the transactions past, but continued to account with great regularity and exactness every quarter afterwards." In her characteristically businesslike manner, the new publisher advised potential advertisers to "send their Advertisements by Wednesday Night, otherwise they cannot be inserted that Week." She also stated that if they did not pay the quarterly advertising rate in advance, their accounts would be discontinued.[8]

If she was a good bookkeeper and businesswoman, Mrs. Timothy was not as good a writer and proof reader. One must recognize, however, that grammars and spelling lexicons were not yet firmly established nor universally applied. In addition, due at least in part to the shortage of type, the typographical appearance of the *Gazette* was uneven.

But the content of Elizabeth Timothy's paper was lively and broad-based. She borrowed accounts from Boston,

Newport, Philadelphia, and such overseas cities as London, Paris, and Constantinople. In reports and commentaries on local news and events, the paper offered a good picture of Charleston and South Carolina life at the time. It carried reprints of addresses by colonial governors; ship arrival and departure announcements; regular columns of "Foreign Affairs" via correspondence; current local events; and at least a page and a half of advertisements. These latter offered commodities, locally produced goods, and products like books, sealing wax, ink, and writing papers from her own shop on King Street.[9]

Despite her limitations as a writer, Timothy made some changes during her six years as *Gazette* editor/publisher. She introduced woodcuts in 1739, usually in connection with notices and advertisements. Her classified advertising section carried blind notices, stipulating "enquire of the Printers," as well as a full complement of regular advertisements. She published occasional special sections in 1740 and 1741, replete with ads and news items, and variously titled them "Postscript," or "Supplement."[10] By design or necessity, she experimented with typography. The *Gazette* went from two- to three-column format in December, 1743, and returned to two-columns in October, 1745, a few months before she turned the paper over to her son.

In addition to a weekly newspaper, Elizabeth Timothy's establishment also produced and sold copies of such official documents as the *Acts Passed by the General Assembly . . . November 10, 1736–April 11, 1739; An Act for the Better Ordering and Governing of Negroes and Other Slaves in This Province* (passed in 1740); and a 1741 *Historical Narrative of the Colony of Georgia*. Other publications included political works and a translation from the French of portions of a treatise on growing and manufacturing indigo.

Staying in business meant printed pleas for payment by negligent subscribers. She offered to exchange goods for subscriptions, and, in turn, advertised these goods for sale in the paper. And she begged in print for rags needed to make newsprint, offering "Ready Money for clean white Linen."[11] Several times during her first year as editor, she printed a public request for better directions to subscribers' country residences so "that they may have less cause of Complaint" at not receiving their papers from the delivery-men she hired.[12] In accordance with the contract with Franklin, however, the notices appeared over the signature of P. Timothy, her son.

The major news story of 1740 was the fire, November 18, which all but destroyed Charleston. The *Gazette*, two days after the event, covered the disaster, which began at 2 P.M. and roared on until almost 8 P.M., when several houses were blown up to prevent further spread of the conflagration. Mrs. Timothy's news accounts in this and subsequent issues further detailed the losses, which included "the most valuable Part of the Town on account of the Buildings and Trade." She reported that two-thirds of the town, including more than 300 houses, storehouses, stables, wharves, and the British foreign post office had been destroyed, along with 200,000 pounds sterling in merchandise. The *Gazette* credited the "diligence of the inhabitants of all ranks, who were very active in their endeavors to extinguish."

The paper also carried two proclamations by the lieutenant governor of the colony, urging citizens to contribute to the relief of the homeless of the community and to render speedy help in extinguishing any subsequent fires. He also advised citizens to give back any articles they might have pilfered during the fire and authorized the posting of militiamen to prevent looting of damaged buildings. As a kind of postscript, the General Assembly issued rules on fire safety and fixed prices on goods and labor needed in rebuilding so that no brickmaker or craftsman could "make the late Calamity a Pretence to extort unreasonable or excessive Prices or Wages."

Serving as a community information vehicle, the *Gazette*, in its postfire editions, was filled with notices of business relocations, pleas for help in finding lost valuables, and assurances by surviving shopkeepers that their customers would be served. William Wright, the gold and silversmith, for example, announced that he had "removed to John's Island and continues to carry on his business," but offered a reward for the return of a gold bar "near a foot in length, and the breadth of a gold button," which had apparently dropped out of his pocket during efforts to save the contents of his store. As might be expected, there were also announcements of fire sales, such as that by Messrs. Binford and Osmond, who moved the remains of their business to Osmond's home "where what Goods they have saved out of the Fire are to be sold very reasonable."[13]

Fires of a different sort raged in the ongoing disputes, which the paper encouraged in its columns. Among the hottest was a series of pro and con essays, between 1740 and 1742, over the Reverend George Whitefield and his interpretation of Anglican doctrine. He was suspended in 1742, with authorities claiming that the discussion, much of it in print, had deteriorated into defamation and vilification.[14] Indeed, fifteen-year-old Peter Timothy was taken to court and charged with libel because of letters over the reverend gentleman's activities.

The bulk of the July 4, 1743, *Gazette* was devoted to an investigation of the management of and motives behind Whitefield's Orphan-House in Georgia. Records were printed, detailing the names of all children taken in, their ages, home colonies, employment while at the home, and conditions under which they were discharged. Letters both supported and attacked Whitefield, with accusers charging mismanagement and un-Christian motives. The August 1 *Gazette* continued the coverage, with excerpts from an earlier Boston *Evening Post* comment on a pamphlet by Whitefield, "A Continuation of the Account of the Orphan-House in Georgia, etc.": "His Account is wondrous satisfying to such as will take his Word for everything." A year later the question remained open, with a letter from "Publicola" charging that Whitefield and his accomplices, "a Knot of Knaves," had bilked money in London for alms-houses, didn't feed their poor charges, and were repeating the crime in Georgia.[15] The matter continued to fester until

1746, when the *Gazette* reported that Whitefield had been cleared of charges regarding the orphan home.

The apparent concern for the welfare of unfortunate human beings exhibited in the orphan-home coverage did not extend to the plight of slaves. Like many of her contemporaries, Mrs. Timothy, who had fled to the new country in search of freedom, accepted as a matter of course the practice of owning and selling slaves. In fact her few woodcuts included illustrations of two slaves standing at auction, one slave running. They were used to call attention to upcoming slave sales, or to head escaped slave notices. The publisher herself owned eight slaves at the time of her death. She accepted and several times ran quite prominently a lengthy advertisement by the Society for Propagating the Gospel in Foreign Parts asking donations to a fund to buy slaves. The idea was that "country-born young Negroes" might be taught to read the Bible and proselytized in the main tenets of Christianity. Then they would be sent as teachers of young Negro and Indian children born in the colonies.[16]

*Gazette* columns played a part both in disrupting and in spreading religious doctrine. Elizabeth Timothy's press served Charleston's religious needs by printing large numbers of sermons. Clergymen apparently felt that they had greater credibility if their works were formally printed. And though not necessarily behind every controversy, the *Gazette* office seems to have been recognized as a catalyst for discussion of the concerns of the town and colony. It was also the outlet for literary and philosophical efforts of Charleston's inhabitants. The publisher invited "any Gentlemen that will please to communicate to us their Sentiments on Subjects beneficial to the Province, in order to be published."[17]

In addition, maintaining the pattern set by her husband, she regularly included promotions for and commentaries on educational, cultural, and literary events, and printed a very modest sampling of literary material. She admitted that some reprinting was due to the times of the year "wherein but little News, properly so-called, may be expected," and promised to "entertain our Readers with Extracts from approved Authors, whose Writings are but little known among us."[18] And so the *Gazette* carried essays from English newspapers and excerpts from and extrapolations on such essays from the *Universal Spectator* as "Of Sincerity," "Of Honesty," and others. Mrs. Timothy also included original poems and essays, some doggerel, some eloquent. Some of these original works centered on the fate of women, constrained by the double standard of behavior in force in the colonies. Poetess E. R. offered her view entitled "The Ladies Complaint." Two poignant stanzas asserted:

> *Men to new Joys and Conquests fly,*
> *And yet no Hazard run,*
> *Whilst we are left, if we deny,*
> *And if we yield, undone.*

And, E. R. urged:

> *Then equal Laws let Custom find,*
> *And neither Sex oppress;*
> *More Freedom give to Womankind,*
> *Or to Mankind give less.*

The response, by "Your Constant Reader, and Incog.," began:

> *Dear Miss, of Custom you complain;*
> *It seems to me you languish,*
> *For some dear, simply homely Swain,*
> *To ease you of some Anguish.*

The debate in verse, to the entertainment and probably the amusement of readers, was taken up again in November in "Verses written by a young Lady, on WOMEN born to be controul'd!":

> *How wretched is a WOMAN'S Fate,*
> *No happy Change her Fortune knows,*
> *Subject to Man in every State*
> *How can she then be free from Woes?*

A "Gentleman" answered, parodying her lines:

> How happy is a Woman's Fate,
> Free from Care, and free from Woe,
> Secure of man in ev'ry State,
> Her Guardian-God below.

And the writer urged:

> Then say not, any Pow'rs ordain,
> that Man should bear the Sway;
> When Reason bids, let Women reign,
> When Reason bids, obey.[19]

And though such feminist complaints were not regular fare, almost every issue had at least one poem, carefully written letter, or essay on a timely topic. At times the works were more ambitious: an extravagantly effusive elegy at the death of Alexander Pope; odes in honor of living Charleston residents who contributions the editor respected; and satiric verses on various topics. Close observation reveals the very apparent hand of Mrs. Timothy's partner, Benjamin Franklin, in much of the essay content of the *Gazette.* Hers may have been only a temporary journalistic career, but the widow Timothy ran a newspaper Charleston could be proud of.

Though she formally turned over the business to her son Peter in May of 1746,[20] Mrs. Timothy continued active in business for a time, and opened her own separate small book and stationery shop next door to the King Street printing office. An advertisement in the *Gazette* October 18, 1746, announced that she would sell "Pocket Bibles, Primmers, Dyche's *Spelling-Books*, Reflections on Courtship and Marriage, *Armstrong's Poems on Health,* ... Bills of lading, Bonds, Mortgages, Bills of Sale, Indentures of Servants and Apprentices, Powers of Attorney, Indemnifying and Arbitration Bonds, Writs, Ink Powder, and Quills, all very cheap."

She kept the book shop through 1747 but *Gazette* advertisements for its wares thereafter do not mention her name as vendor. It is not clear just where she spent her remaining active years.

When Elizabeth Timothy died in May, 1757,[21] she left a journalistic legacy in Charleston. She had not made major breakthroughs in technology. She had not contributed major innovations in editing or publishing. But she had continued a paper at a time when a growing community needed it. And she had done so to the satisfaction of one of the most influential newspapermen of her time.

She bequeathed her books of account and all that was owed her to Peter. In the years she had edited in his name, she had been giving him the example of hard work and devotion. To her three daughters she left three houses, eight slaves, land, money, furniture and clothing.[22] To the *Gazette* and the people of Charleston, she left her contribution to the history of the colony and her example of what women editors could do.

Indeed, upon Peter's death in 1781, after he had been taken prisoner by the British, his widow Ann Donavan Timothy followed her mother-in-law's example and ran the press and the *Gazette* until her own death in 1791.[23]

Mrs. Timothy's example is remembered into the current century. In 1975 ceremonies in the printing museum at Charles Towne Landing, site of the first South Carolina colony, Women in Communications, Inc., recognized this first American female newspaper publisher by erecting a plaque in her honor.[24] It was fitting that such a commemoration should be made just as the United States was preparing to celebrate the 200th anniversary of its independence, promoted at least in part by journalists like Elizabeth Timothy.

S. M.

# 2

# MARY KATHERINE GODDARD
*Colonial Publisher and Postmistress*
[1738–1816]

><><

In the early snows of January, 1777, the beleaguered Continental Congress commissioned the first official printing of the cherished Declaration of Independence. Because the body had moved its headquarters to Baltimore, the Congress chose Baltimore's capable printer, and also its first continental postmistress, to print the historic document. Mary Katherine Goddard, who had spent fifteen years in her mother's and then brother's print shops, prepared the document, and then took from her pocket the money needed to pay post riders to distribute it throughout the colonies.

Almost forty years later she would die a dispossessed woman, having lost her newspaper to a brilliant but unstable brother and her post-office position to a male patronage winner. Between those events, she would provide the stability and sometimes the finance behind the fledgling continental postal system; more often than not, she would be the editor/printer, in fact, though not always in the official imprint acknowledgement, of colonial newspapers in three states. In these capacities she would show herself an able business executive as well as a craftsman whose manual labor contributed greatly to the success of her operation. She would also bring the power of the press to support the Revolutionary cause and would take patriots to court to test the freedom of the press. And she would demonstrate the dogged determination of colonial women to be loyal to their menfolk while very often receiving limited or no credit for the work they themselves did.

## Mary Katherine Goddard

Born June 16, 1738,[1] Mary Katherine Goddard began preparing for her journalistic career in her physician father's study, being taught to read and figure by her well-educated mother. She continued in the New London, Rhode Island, public school, where she and other girls read Latin and French and studied watered-down mathematics and sciences when the boys did not need the facilities.

When her father, Giles Goddard, who was also postmaster of New London, became incapacitated by gout in 1755, her mother, Sarah Updike Goddard, assumed the duties of postmistress and also finalized arrangements to apprentice an only son, William, to printer James Parker of New Haven.[2] This foresight was eventually to benefit the Goddard family as well as the young American colonies.

Giles' death in 1757 left Sarah financially secure, enabling her to remove to Providence in 1762 to finance the establishment of twenty-two-year-old William's first newspaper. The *Providence Gazette, and Country Journal*[3] carried his imprint but displayed from the start his mother's business sense and his sister's steadiness.

Mary Katherine Goddard began her journalistic apprenticeship in William's establishment as an unpaid twenty-four-year-old helper "more from sheer exhuberance and pleasure than from necessity."[4] In the adventure she was to observe her mother's management practices, lively spirit, and deep loyalty to family and community. And she was to learn traits that, more than once, would bring ailing newspapers from the brink of ruin.

Despite the concerted efforts of the three Goddards to build a steady and healthy circulation for this early Providence paper, lagging circulation caused a temporary closing of the paper in May, 1765. The circulation problem, however, was a timely release for William, impatient as he was to be on the move. Mother and daughter maintained the printing office under the title Sarah Goddard and Company while he began a job-hopping career made possible by the stability of his mother and sister. They printed broadsides, pamphlets, and stationery. They also served the business sector. As a busy seaport with a population of around 3,500,

Providence had a variety of businesses. The Goddard shop printed legal blanks, which eliminated the time-consuming process of hand-copying such forms, and in November, 1762, advertised: "Policies of Insurance, Portage Bills, Bills of Lading and Sale, and Letters of Attorney, Administration Bonds, common Bonds, Deeds, Writs, and Executions; and Kinds of Blanks used in this Colony, neatly printed, and sold as cheap as at any Printing-Office in New England."

Another item popular with local housewives and farmers was the almanac. Starting in the fall of 1762 William had acquired, through Benjamin West, "An Almanack, for the Year of our Lord Christ, 1763 ... calculated for the Meridian of Providence." These works of West, sold from Providence to Halifax, not only provided sunrise and sunset, phases of the moon, and tide information but also came with alternate blank pages for the keeping of a daily journal.[5] The Goddard women continued the almanac along with their other services and frequently did the job printing. Sarah also ran the Providence post office.[6]

Although the paper had been officially discontinued in May, a special issue entitled *A Providence Gazette Extraordinary* appeared August 24, 1765. It carried the slogan *"Vox Populi, Vox Dei,"* and the imprint "S. & W. Goddard," though by this time William was involved with the antitax broadsides in the New York-based *Constitutional Courant.*

The March 12, 1766, issue bearing the imprint of William Goddard, was called the *Providence Gazette Extraordinary and Supplement,* and was, ostensibly, directed at reviving the *Gazette.* The entire first page was an advertisement seeking 800 subscribers. It offered to trade subscriptions for farm produce or linen rags and old sail cloth to be made into paper at the mill near Providence, in which William was a partner. The shortage of newsprint was to continue, bringing the family into yet another paper mill investment in Elkridge Landing, Maryland. Mary Katherine would buy into and manage this operation in 1778 and 1779, as part of her printing business in that state.[7]

The reestablished *Gazette* appeared with the imprint "Sarah Goddard and Co." until January, 1767, when the phrase "in the absence of William Goddard" was added. There were several possible explanations for the phrase. The two women may have wanted to call attention to the fact that they were perfectly capable of conducting the business on their own. They may have wanted to give a signal to William's political enemies that the irascible fellow was not often in the *Gazette* shop, and that, hence, his creditors and critics should not seek retribution from Sarah Goddard and Co. Or, despite continuing evidence of family loyalty and long-suffering, it may have been an expression of good-riddance. Whatever the motivation, the statement did not signify rupture of family ties. Indeed, on January 24, 1767, a reprinted advertisement in the *Gazette* announced the appearance of *The Pennsylvania Chronicle, and Universal Advertiser,* William's latest effort. The first issue, January 26, 1767, was on the largest scale yet attempted in America,[8] a large folio with four columns instead of the usual three.

William's poor management and worse personal relationships with silent partners Joseph Galloway, a supporter of the Stamp Act, and Thomas Wharton, a Quaker, were soon more than he could cope with. In May, 1768, they urged William to sell the *Gazette,* which was doing well, in conjunction with the printing concern and to bring his mother and sister to Philadelphia. Sarah refused and turned down the offer of a house and bookstore of her own near the Philadelphia paper. She was persuaded to leave only after William personally entreated her in Providence. Selling the shop and newspaper to John Carter, Sarah's partner since September, 1767, William returned to Philadelphia. Summoned with little consideration of their wishes or needs, the Goddard women arrived in November, 1768, to manage and operate his newly established *Pennsylvania Chronicle, and Universal Advertiser,* which was to be Philadelphia's best edited pre-Revolution newspaper. The year after the move Sarah died at about the age of seventy, and the task of supporting and moderating fell to Mary Katherine.

William's irascible personality disrupted possibilities for friendship with Benjamin Franklin and other leaders of the burgeoning patriot movement. Lacking friends and besieged by creditors, he left his sister in charge of the *Chronicle* and took off for Baltimore in 1772 to start a third paper. It is evidence of his sister's skill as a journalist and of her business acumen that he intended to operate the two papers simultaneously.

The *Maryland Journal and Baltimore Advertiser*, the third newspaper established in Maryland and the first for the city, appeared August 20, 1773. William cited ill health as the cause of irregular publication during the paper's early months, and by February 17, 1774, his sister had completed the sale of the *Chronicle* and had come from Philadelphia to take over the *Journal*, a responsibility she would maintain for almost ten years. William resumed his job hopping, this time to establish an American postal system that would rival and replace the British system.

Threat of war offered Mary Katherine a real challenge. Because good printer's assistants were hard to find and keep, she often ran the shop and the presses alone. But the *Journal* appeared on a regular basis with few interruptions. Due to a shortage of folio sized sheets, the paper often appeared on whatever small sheets were available. Upon William's release from debtors' prison, a result of financial involvements from the *Chronicle*, *Journal*, and establishment of the post office, a deal was struck, and the name 'M. K. Goddard" appeared alone in the colophon from March, 1775, on. The paper prospered under her direction and, on November 16, 1779, she told her readers that the *Journal* was circulated as widely as any on the continent. Isaiah Thomas, premier historian of the early American press, called her "an expert and correct compositor of types."[9]

Despite the vicissitudes of the Revolutionary War years and the precarious position in which newspapers sometimes found themselves, the Goddard *Journal* appeared throughout the conflict. It was the only paper in Baltimore between July 1779 and May 1783 and was called by historians "second to none among the newspapers of the colonies."[10]

The fearless editor reported at length June 30, 1774, on

British reaction to American protests and on the blockade of Boston Harbor. Her news and commentary attacked the cruelty of British soldiers and bolstered the courage of the Patriots.

"The British behaved with savage barbarity," she wrote on June 7, 1775. That she saw the role women could play in the war was apparent in an April 5, 1775, essay, "A Friend to Liberty and the Fair," which urged women to practice frugality and to raise flax and wool, making for greater independence from Europe.

Wartime pressures on colonial pocketbooks often made it hard for subscribers to pay. So, on December 15, 1778, the publisher reminded her readers of her willingness to accept cash or goods, including "Beef, Pork, or any Kind of Animal Food, Butter, Hog's Lard, Tallow, Bees-Wax, Flour, Wheat, Rye, Indian Corn ... tann'd Sheepskins, brown Linen ... and Cotton Rags."

Mary Katherine also opened the columns of the *Journal* to patriot propagandists. Thomas Paine's "Common Sense" appeared in two installments. She scooped rival printers by printing for distribution to the colonies the first official copy of the Declaration of Independence. Authorized by Congress on January 18, 1777, with the names of those who had signed it, the copies from her press were signed by John Hancock, president of the Continental Congress and Charles Thomson, secretary, and are collectors' items today.[11]

Six months earlier, she had defended the freedom of the press by taking a reader to court. George Sommerville, angered by contents of a story, entered her office "and abused her with threats and indecent language." On June 3, 1776, the Baltimore County Committee censured his conduct as having a "direct tendency to influence the Freedom of the Press, which in every free country should be inviolably maintained."[12]

William returned briefly to Baltimore in January, 1777, ostensibly to help his sister with the *Journal*, although his name did not appear, perhaps to protect him from further debts he had incurred during his absence. His return was less an asset than a liability. The *Journal* and the entire printing operation prospered under Mary Katherine Goddard's leadership and was solvent when, in 1779, William announced the formation of a partnership with Colonel Eleazar Oswald to administer a bookselling and stationery business. It was not, he said, their intent to rival Mary Katherine's control of the paper, but rather to print and sell inexpensive European classics. The plan went nowhere.[13]

The year before she sold her interest in the paper to her brother, she responded to the urgings of "several respectable characters" and her own "sincere inclinations to render her paper more extensively beneficial to the Public" by going semiweekly. The *Journal* appeared regularly on Tuesdays and Fridays, beginning March 14, 1783.

Like many other contemporary printer/editors, Mary Katherine Goddard was postmistress, appointed to that position in Baltimore in 1775 by her brother. William Goddard had been instrumental in founding the Constitutional Post Office, one of the many involvements which took him out of the family's printing and publishing shops for years at a time. Mary Katherine was postmistress until 1789, the first woman ever appointed to a federal office.[14] As might be expected, she used the *Journal* to notify readers of changes in daily and weekly post schedules, list unclaimed letters, and promulgate Baltimore Post Office regulations. Her innovativeness and sense of public interest led her, in 1784, to establish a postal delivery service. An advertisement for a mailman ran in the Maryland *Journal* December 30, 1783.

But hard work and loyal service were at the mercy of political considerations, and when George Washington's new government came to power in 1789, a newly appointed postmaster general, Samuel Osgood, sent Miss Goddard a brief note, dismissing her in favor of a John White of Annapolis. Osgood made a feeble explanation to 200 of Baltimore's leading citizens, who signed a November 12, 1789, petition for her reinstatement. The postal district was to be enlarged, he said, and the travel necessary to oversee it all might be too strenuous and, therefore, inappropriate for a woman. Though the 51-year-old postmistress/publisher had handled the presses, loaded books and boxes at the *Journal* and at her shop next-door, and personally supervised the early operation of the postal delivery system she pioneered, she was deemed inadequate.[15]

Her petition to the United States Senate, January 29, 1790, argued rightly that the position was taken from her just as it was becoming lucrative: she herself had advanced pay from her own purse to post riders during several years of wartime hardships. She had not been reimbursed, and her services had gone unpaid until the war ended because there was no money in the Continental treasury. And, she reasoned, there was no hint of malfeasance or incompetence. Indeed, as Ebenezer Hazard, the postmaster general, wrote to General Gates in praise of her work as postmistress, she had been a "careful and conscientious public servant."[16]

But though she was not reinstated, even following White's death after only a few months in office, Miss Goddard was to remain active in Baltimore until age 72. She retained her dry goods and stationery business, started a bookstore in 1796, and retired from business only six years before her death, August 12, 1816. In her will, she freed a black slave, Belinda Starling, a woman who was companion to her for many years, and gave her "all the property of which I may die Possessed [sic] all of which I do to recompense the faithful performance of duties to me."[17]

It is an ironic, though somehow fitting, commentary on the role Mary Katherine Goddard, as a woman, was assigned that her brother felt quite justified in forcing her to sell her interest in the *Maryland Journal* in 1784, after she had made it a prosperous and prestigious institution.

The arrangement is all the more regrettable when one considers the many storms she weathered in the family enterprises she ran for her brother. At the age when her contemporaries were settling back to the well-deserved rewards of their labors, she had her crowning achievement taken away from her. It must have been especially galling to her to watch her brother repeat his earlier business patterns: having married a landed woman, he took a partner, ran the *Journal* eight more years, and sold it to pay off debts incurred in ill-advised speculation.

Her last years were not much rewarded by either the brother she supported so long and so loyally nor by the country she served so ably. But regardless of historians' neglect, a careful rereading of the record gives a place of honor to this colonial printer/publisher who served Maryland in a way and to a degree unequalled by any woman of her period in any other American community. The irony, however, is that, as in the case of many great women, one must search the records of the man with whom she was associated to find evidence of her accomplishments. And mentions made of these accomplishments are often tossed off lightly, overshadowed by attention to male successes.

S. M.

## 3

# ANNE NEWPORT ROYALL
*Travel Correspondent and Washington Editor*
[1769–1854]

Legends will always linger about the life of Anne Newport Royall. More than a century after her death the most-often-told anecdote is that she trapped President John Quincy Adams, swimming in the Potomac River, by sitting on his clothes until she got her interview. Even President Harry Truman repeated the old tale to author John Hersey, who in turn passed it on to posterity.[1] But like other stories about Mrs. Royall, that one is not true. While Mrs. Royall, being a persistent reporter, is known to have done some bold things, it is unlikely that she would have done anything to embarrass her good friend, President Adams.[2]

Her life spanned eighty-five years, from her birth before the Revolutionary War to her death during the presidency of Franklin Pierce. Her career in journalism, however, did not actually start until she was fifty-five years old—beyond the mortality age of most persons of her day. In fact, the first of her ten books, describing life and manners in the United States, did not appear until two years later in 1826.

Indeed she was sixty-two when in 1831, she turned newspaper publisher in the nation's capital with her *Paul Pry*, later called *The Huntress*, papers which endured for twenty-three years until she died. Frank Luther Mott called her lively publications "forerunners of the modern Washington gossip column."[3] *Notable American Women* has pointed out that she is "sometimes termed the first American newspaperwoman"—that is the first woman to initiate a career as a reporter and editor and not merely to inherit one as a widow. Certainly she must be recognized as one of the first, if not the very first, self-made women journalists with a national reputation.

Mrs. Royall's travel reports on early nineteenth-century America remain among the gems of journalism of that period, of importance still to any student of social history. A tiny lone woman, she journeyed intrepidly by stagecoach and steamer, by horseback and on foot, to almost every settlement of any importance in the United States. Often hungry and cold, sometimes destitute, she would wangle a tavern room, meal, or her travel fare from compassionate souls, perhaps with the promise of a mention in a forthcoming book.

Mrs. Royall was exceptionally well-read, and always curious, observing, and perceptive. Everywhere she went, she took prodigious notes and wrote about her impressions of contemporary society in what today would be called personalized feature style. She relished talking with all kinds of people—but was especially proud that she had interviewed every president from John Quincy Adams to Franklin Pierce.[4]

She was ever the crusader in behalf of truth and liberty as she saw it. She campaigned against graft and corruption in the federal government. She defended Sunday transportation of the mails, in opposition to Sunday Blue Laws, nonpartisan tariff regulations, tolerance for Roman Catholics, sound money, internal improvements, territorial expansion, states' rights in the matter of slavery, free public education, and the rights of Indians. She carried on a perennial battle against certain fundamentalist churches that promoted a church and state party. "I do not work for money," was her watchword. "I work for the benefit of my country."[5]

In 1829, as a result of derogatory words spoken against some evangelists who were harassing her, she was brought to trial under an obsolete law as a common scold. Convicted, she was punished with a fine instead of the traditional ducking; if two newspapermen had not come forth with money, in the name of freedom of the press, President Andrew Jackson would have done so.[6]

## Anne Newport Royall

Mrs. Royall was born in Baltimore, the eldest of two daughters of Mary and William Newport, on June 11, 1769. Little is known about her father, who apparently was a farmer and perhaps a trader. Although his child was "called after Queen Anne," there seems no real evidence that he was either a Tory or an illegitimate son of the Maryland Calverts, or of Stuart royal blood, as early biographies suggested.[7] Her mother was bright and industrious, although illiterate, like most women in the late eighteenth century.

Newport moved his family to the rough frontier of Western Pennsylvania when Anne was about three years old, perhaps in search of cheap land. There they lived in the wilderness, eking out a living and escaping Indian raids. After a time Newport died or disappeared, and his widow married a man named Butler and had another child, James. The Butler family was living in Hanna's Town at the time of the Indian attack on July 13, 1782, and mother and children survived in Fort Shields; but Butler seems to have died either during or before the attack.

Sometime after that the disillusioned widow Butler set out on foot with other refugees for the more promising land of the Shenandoah Valley. She took thirteen-year-old Anne and her stepbrother but left behind her other daughter, Mary, in the care of another family.

Their long and weary march ended near Staunton, Virginia, where Mrs. Butler found work as a housekeeper on a farm. In this class-conscious Upper Valley area, where her mother was a servant, Anne was relegated quickly from the democracy of the frontier to second-class citizenship. Ever after, Mrs. Royall's life was influenced by this experience during her sensitive teenage years. Her aggressive and defensive personality, and some of her later misgivings about the Christian church, were rooted there. During these years when she was ostracized and lonely, she buried herself in reading.

After about 5 years, probably seeking a better life, Mrs. Butler again set out penniless—this time arriving in Botetourt County, Virginia, after 115 miles by foot over the Allegheny Mountains. Anne was 18 at the time, and described as thin, less than 5 feet tall, with eager intelligence her most endearing quality. Atop Peters Mountain near Sweet Springs, Mrs. Butler found employment again as housekeeper in the manor of a well-to-do bachelor, Major William Royall. Neighbors knew him as a gentleman farmer of independent means, a Revolutionary War hero, a dedicated Mason, a somewhat eccentric scholar who read Rousseau, Voltaire, Jefferson, and Paine, rather than tend his large plantation.

Young Anne soon discovered the major's fine personal library and learned that the master of this household did not treat her as a servant's daughter, but rather as a pupil worthy of instruction. In fact, Royall himself became her tutor, and in time Anne had an education, especially in literature and history, far exceeding that of most women of her day. He also instructed her in Freemasonry, which in his view was preferable to the organized church; Royall taught that the Masons lived by the simple teachings of Christ rather than by dogmatic preachings. Anne accepted Royall's creed so well that throughout her later career in journalism, she promoted Masonry while distrusting orthodox religion.

As months of companionship slipped into years, the middle-aged major and his protegé were seen frequently together, not only reading in the library, but galloping horses across the country and sipping wine by the fire. Gossip grew among the neighbors and friends and relatives who visited the mountain lair. Finally a preacher riding the circuit recorded a marriage performed on November 18, 1797, between William Royall and Anne Newport. The groom was in his middle fifties and the bride was 28. While the couple had some common interests, their marriage had drawbacks. Royall had a reputation for drinking, and little practical interest in business. His young bride dreamed of exploring the real world beyond their library and Sweet Springs.

Royall spoke of moving to the bustling settlement of Charleston, Virginia, in Kanawha County, which had impressed him on a visit there. But no buyer could be found for the land on Peters Mountain. Time passed and the major engulfed himself with more reading and whiskey. Meanwhile Anne lost the young companionship of her stepbrother, James Butler, who went off to Kentucky, seeking his fortune. Burdened with running the plantation, Mrs. Royall apparently paid little attention to the fact that her aging and failing husband was discussing whimsical changes in his will, from time to time favoring various relatives. In 1812 Royall died in his bed, with a new carriage he had bought to move them to Charleston still waiting outside. In his last days he had been often intoxicated, unreasonable, and even violent. But he left behind what Anne Royall always declared to be his final true will, attested by her mother and a friend.[8] The widow Royall, just forty-three, appearing to be the heiress to a fortune, decisively arranged for her plantation to go up for auction—and set out to sample life beyond Botetourt County, without waiting for the sale. At last her carriage headed down the mountainside, with several slaves and a few treasured possessions.

Once in Charleston, she entered into partnership to build a hostelry—an investment that started well. But almost immediately this bright beginning was dashed when she found herself defending various lawsuits against the estate of William Royall. Primarily she faced relatives who claimed that they were the true heirs, and that the accepted will really was a forgery. Further, they said, Major Royall had cohabited with his wife before their marriage, and in later years he had no affection for her.[9] Such assertions the widow denied. Meanwhile, Mrs. Royall also learned that her plantation had been auctioned off for a mere $500—a good portion of that had been claimed by a creditor. Also she was forced to dispose of most of her assets lest avenging relatives claim them.

In the following years Mrs. Royall was to fight litigation, including creditors who would have put her in debtors' prison if they could. She was to fight a pitiful battle for her right to a Revolutionary War widow's pension. And despite all her harassment, frustration, and destitution, she was to travel the raw United States of those early times, armed with little than immense courage. She would barely be supported by her dwindling funds, the charity of people she encountered, and a few advance subscriptions to books she proposed to write.

After some months she was to discover, through letters she was sending for her own intelligent amusement, that she had a talent for interviewing, observing, and writing. Eventually it would occur to her that she might earn a living by publishing her letters and reports as books, telling less-travelled citizens what various parts of America were like.

Her idea was not a lot different from that author John Gunther applied to his world travels in the twentieth century. Those less fortunate than he were treated to his versions of *Inside Europe, Inside Asia,* et cetera.

Thus it was that during the winter of 1817, Mrs. Royall, already forty-eight, left her legal miseries behind in Charleston and went off adventurously to investigate the sunny land of the newly annexed Alabama Territory. At first she had no thought of being a journalist. Accompanied by only one slave, she set off on horseback, traversing the muddy and snowy roads and fording the streams. The ride across Kentucky alone took seventeen days, mostly through "gloomy, lonesome woods from which the light was excluded by lofty timber." Then across Tennessee with its "chocolate-covered soil," a land where she found native son Andrew Jackson, recent hero of the Battle of New Orleans, to be everywhere "the idol." And with the wit which came to characterize her writing she later recalled: "I am afraid that they (citizens of Tennessee) indulge too great a fondness for whiskey. When I was in Virginia it was much whiskey; in Ohio, too much whiskey; in Tennessee it is too, too much whiskey."[10]

Despite the rigors of journey and weather, Anne Royall arrived in Alabama Territory and settled for a week in Huntsville; she was soon out admiring the "great splendor" of wealthy planters' homes; researching the history of Huntsville which "took its name from Captain Hunt who built the first cabin on the bluff"; and examining current developments, such as the vast 50,000 acres of land for sale westward along the Tennessee Valley. Cherokee Indians had recently yielded their ancient homeland and retreated to an area bordering the Arkansas and White Rivers. Settlers poured into Huntsville from all over the country. And at Talbot's Tavern Mrs. Royall talked with General John Coffee, Jackson's close friend, whom the reporter described as "about 200 weight, six feet in height, 35 or 36 years of age." And added: "His black hair is carelessly thrown to one side in front and displays one of the finest foreheads in nature."[11]

Next she galloped off to Melton's Bluff (now extinct) on the Tennessee River near Jackson's plantation. Upon hearing of a nearby encampment of Indians, she rushed to the site in a canoe, believing wrongly that missionaries had taught them English. When even her efforts at sign language failed, she still described all she could observe and smoked a friendly peace pipe with them. Later, she climbed a hill above the river to visit "Old Hickory's" plantation. She not only talked with the overseer but studied the slaves toiling in the fields, watched the cotton gin at work, and inspected the Negro cabins. "The cabins," she wrote, "were warm and comfortable, and well stored with provisions, General Jackson being one of the best Masters," she wrote. Her real thrill at Melton's Bluff came when Andrew Jackson himself dropped by her tavern fireside one night to chat with everybody. "There is a great deal of dignity about him. He related hardships endured by his men, but never breathed a word of his own," she remembered.[12]

Despite legal interludes, fighting for her widow's rights in Virginia, Mrs. Royall, aided by a small dole on her dower, wandered about warm and hospitable Alabama for the next four years, witnessing the Territory turn state and observing the aftermath of the Panic of 1819. Her main headquarters were a boardinghouse in booming Huntsville.

Meanwhile heirs had succeeded in breaking Major Royall's will and denying all inheritance to her. Anne Royall, however, was to remain loyal to her husband's memory; she had been loath to admit in court about his addiction to alcohol, a habit she never shared during her long life; instead she always was to praise his scholarship and patriotism.

By 1823 Mrs. Royall had the idea of collecting her letters for publication, although her book, *Letters from Alabama*, did not actually appear until 1830. These had been addressed to a young friend, Matthew Dunbar, a Charleston lawyer and loyal defender whom she regarded almost as a son. (The studious biographer of Mrs. Royall, Bessie Rowland James, disavowed earlier implications that young Dunbar was her lover.) While editing the letters Dunbar mailed back, the impoverished widow had the idea of earning a living by travel writing. She had discovered her talents. Her new scheme was to collect subscriptions in advance of projected books. Initially she would go to Pennsylvania, New York, and New England, and describe the East for the folks out West. She had a title ready: *Sketches of History: Life and Manners in the United States*. It was to take three years to achieve the printing of this first book.

First, however, she had some business to attend checking on matters back in Virginia, and seeing her mother, Mary Butler, and stepbrother, James, both now living in the great Queen City of the West, Cincinnati, Ohio. Attorney Dunbar did not advise her to linger during her quiet visit in Charleston, where subpoenas for her arrest over her debts were waiting. And in Cincinnati her merchant brother was bankrupt, ready to move to cheap land in Indiana.

In 1824 Anne Royall was to be found in Washington or nearby, delaying her travels while fighting for her rights as a Revolutionary War widow. She wrote of Alexandria, Georgetown, and her experiences in the nation's capital. At first the pension bureau claimed to find no record of Major Royall's military record. Angry and hurt, she managed to gather documents and affidavits, only to be told next that only widows married prior to 1794 were qualified. It would take an amendment by Congress changing the wedding-date limitation on Revolutionary War brides to recognize her claim!

A shabby figure, usually garbed in her familiar worn black dress, Mrs. Royall was to be seen about the nation's capital talking about her case with Congressmen and collecting subscriptions and letters of introduction for travel. She explored the wonders of the city and Hill. She made the acquaintance of John Quincy Adams, Secretary of State, who won her respect at once. She called him "a profound scholar ... a consummate gentleman ... a truly great man." He was to become her lifelong friend. He not only contributed money to her literary cause but sent her off to call on his wife, Louisa. Afterwards she wrote of her reception of Mrs. Adams: "You do not have to stand and wait here. The rich and poor meet with a cordial welcome." Anne Royall decided that she was "the most accomplished American lady I have seen."[13]

Her journalistic daring-do was demonstrated during this Washington visit when she invaded the hotel suite of French hero General Marquis de Lafayette. Somehow she outwitted the guard posted at his door and received a cordial reception from the general; in fact, she not only got a story but also a testimonial letter from Lafayette, a good brother Mason of her late husband, praising Major Royall's war service. The impressive letter was to be most helpful in her travels.

Still nearly penniless she left by stagecoach for Baltimore, wearing a farewell shawl which Louisa Adams had draped over her slight shoulders. From then on she was to continue touring, coming back and forth to Washington as her base, until it became her permanent home in 1830. Always "subscriptioneering," she eagerly investigated everything in her path—people high and low, of varying customs, common places, politics, cultural events, historical sites, businesses, and factories. Her curiosity had no bounds, and her gift for making reportorial notes on paper was astounding. No matter how weary, hungry, cold or bereft, she kept going.

With luck she skimped along on free lodgings and meals. In New York she was overwhelmed at the goodness of the Masons, who honored her with a benefit in Chatham Garden Theater; they seated this brother's fragile widow in a box seat and afterwards handed her $180 to continue her travels.

A sample of her varied activities in these early months of touring included: an interview in Albany with New York Governor DeWitt Clinton, whose good mind she praised; in Springfield, Massachusetts, a tour of the United States Arsenal, observing men at work on their machinery; an inspection of a company manufacturing paper in Hartford, Connecticut; a visit to a pioneer school for deaf mutes and a talk with Lydia Sigourney, the popular women's author.

In Boston she sought out the great landmarks, worshipping at the Old South Church; observing the Boston's Alms House working farm for the poor and the labor training program at the state prison. She attended a lecture at Harvard College and made a sidetrip to learn more about Salem's witchcraft days. The high point in Boston, however, was tea with ex-President Adams, then in his ninetieth year. Her readers were to learn of his amiability, and courtesy, and his graciously appointed home.

In several cities she pounded the streets, searching for a publisher for her proposed *Sketches*. Finally in New Haven, Connecticut, a printing by the author was arranged on credit. In May of 1826, when Mrs. Royall was fifty-seven, her first book appeared. Following a frequent custom of the day, the work did not carry the female author's name but used a polite byline; hers was: By a Traveller. Newspaper reviews, however, were soon acknowledging Anne Royall as the true bright and spirited Traveller. Many were favorable, and several hailed her as the "Mrs. Walter Scott of America."[14] The book sold well, and Mrs. Royall was proud of her recognition. Almost at once she turned to her next travel book, which became three volumes, all under the ominous title, *Black Books*. The newly successful author, who had been a battered beggar, now decided to speak out about persons and places that annoyed her. It was the beginning of Mrs. Royall's tongue-lashing style that earned her a reputation as a shrew.

As years went on, only special persons such as John Quincy Adams were to have the insight to look beyond the rough exterior and see her good heart, basic intelligence, and crusading sense of justice. In his diary he wrote: "Mrs. Royall continues to make herself vexious to many persons, tolerated by some and feared by others, by her deportment and books; treating all with a familiarity which often passes for impudence, insulting those who treat her with civility, and then lampooning them in her books. Stripped of all her sex's delicacy, but unable to forfeit its privilege of gentle treatment from the other, she goes about like a virago in enchanted armor, and redeems herself from the cravings of indigence by the notoriety of her eccentricities and the forced currency they give to her publications."[15]

As she travelled across the United States, the famous authoress Royall was apt to meet with extreme admiration or hatred. Increasingly she became embroiled in controversy over the development of third political parties which were anti-Mason or evangelical. Although she believed firmly in God, she believed in the American principle of separation of church and state. To the evangelical or anti-Mason leaders of the period, Mrs. Royall was an arch enemy. She retaliated with caustic words, whether it was on a streetcorner or stagecoach or in a book. In Burlington, Vermont, one vexed man shoved her on both shoulders away from his door and down ten feet of stairs; she was five weeks recovering from a fractured leg and bruises. When she returned, still disabled, to Washington for a spell, she was carried onto the floor of the Senate to watch the debates and noted with satisfaction that some Congressmen displayed copies of her *Black Book*. Before long she was back limping along Pennsylvania Avenue and checking the news in various departments of the federal government.

In 1829 she attended the inauguration festivities of the people's hero, Andrew Jackson, and chatted with some of the wagonloads of the plain folk who deluged Washington to celebrate the nonaristocratic president. That summer brought her notorious trial as a common scold or public nuisance. A group of evangelists had taken to praying for Mrs. Royall's misguided soul under the windows of her rooming house. They brought tracts to her door, offering her salvation. Some of their children threw stones at her windows. Finally all patience snapped and her temper was unleashed.

The evangelists said her words were obscene, as they would testify. Suit was brought against her, and despite Mrs. Royall's outstanding character witnesses, including Secretary of State John Eaton, the jury found her guilty. The judge spared the sixty-year-old woman a ducking, but fined her $10 and ordered a bond posted for $100 to guarantee she would keep the peace for one year. Although President Jackson had dispatched friends to the courthouse, two re-porters from the *National Intelligencer* stepped forth first with the money and a guarantee of her future conduct. During the trial James Gordon Bennett, then a Washington reporter and later founder of the New York *Herald*, sat beside her for support.

The much publicized trial added to Anne Royall's reputation as a colorful character and also to the sale of her travel books. In all she completed ten volumes, including two volumes of *Pennsylvania*, three volumes of *Southern Tour*, as well as her *Sketches* and *Letters from Alabama*, and *Black Books*, before settling in Washington. But the wear of travel had outdone the glamour of it by 1830 when she located in the capital to turn newspaper publisher. With the help of a longtime friend named Sally Stack, Mrs. Royall collected a few funds, found an old press and some type, both discards, and employed a tramp printer and two orphan boys as printer's devils.

The first issue of the four-page, four-column *Paul Pry* was produced in the Royall kitchen in Bank House, a room-ing house so-named because the building once held the Bank of the United States, not far from Capitol Hill. The paper's name was given by a neighborhood carrier boy. In appearance it was rather standard for its day, with twelve-point roman type and a column width of eighteen picas.

## Anne Newport Royall

In content *Paul Pry* carried the usual news from the government, reprints of political commentary, social news, joke fillers, and poetry. In time advertising filled up to one-third of her papers. Mrs. Royall's own writing, sometimes quite peppery, was what livened the paper, including her replies to Letters to the Editor. From the start it was evident that she would not be merely a "clippings or scissors editor," who relied heavily on reprints in place of local news. Her reports were generally personal, even gossipy at times, rather than merely factual. But it was the philosophy behind *Paul Pry*, announced in that first issue on December 3, 1831, that mattered: "The welfare and happiness of our country are our politics. We shall expose all and every species of political evil, and religious fraud, without fear or affection. We shall patronize merit of whatsoever country, sect, or politics. We shall advocate liberty of press, the liberty of speech, and the liberty of conscience." Anne Royall had said that nobody could buy her integrity. In an age of the widely-accepted partisan press, when many editors were paid fronts for political parties, her independence was brave.

*Paul Pry* was soon marked by its editor's strong feelings for and against causes, expressed in lavish praise or fierce tirades. (Flattery and invectives were not unusual, however, in pre–Civil War journalism.) Anti-Masons were trounced in many issues.

One of her early exposés demanded the firing of the clerk of the House of Representatives because of his support of payroll padding and nepotism. In other issues the watchdog editor detailed how various governmental employees were cheating on their jobs or passing out favors. On Capitol Hill editor Royall was soon known as either a fearless journalist or a troublemaker, pointing out the inadequacies of the Bank of the United States as well as the exorbitant price of flannel. As for the cholera epidemic in Washington in 1832, Mrs. Royall told the city government it was high time to put in sewers and drain the filthy marshes! In another campaign she criticized the United States Post Office for incompetencies and abuse of privileges, and, partly as a result of her work, Postmaster General William T. Barry resigned. The movement for trade unions in America brought her applause as a boost for workers.

When Bank House was sold, she lost her free rooms and friend Sally Stack helped scrounge up another place to live. *Paul Pry* pleaded for paid-up subscriptions and somehow kept coming off the press, while widow Royall kept seeking her pension. On November 19, 1836, *Paul Pry* closed down, being out of cash, but just two weeks later the same paper bounded back as *The Huntress*. The farewell editorial in *Paul Pry* typified the emotional style of Mrs. Royall. She flayed those who failed to support the paper and lauded her many accomplishments. Speaking of the public's "ingratitude" and "shameful neglect," she declared that citizens should "remember this widow, whose husband spent seven years for you on the field of revolutionary battles," because she herself had been "always in the van of the editorial corps, and attacked the enemies of its country in their strongholds."

Almost seventy, she next took on the cause of Richard White, charged with setting fire to the Treasury building; she was convinced of his innocence and felt vindicated when President Zachary Taylor pardoned him in 1841. Not surprisingly the underdog's champion felt sympathy for Indians as America's vast expansion shoved them off their ancient lands; for example she spoke out after Black Hawk and his starving band were defeated and after the Cherokees were driven from Georgia. She was *for* expansion, but within reasonable limits.

Old soldier William Henry Harrison of Indiana Territory drew her moderate support for the election of 1840. As was her custom, she paid a congratulatory call on America's new president, who was to hold a very brief term; two weeks after taking office Harrison was dead from pneumonia, having sworn his oath outdoors in freezing temperature.

In the 1840s, as the women's suffrage movement began rumbling, it is amazing to note that Mrs. Royall, the epitome of an independent soul, opposed equal suffrage and also even opposed her colleague, the female editor-suffragist Amelia Bloomer, whose bloomer costume for women the long-skirted editor thought unbecoming and immodest. The fight to win Texas over from Mexico brought support from *The Huntress,* who called for military volunteers; and when the former General, Sam Houston, came to Washington as the victorious senator from the new state of Texas in 1846, she relished her interview with him. When the dispute arose in 1848 over the issue of slavery in Oregon Territory, the bright-eyed seventy-nine-year-old reporter was in the Senate to witness Daniel Webster rendering his triumphal oration for abolition.

To her last days money problems hounded her very existence. As she grew older and more feeble, she sought more advertising revenue and used more reprints since there was no international copyright to worry her. She took pride in clipping such quality writing as that by Charles Dickens. She was ever more grateful for donations of kindling, food, or clothing. Although she hobbled around Washington far less, she tried to take in newsy happenings; she visited the new daguerreotype galleries and sat for a picture herself. However, no likeness of her of any kind has ever been found.[16]

When she was in her eightieth year in July, 1848, Congress at long last voted a change in the pension laws which would provide widow Royall with the sum of forty dollars a month. She was overjoyed, though her dear friend Representative John Quincy Adams of Massachusetts, who had faithfully fought for that goal year after year, missed her moment of glory; he had collapsed in his House seat and died the previous February. The widow's new mite helped support her in a little cottage that she and Mrs. Stack had found.

As the national controversy over the morality and economics of slavery mounted, the octogenarian Anne Royall worried over possible civil war in her country. She attended the Senate debate over Henry Clay's compromise resolutions—which were to preserve the Union for a time. Among her last big social occasions were the "levees," parties given by Presidents Zachary Taylor and his successor, Millard Fillmore.

The year 1853, when she was eighty-four, brought many days of weakness and illness for her. She could not take long walks or climb stairs. But when unfailing Sally Stack fell ill while doctoring Anne Royall, the aged editor hired a hack and herself delivered the paper to subscribers.

The last issue of *The Huntress* appeared on July 24, 1854, two months before her death; she was still able to scold certain politicians as "poor dupes" for their "empty-headed knavery," and she had a final "prayer . . . that the Union of these States may be eternal."

With an unabashed lack of pride, the exhausted crusader admitted that she had "but thirty-one cents in the world and for the first time since we have resided in this city—thirty years—we were unable to pay our last month's rent, only six dollars." Yet, undefeated, she put her "trust in Heaven" and also in a "miraculous" new medicine, "Dr. Morse's invigorating elixir."

On Sunday, October 1, 1854, she died. Her services were conducted by the Masons in Grace Episcopal Church, and her body was laid to rest in an unmarked grave in Congressional Cemetery.

In the early years after her death Anne Newport Royall was often disparaged as a half-comic figure. Then more careful research began to put her into perspective. In the history of journalism her record came to be viewed as one compiled by a woman of exceptional ability and rare courage. Now she is respected and admired both for her excellent roving correspondent's reports on early America and her fearless integrity as a newpaper writer and editor.

M. G. S.

# 4

# SARAH JOSEPHA HALE
*First Women's Magazine Editor*
[1788–1879]

> Mary had a little lamb,
> Its fleece was white as snow,
> And everywhere that Mary went
> The lamb was sure to go.

Generations of American children have beamed their delight, reciting this favorite old nursery rhyme, and probably will keep doing so forever.

But, quick, who can name the author of that perennial verse? It was Sarah Josepha Buell Hale, one of the most distinguished women in American history, but her true fame had nothing to do with her hobby of writing children's poetry.

For forty remarkable years, from 1837 to 1877, Mrs. Hale was the widely respected first woman editor of the first important and lasting women's magazine in America, *Godey's Lady's Book*, that nineteenth century Bible of morals, fashions, literature, entertainment, and general instruction.[1] Before that she edited the less-remembered *Boston Ladies' Magazine*, which thrived from 1828 through 1836. And she was the first American woman to publish a successful novel, *Northwood: A New England Tale*, in 1827.[2] Indeed, this pioneering journalist established a record with her accomplishments in many worthy national causes, which came to fruition largely because of her drive and determination.

Yet the dynamo known as Sarah Hale looked more like a life-sized China doll so popular in that period, with her porcelain complexion, lovely eyes, dark curls, and lace-trimmed silks. Her quiet manner suggested that she could have written, at most, "Mary's Little Lamb."

Her life spanned nineteen presidents, from her birth in 1788, before George Washington was yet elected first president, into the administration of Rutherford B. Hayes. She retired only a year before she died at 90, and in her final editorial, in *Godey's Lady's Book*, that December, 1877, "bid farewell to my countrywomen, with the hope that this work of half a century may be blessed to the furtherance of their happiness and usefulness in their Divinely-appointed sphere."[3]

During her unusually long and active career, Mrs. Hale, an ardent patriot, instigated the creation of Thanksgiving as a permanent nationwide holiday. For years she had campaigned to persuade several presidents to issue such a proclamation, and finally succeeded with Abraham Lincoln in 1864.[4] The daughter of a Revolutionary soldier, she spearheaded national movements to raise money for completing Bunker Hill Monument and also for preserving President Washington's home at Mt. Vernon as a memorial.

Using her influence as the respected editor of a popular, widely circulated magazine, she was among the first persons in the nation to take up the cudgel for women to obtain such things as equal elementary education, vocational training, higher education, property rights, career opportunities, day nurseries, kindergartens, public playgrounds, and public health centers.[5]

To mention a few of her other interests: She undertook an uphill campaign for stormy Elizabeth Blackwell, the nation's first woman physician, for her right to secure a medical education and be allowed to practice. She encouraged Matthew Vassar to develop the first American women's college. Despite opposition from angry profiteers who were cheating them with shabby jobs and rooms,[6] she founded the first Seaman's Aid Society in Boston's "Shanty Town" to better the lot of sailors' wives and children left behind when the men went to sea.

Mrs. Hale's various works came at a time when it was

generally considered improper for a woman to set foot outside her home and mix in the public fray. She did shy away from politics, however, including the suffrage movement. Although she was a contemporary of such leading feminists as Margaret Fuller, Elizabeth Cady Stanton, Lucretia Mott, and Susan B. Anthony, Sarah Hale was never one of their circle. "The Lady Editor" was always guarded in her approach to women's progress.

From the start of her journalism career in 1828, she said that her aim was merely "female improvement," and she obviously preferred to bore gently from within the women's magazine regarding any serious social change for women. It was never her style to rile men, who unquestionably controlled the purse strings of journalism and the nation in Sarah Hale's day.[7]

From 1837 to 1877 she worked in harmony with her publisher, the less-educated, bragging, self-made Louis Antoine Godey, who had named *Godey's Lady's Book* for himself. And Godey regarded the soft-spoken Mrs. Hale, with her elegant appearance and refined manner, as the epitome of a lady; he proudly advertised on the magazine's back cover that "her name alone is sufficient guarantee for the propriety" of the magazine.

Today her identity has been all but lost except to journalists, historians, and antique collectors poking about for the rare old hand-colored *Godey* illustrations for framing. In 1928, only fifty years after her death, Sarah Hale's name appeared in Richardson Wright's *Forgotten Ladies*, a book about women who once shaped the course of history but had been forgotten. In 1970 her once-celebrated novel, *Northwood*, was reprinted, and the introduction commented that few persons "recognize" her name.

Who was this Sarah Hale, so primly beautiful in the old paintings and daguerreotypes left to posterity?

Her career as a journalist did not really start until she was nearly forty, an impoverished widow with five children to support. Before then, she had hardly set foot outside Newport, the sheltered New Hampshire village where she was born, reared, and started married life.

She was born Sarah Josepha Buell on October 24, 1788, on an isolated farm several miles outside the town. Her father, Captain Gordon Buell, who suffered from injuries received during the Revolutionary War, had settled his family on a 400-acre tract of rocky, remote land on East Mountain, overlooking the Sugar River. The land was a gift from his grandfather, Deacon Daniel Buell.

Sarah's mother was Martha Whittlesey, by all accounts an unusually bright and advanced woman for postcolonial days when half of American women were illiterate and only a few had an academic education. It is known that Mrs. Buell was well read and encouraged Sarah to read. By eighteen, young Sarah had become a township schoolteacher, riding horseback over rough roads through rain and snow.

Also significant in her development was an older brother, Horatio Gates Buell, who later became a distinguished New York lawyer and judge. During his vacations from Dartmouth College (Class of 1809) he tutored his sister in subjects such as philosophy, science, mathematics, and Latin. He did this in response to her eagerness to learn, her envy of his opportunity for a higher education. There were no colleges for women in the United States at the turn of the nineteenth century, and females were not admitted to the male institutions.

By 1811, Sarah Buell, twenty-three and unmarried, was considered almost an "old maid" when she met David Hale, a young lawyer starting practice in Newport. Her father, who by then had a tavern, "Rising Sun," on the main road from Keene to Hanover, gave his approval to the match and in 1813 the couple was married and settled in the village.

After her hard years of township teaching, Sarah Hale found herself, according to all references in her own writings and critical research by others, in an easy-going, happy marriage. David Hale encouraged Sarah's education. During regular long evenings of study he instructed his wife in such subjects as botany, French, geology, and mineralogy, although she devoted most of her time to her husband and four children. Then in 1822, her idyll came to a sudden end when David Hale died from pneumonia. A fifth child was born two weeks later, and soon thereafter, widow Hale opened a millinery shop, one of the era's respectable livelihoods for a woman needing to support her family.

Assuaging her grief, she began writing poetry about her sense of lost fulfillment as a woman. In 1823 these verses were published, thanks to the sponsorship of her late husband's brother Masons, as *The Genius of Oblivion* by "A Lady of New Hampshire." Although the work was rather dull, some of it in the classical tradition of Dryden, it was apparently therapeutic for Mrs. Hale and gave her confidence in writing. This first book also revealed her philosophy about the differing roles of men and women, which was to alter only a little with the passage of her long life:

> *"Man rides the wave and rules the flame . . .*
> *Woman may dearer empire claim,*
> *The heart, her throne."*[8]

Hardly radical feminism!

In fact, Mrs. Hale even belittled the famous tract by English feminist Mary Wollstonecraft, *Vindication of the Rights of Women*, in another poem in her book. Ironically, Mrs. Hale was later to spend most of her half century in journalism promoting some of the same themes Miss Wollstonecraft emphasized—education and employment for women. Their difference in approach, however, was one of quiet persuasion versus loud agitation.

Shortly after *The Genius of Oblivion* appeared, Sarah Hale was so taken with the idea of a literary career, she dove into writing a novel. It was one of the first American writings to explore the regional differences between North and South, and it dealt openly with the problem of slavery. *Northwood*, published in 1827, is still of interest to historians, and was popular enough to be read widely in America and in England, France, and Germany.[9]

It was really *Northwood* that launched Sarah Hale into her career as a magazine editor for the next fifty years. Her book attracted the attention of a Boston publishing firm interested in founding a "ladies' magazine." Mrs. Hale was offered the editorship. Thus at forty she entered journalism with "the first literary work exclusively devoted to women ever published in America." She moved her brood to Boston by stage coach.[10]

*Ladies' Magazine* appeared in January, 1828. Its opening editorial words were assuring to early-nineteenth-century male society: "Husbands may rest assured that nothing found on these pages . . . shall cause her (the wife) to be less assiduous in preparing his reception . . . or to usurp station . . . or to encroach on the prerogatives of men."[11]

But in the very same issue the adroit Mrs. Hale also carried a report of a lecture by an Episcopalian minister, the Reverend Charles Burroughs, expounding the need to broaden women's education. Thus Mrs. Hale initiated her journalistic career, obliquely advancing her innovative ideas under careful wrappings.

From the first she abandoned one journalistic convention of the day, that of freely "borrowing" materials from English periodicals, and called for original American contributions instead. For a few issues she wrote much of the magazine herself, while seeking out quality essays, fiction, and poetry to publish. And in all ways she began to promote the need for women's education, including "female seminaries."

In 1830 some of her poetry, which had been written mostly to entertain her own children and for her publisher's other magazine, *Juvenile Miscellany*, was published as a book, *Poems for Our Children*, Among these was her never-to-be-forgotten "Mary's Lamb." Later challenges to Mrs. Hale's authorship of the nursery rhyme were well-refuted in a chapter of a major biography, *The Lady of Godey's* by Ruth E. Finley.

Shortly after Mrs. Hale's book appeared, composer Lowell Mason set many of the verses to music, and in 1831 the *Boston Lyre* by Hale and Mason was introduced to schoolchildren. Meanwhile, "Mary's Lamb" found its way into *McGuffey's Reader*.

Far from the realms of strict women's magazine journalism, Mrs. Hale also began pursuing the wide world around her in Boston, shortly after her arrival there. In walks about the slum-ridden waterfront, she worried over the wives and children sailors left behind during their long spells at sea. These forgotten families were often ill-housed, ill-fed, and ill-clothed. They were at the mercy of unscrupulous merchants and employers of all kinds.

By 1833 the "lady editor" had an answer: why not found a Seaman's Aid Society? Amidst some flak from sweatshop owners, she proposed that the women operate their own independent sewing business and divide the profits. Guiding the Society, she even initiated plans for an industrial training school, a day nursery, free library, and decent housing. Perhaps without the warm friendship of daring Dr. Oliver Wendell Holmes, who took his meals at the same boardinghouse as Sarah Hale, she might not have spoken out so sharply that early as a newcomer to Boston. But during their years of association he apparently stirred her interests in public health and other social concerns.[12]

During her years in Boston, before Louis Antoine Godey bought out *Ladies' Magazine* and claimed the fabulous Mrs. Hale as editor of *Godey's Lady's Book* in Philadelphia, Mrs. Hale accomplished many things with her public activities. Outstanding among these was her campaign to save Bunker Hill Monument, although it did not come to fruition for more than a decade.

Because money ran out, the project honoring Revolutionary War heroes had collapsed after Daniel Webster laid the cornerstone in 1825. Bunker Hill was merely a disaster of unfinished rubble when the new editor arrived. It was Mrs. Hale's famous week-long Woman's Monument Fair of Boston, in September, 1840, that really raised the funds to restore the project. Women from as far away as the Carolinas and Ohio contributed homemade goods such as jellies, pickles, embroidery, quilts, and knitted works for sale at the exposition. Thousands of people poured into Quincy Hall—and nearly $30,000 were raised. The effort for "completion of one of the most sacred memories of our nation's gratitude" was a "perfect success," wrote Mrs. Hale in

*Godey's*, thanks to "the efficiency of female industry and influence."[13]

Finally in 1843, when the monument was actually completed, Webster dedicated the monument amidst tumultuous fanfare. It was widely acknowledged that Mrs. Hale's amazing hand had organized the women of America to achieve the triumph.

Already back in 1836, Godey had merged *Ladies' Magazine* with *Godey's Lady's Book*, and by January, 1837, Mrs. Hale was the functioning editor. But because her youngest son was still at Harvard University, the publisher permitted her to work in Boston and delay her actual move to Philadelphia for four years.

In *Godey's* Mrs. Hale espoused the traditional ideas about the roles of men and women which had been her trademark in *Ladies' Magazine*. Men were marked by a degree of depravity or temptation to sin, unlike women who were a purer breed. And "woman's sphere" continued to be primarily wifehood, motherhood, and homemaking. She warned against seeking equality with men.[14]

By the time Mrs. Hale, 53, took the helm in Philadelphia in 1841, she was acknowledged as a powerful arbiter of tastes and morals in the American household, a kind of Ann Landers and Amy Vanderbilt in one auspicious person. *Godey's* circulation was climbing steadily, and by 1851 was to reach 63,000, twice that of any rival magazine. By the Civil War it reached 150,000, "extraordinary" for those times.[15]

Through these salad days for both Sarah Hale and *Godey's*, principal authors were published in the magazine. These included Horace Greeley, Edgar Allen Poe, Washington Irving, Henry Wadsworth Longfellow, John Greenleaf Whittier, Ralph Waldo Emerson, William C. Bryant, Mary Virginia Terhune, and Harriet Beecher Stowe, among others.

As with *Ladies' Magazine*, her success formula for *Godey's* was the forerunner for what has since characterized the American women's magazine. Along with the fiction and essays came the lavish fashion color illustrations, and information on the latest needlework, recipes, designs for home building and furnishings, gardening, book reviews, and advice on etiquette—all forerunners of the modern magazine's departments. There was enough piffle that conservative readers at the time, or for years afterwards, never questioned whether Sarah Hale might be rocking the boat of Victorianism or questioning woman's place as firmly at home.

Her unceasing bits of propaganda for women's advancement were slyly stuck amidst the whipped cream and ruffles, the crochetted knick-knacks, and sentimental poetry.

Mrs. Hale was also a practical woman when it came to any improvements for women or mankind in general. For example, she called for the invention of a mechanical contrivance to launder clothes while most women were resignedly pounding their washboards; and she sent one of her magazine reporters off on a trip to Niagara Falls to sample firsthand the safety and comfort of the new steam railroad.

Of course she glorified "domestic science," and she insisted that "the art of conducting the ... house with order, prudence, and as far as possible, elegance, was something that every woman should understand."[16] But she preached away, in almost every issue, on the need for women's seminaries and colleges. On that she never gave up. When she was eighty-four, in July, 1872, she devoted part of her editorial column to complaining that great English universities like Oxford and Cambridge were giving advanced degrees to women while some colleges in America were still "hesitating."

Already in the 1850s she had lessened her emphasis on women's sphere being restricted as a wife, or maybe a schoolteacher or medical missionary. She had the foresight to understand that industrialization and urbanization were forcing more women into the labor market. Women should be trained to sustain themselves in case of necessity, she suggested. In an editorial of July, 1853, this time concerning untrained women, Mrs. Hale was also ahead of her time when she proposed women might work as waitresses and typesetters. "Indeed, where in this Republican land shall her (woman's) field of work be fixed (limited)?" she slyly asked.

It was during this period that she gave her support to Elizabeth Blackwell, M.D., America's first woman physician. Cleverly, she selected a male physician, Dr. William Cornell, to write for *Godey's* in January, 1853, arguing that women were just as qualified as men to be "the best of physicians." Then the editor went to bat for women's medical colleges, compromising with her adversaries, agreeing that it was unthinkable for girls to be trained in these delicate matters along with boys. She also pointed out carefully what welcome Christian service such women doctors could render in the foreign missionary field, especially where women in secluded societies were forbidden examination by male doctors. Even numerous women in America suffered danger and pain rather than ignore scruples of delicacy and allow medical men to examine them, explained Sarah Hale, ever drumming on persuasion rather than agitation.[17]

She also suggested that the ladylike pallor so popular in the midnineteenth century, like a tight corset, was really not healthy, and that clothes were made for comfort, and bodies for exercise. She recommended outdoor sports and calisthenics. Even the picnic, coming into strong popularity, should be a useful occasion, in her opinion, for easy dress and movement such as hiking.

Note that Mrs. Hale disliked the word "female" as an "animal epithet" and campaigned for use of "the beautiful word, woman." Indeed, she persuaded Matthew Vassar to drop the word from the original name, Vassar (Female) College.[18]

In addition to editing the magazines, Mrs. Hale wrote or edited a number of books. The most outstanding included: *Traits of American Life* (1835), a description of various American personality types in local color vignettes; *Woman's Record* (1853), an ambitious biographical encyclopedia containing some 2,500 names from Eve to

Mrs. Hale herself; and *Manners or Happy Homes and Good Society All the Year Around* (1867), Sarah Hale's view of woman's role, written when she was seventy-nine.

The 900-page *Woman's Record,* subtitled *Sketches of All Distinguished Women from Creation,* attempts to identify every important woman and her accomplishment in history; it remains of substantial interest and stands as another singular monument to Mrs. Hale.

In her later years, she lived with her daughter, Frances Hale Hunter, wife of a Philadelphia physician, and worked from a home study. In December, 1877, her ninetieth year, she retired, and sixteen months later she died peacefully in her own bed.

Godey, himself, who was sixteen years younger, died shortly after he sold the magazine in 1877. *Godey's* actually lasted another twenty years, but never reached its peak again, which declined steadily after the Civil War. Godey, who had firmly banned all politically controversial topics from his magazine, ignored the war, including the call for Union nurses. Most people felt he did not want to offend his large Southern readership, although distribution was temporarily suspended in the South. And other magazines, such as *Peterson's Magazine, Atlantic,* and *Harper's,* had given him lively competition.

Sarah Hale seems to have been nationally revered to the end. The Hunter family remembers a constant stream of visitors to her room. And by the time she edited her farewell issue the status of women had vastly changed. The dainty quill pen of Sarah Hale had quietly helped to open many new opportunities for women, undreamed of when her career began.

Although critic Vernon Louis Parrington disparaged all the "cambric tea"[19] on which Sarah Hale fed her reading public, Helen Beal Woodward, disagreed; she noted that the cambric tea was, after all, "heavily slugged with the benzedrine of feminism."[20] Doubtless *Godey's* editor had, as biographer Finley wrote, "speeded the thought and progress of women of her time." The late pioneering historian of American journalism, Frank Luther Mott, observed that

Sarah Hale was not only a "notable literary figure" in her day, but that under her editorship *Godey's Lady's Book* was "transformed from a mediocre miscellany to a literary magazine of great importance."[21]

M. G. S.

# 5

## MARGARET FULLER
### *Critic and Foreign Correspondent*
### [1810–1850]

><><

That oracular editor of the New York *Tribune,* Horace Greeley, one of the giants of journalism in the nineteenth century, called Margaret Fuller "the most remarkable, and in some respects, the greatest, woman America has yet known."[1] She was an accomplished scholar, the country's first woman literary critic, and the first woman foreign correspondent. Miss Fuller, who was what is often termed "a walking encyclopedia," had an impressive classical education and was widely described by 1840 as "the most learned woman in the United States."[2] But it was "Uncle Horace," as an admiring American public called him, who claimed credit for pulling his protegé down out of the clouds and making an earthy journalist out of her.

She died tragically before her time at the age of forty in 1850, with perhaps her most promising work still ahead. Fortunately her writings are preserved in many books, including posthumous collections. A legendary figure of American letters, she has been the subject of numerous biographies and critical studies.

Sarah Margaret Fuller was born May 23, 1810, in Cambridgeport, Massachusetts, the oldest child of Margaret Crane and Timothy Fuller. Margaret's mother, a schoolteacher before her marriage, was a fragile, retiring woman, who bore nine children within sixteen years; apparently she was devoted to her husband, whose brilliance and iron will dominated their family life. Margaret's father was a prominent lawyer and politician, a member of the Massachusetts Senate and the United States Congress. At one time he pinned his ambitions for advancement, such as an appointment to a foreign ambassadorship, on his friend, John Quincy Adams; but later Fuller's high hopes were bitterly dashed.

A Unitarian and a Jeffersonian, he came by his rugged individualism naturally. Timothy Fuller's father, a country preacher, was so fiercely independent that he expounded Tory views from his pulpit during the Revolutionary War. When his congregation, including some patriotic Minute Men, forced him out of the church, he was not at all ashamed, but instead sued to recover his salary; even after he lost his case, he remained staunchly in the same community and reared his family on a farm. Son Timothy Fuller had to work his way through Harvard, but he graduated with honors in 1801.

Nine years later, as a practicing young lawyer, Fuller was disappointed that his first-born child was a girl. It was quickly evident, however, that Margaret was a prodigy, and so he undertook to compensate for his lack of a son, with overwhelming dedication, by giving her the rigorous classical education in the early nineteenth century usually thought worthy only of a boy. Taking charge of her life almost immediately out of infancy, the strict father saw to it that she was reading Latin by age six, including works by Virgil, Horace, and Ovid, and by age eight, Shakespeare. When not forced into her tortuous program of study, she was expected to be reading in her father's library of classics —authors like Smollett, Fielding, Cervantes and Molière. And in time she mastered Greek, Italian, French, and German. Trembling, sometimes late into the night, little Margaret was expected to recite before her father with gruelling perfection.

Small wonder that years later the grown Margaret was to look back in her diaries to recall a childhood filled with shrieking nightmares in which she was drowned in pools of blood, attacked by giants, or trampled by horses. With the best of intentions, in the tradition of fanatical Puritanical commitment, Fuller nearly drilled his young daughter to death.

When Margaret was fourteen, pale, harried, and sickly, he finally acknowledged that she might be wanting in recreational activities and peer companionship. He sent her forty miles away to a boarding school operated by the Misses Prescott. As might be expected, she was not prepared to relate to girls her own age. She was an arrogant leader who demanded loyal followers. She was tense, highstrung, and quarrelsome, and she even jealously slandered other students. Finally, she was summoned by the school administrators for a conference on her troublesome ways.

Fortunately the traumatic scene of confrontation led to a change of spirit in Margaret, largely as a result of guidance from a wise and compassionate teacher. After a period when Margaret was at first so contrite that she fell ill, and into a depression, she rallied enough to ask forgiveness from her schoolmates, and to set about drastically reforming herself. The resounding impact of this adolescent experience was later told in her autobiographical tale, "Mariana."

When she returned home after two years, a mature sixteen, Margaret soon found a place in Cambridge social life. Her unusual intelligence and knowledge, so readily expressed in her facile conversation, quickly won respect, especially among the young men of the Harvard Class of 1829, including the blossoming scholars Frederick Henry Hedge and James Freeman Clarke.

It was during that summer of 1826 that Timothy Fuller had the distinct honor of giving a memorable party in his own home for President Adams. Margaret, looking more like eighteen, attended, wearing a fine silk dress; her long blonde hair and compelling big eyes saved her from the otherwise plain appearance which she was to resent all her life. Ever mindful of her physical shortcomings, she was grateful when the popular wife of one Harvard professor, Mrs. Farrar, author of a book, *Manual for Young Ladies*, undertook to help polish Margaret's appearance and manners.

Actually the young Miss Fuller had begun to flourish in Cambridge intellectual groups when, abruptly in 1833,

Timothy Fuller moved his family to an isolated farm near Groton, Massachusetts. Unfortunately, Fuller had felt his career was at an end and he was ready for retirement at fifty-five. The election of Andrew Jackson had ruined his political aspirations, and the income from his law practice was never sizable, due largely to his strident personality. Thus he went to a tiny kingdom in exile where he was absolute ruler.

At twenty-three, in the prime of developing life, Margaret was crushed. She was cut off from Cambridge's bright world of culture and conversation to be buried in a rural village. She was left in loneliness, expected as the eldest and unmarried daughter to help run a house and farm, to tutor her younger and duller brothers and sisters. Her social and intellectual life had been sadly transformed.

Driven and discontented, she fell seriously ill with brain fever after just two years on the farm. Her mother managed to nurse her back to health, and even her father broke from his Puritanical stoicism long enough to show his concern and later his joy at her recovery; Margaret basked in the warm sunshine of this long-overdue and unexpected appreciation as her father's favorite child. Then, just as suddenly, Timothy Fuller died in 1835 from Asiatic cholera. Both Mrs. Fuller and Margaret were grief-stricken. But the eldest child knew she had to assume the position as head of the family, because her mother was not capable. Thus entrapped, Margaret, whose interests in life were in literature, languages, and the arts, suddenly began to instruct herself in practical business matters and to face the facts of the family's limited inheritance.

Meanwhile, her father's death led Margaret to a serious reevaluation of her position in religion. Already back in 1831 on a Sunday walk through the fields after church, she had a profound mystical experience, a sort of vision of being at one with God. "From that day on, she was never completely engaged in self," the biographer Wade has said, because a certain "meekness and love and patience" came to her.[3] During her period of grieving after 1835, she took consolation in the study of religion, especially Christianity.

In the summer of 1836 Margaret visited Ralph Waldo Emerson for several weeks, further exploring her personal philosophy. The Sage of Concord was much impressed by the gifted Miss Fuller, as his devoted friendship for the next fourteen years of her brief life was to prove.

With the need for money ever more apparent for the Fuller family, Margaret next accepted a position teaching languages at the progressive Temple School in Boston. This was Amos Bronson Alcott's famous, although short-lived, experiment in education. It was soon rejected as too radical for its day. For Alcott, personal development and self-knowledge were regarded as just as important as memorizing facts; and self-government was emphasized. When Alcott accepted a Negro pupil, his handful of supporting parents withdrew their children indignantly from the ill-fated school.

During her year in Boston, Margaret grew enthusiastic over Alcott's theories and regarded him as a fine educator. She also became acquainted with the distinguished preacher, Dr. William Ellery Channing, and often attended his Unitarian Church and read German literature and philosophy with him. He became another lifelong friend. In 1837 Margaret was offered a teaching post at the handsomely appointed new Greene Street School in Providence, Rhode Island, at the unprecedented high salary, for a woman at that time, of $1,000 a year. With only four hours of daily teaching expected of her, she found time to pursue her own studies again, as well as provide a better income for her family.

For the next two years, Margaret reigned in the Providence school as its "lady superior" and "guiding genius." She even managed to slip some of Alcott's ideas into her new environment.[4] It was also here that she heard an influential speech by John Neal, the novelist, on "the destiny and vocation of women in America," which nudged her to further "thinking along feminist lines." His talk helped to plant the seed for her classic book written just a few years later, *Woman in the Nineteenth Century.*[5]

Although Miss Fuller enjoyed exploring Providence, meeting new people, and exploring interests there, she frequently returned to see old friends and attend cultural events in her beloved Boston. She also kept busy translating Johann Eckermann's *Conversations with Goethe* for publication in a new library of foreign classics in English, edited by George Ripley. She was one of the few Americans living at that time who had an excellent command of German.

At the end of her two years in Providence, with her health showing strains from overwork, Margaret Fuller decided that teaching young children was not her annointed work. With some sadness, because she did enjoy her pupils, she said farewell and headed back to Boston. That summer of 1839 she rented a house in suburban Jamaica Plain and resolved to launch her fond new scheme of earning a living by free-lance writing and tutoring.

The times were ripe for Margaret to thrive in her career, during the golden 1840s of New England, especially in Boston. Transcendentalism was on the rise, an idealistic philosophy promoting the betterment of mankind, and its inner circle were her close friends. These Transcendentalists, Alcott, Channing, George and Sarah Dana Ripley, Theodore Parker, Elizabeth Peabody, Clarke, and the leading luminaries, Emerson and Thoreau, were broadly bound together by such beliefs as the innate goodness of man, the unity of all creation, and the importance of intuition and insight over mere logic and reason. Their eclectic sources included the German philosophers, Thomas Carlyle, Emmanuel Swedenborg, as well as Platonism, Neoplatonism, and Oriental scriptures. The group met together and held endless erudite discussions. Margaret was drawn into the elite circle at once and soon was appointed chief editor of their new literary magazine, *The Dial.*

In the winter of 1839 she began the celebrated program of "Conversations," which was to last five years. These were scintillating classes for women held in private homes, discussing and reading papers. Topics related to religion, philosophy, literature, and the arts, with Margaret presiding as the very Sibyl of the salon. Some of Boston's best families sent their mothers, wives, and daughters to attend and absorb the class's atmosphere. The classes, Miss Fuller declared, were designed to teach women to organize their thoughts and to speak clearly and precisely in expressing ideas. Not everyone approved of this "female pedantry," certainly not anyone who believed ladies should not be sullied by public matters, contemporary issues and politics, or voicing opinions outside their own parlors.[6]

For Margaret the "Conversations" created the stimulus which led her to write a piece of journalistic dynamite. Originally published as a magazine article in *The Dial*, her famous work on women's rights was first entitled, "The Great Lawsuit: Man versus Men, Woman versus Women." The first ripples from her article were somewhat contained, since the Transcendentalist magazine had a limited number of readers, many of whom already believed in equality of the sexes. The real shock waves came when she expanded the manuscript into book form later in 1845 and the popular market was flooded with her pioneering bible on feminism.

A rather mild tract for later generations, *Woman in the Nineteenth Century* argued that women were downtrodden and should receive an education and the same rights as men in order to develop their characters. "We would have every path laid open to Woman as Freely as to Man," she wrote, arguing that "inward and outward freedom for Woman as much as for Man shall be acknowledged as a right, not yielded as a concession." Rejecting rigid role-playing for the sexes, she declared, "Penelope is no more meant for a baker or weaver solely, than Ulysses for a cattle-herd."[7]

It was the first such book in America, however, and the first in English since the publication in England in 1792 of Mary Wollstonecraft's *A Vindication of the Rights of Women*. There had been limited attention to that work across the ocean in the United States. Before Margaret's controversial book on women's rights caused a public storm, however, her first and milder book published only the year before, as well as her work with *The Dial*, had caught the eye of editor Horace Greeley. Her *Summer on the Lakes*, accounting her experiences on a trip to the rolling prairies and farmlands of the new frontier West, including Illinois and Wisconsin, had greatly impressed him.

Her journalistic capacities for detailed observations and interviewing were displayed in her keen and colorful stories about her travels by horsedrawn wagons, boats, and hiking; and she talked with all kinds of ordinary folks, including deprived American Indians and the poor and anxious immigrants from Holland, Germany, and Ireland. Margaret had gotten away from the hothouse world of New England Transcendentalists and sat about campfires, climbed cliffs, shot the rapids in a canoe, laughed and lived.

Greeley, with his decisive eye for talent, asked this stirring Margaret Fuller to serve as the first woman literary critic on his *New York Tribune* staff. Indeed, he even invited her to move right into his own spacious home on Turtle Bay overlooking East River. And Mrs. Greeley regarded her houseguest as "the new goddess of intellect."[8]

In accepting Greeley's offer, Margaret Fuller was entering the rawer world of New York journalism and moving sharply away from "the Boston zanies," as the Transcendalists were unflatteringly called.[9] Her teas and talks were about to be replaced by active investigative journalism, even the coverage of war.

But there had always been an edge of realism in Margaret, who as a child resented being trapped in a too-bookish world, and who, as a young magazine editor, refused to follow the Transcendentalists all the way in their Utopian Brook Farm. She had had enough back-to-nature and manual labor on the old Groton farm experiment with her family. She placated her friends by short visits to their farms, which is how Nathaniel Hawthorne was able to study her and later model his unflattering character, Xenobia, on Margaret for his weakly disguised novel about Brook Farm. Her friends felt he maligned her memory and never forgave him.[10]

Thus, in 1844, Margaret, the brainy woman who was

widely reputed to know everything, reported to the *Tribune's* grubby third-floor office. Somewhat hesitant among the paper's tough male staff, she began her training under the merciless blue pencil of Greeley and the other editors. At first she felt insulted, but Margaret soon learned to write and rewrite.

Before she met Greeley, one of his biographers has declared, "she lived in a realm of introspection and disembodied ideas." Greeley told her that the fault with her writing was her study of "too much grandiose German," which at times made her newspaper copy "ponderous and fuzzy."[11]

For the first time she was "thrown into the world's daily stream," because her leader now was a man imbedded in social concerns, a crusader and reformer. Her perceptions were soon sharpened, and her writing was refined and enlivened with the hard-hitting stories assigned to her.[12] Greeley packed her off to interview women prisoners at Sing Sing about their lives and prison conditions and to observe the theories of penology in actual application. By her own offer she returned to spend a Christmas holiday among the "fallen women" there, and also addressed inmates in the chapel. Much to Greeley's delight she took as her focus the current notion: "Women, once lost, are far worse than abandoned men, and cannot be restored."[13] Nonsense, said Margaret, women were as capable as men of reform and new life. Greeley praised his star reporter for her dedicated hours with "the most degenerated and outcast of her sex"; where others might "deplore," his Margaret would "redeem," he said.[14] Swelling in pride, Greeley sent her off to Blackwell's Island and into the city's hospitals to study conditions there, too.

In part as a result of her general journalistic training, Margaret burst forth as the leading American literary critic of her day, second to no one and equalled only by Edgar Allen Poe. Contemporary critics, looking back over her work, have praised it as "penetrating," "original," and "honest"; she eschewed the "pussy-footing and puffing" characteristic of the times.[15]

Without fear or favor, she produced critical analyses of

works by such major figures as Elizabeth Barrett Browning, Alfred Tennyson, Henry Wadsworth Longfellow, Ralph Waldo Emerson, Nathaniel Hawthorne, James Russell Lowell, and William Cullen Bryant. Her decision to speak her mind was all the more remarkable in a day when displeasing reviews could be dangerous for newspapers. Earlier Greeley had to pay James Fenimore Cooper $200 damages for an unfavorable review of *Leatherstocking Tales.* Yet she bearded literary lions like Longfellow, Lowell, and Bryant; on the other hand she was among the earliest to perceive the lasting significance of Hawthorne and Mrs. Browning.

With her own rich background in languages and literature, she also did much to introduce such foreign authors as Goethe, Balzac, and George Sand to American readers. Today her work is "regarded as one of the high water marks in American criticism before 1850."[16]

So celebrated a figure was Greeley's houseguest, so overwhelming the number of admiring callers, that Margaret sometimes had difficulty getting to the *Tribune* office and meeting her deadlines. Greeley, however, who certainly did "adore" her, as did his little son, "Pickie," tried to be tolerant of this failing and also of her headaches and sickly spells.[17]

Greeley promoted Margaret Fuller in numerous ways: attending social functions with her, conversing long hours into the night in his home with her, backing the publication of her book on women's rights, and seeing that her articles were prominently positioned in the *Tribune.* Yet he loved to tease her. "Let them (women) be Sea Captains if they will!" he would ring out, quoting *Woman of the Nineteenth Century.*[18] Greeley's biographer, Hale, said that "Uncle Horace" felt very strong emotional as well as intellectual ties with Margaret, the more so because he and his wife, Mary, were not especially compatible.

Nonetheless, during this period Margaret had what critics generally agree to be the first important romance in her love-deprived life. The romance was with James Nathan, a young businessman. Unfortunately he proved to be a cad, whose true interest was in using her influential name and position and later even in attempting to extract money in exchange for returning her passionate love letters.

The Nathan affair was a humiliating experience for Margaret who, in her usual generous way, had blindly devoted herself to someone for whom she cared. She was saved from slumping into another depression by her many friends; it was Greeley himself who encouraged her, in the summer of 1846, to take her long-dreamed-of first trip to Europe. In fact he appointed her "the first woman foreign correspondent in America," which meant welcome financial assistance, and promised that her job as literary critic would await her return.[19] That same year her much-respected work, *Papers on Literature and Art*, a collection of *Tribune* writing, also appeared.

Sailing on the *Cambria*, Margaret landed in England and was welcomed at once among intellectuals there and in Scotland. She talked with notables, such as Thomas Carlyle, and saw the usual tourist sights, castles, zoos, gardens, famous birthplaces, and attended lectures, theater, concerts, museums, and art galleries; she talked with myriads of natives and even rode down to see a coalmine. Then she was on to France and Italy, where she had similar adventures, including her visit to the French feminist and novelist, George Sand and her lover, the musician, Frederic Chopin. Many of her adventures were the subjects of her lively "letters," as news correspondence was then often called, in the *Tribune*. Most of these were later collected posthumously in *At Home and Abroad*, edited by her brother, Arthur Buckminster Fuller.

It was in Rome that she met the handsome Marchese Giovanni Angelo d'Ossoli, ten years her junior, who became her lover in 1847. At 37, Margaret Fuller, who had been dismissed by many people as an unattractive spinster, seemed suddenly and miraculously lovely, transformed in appearance and manner by a man who truly seemed to love and appreciate her. Alas, Ossoli, however noble in lineage and goodness, was an impoverished soldier; Margaret's writings for the *Tribune* had to provide the stable economic support. Alas also, for his family, who were Italian and

Catholic, that Margaret was an American and Unitarian. So their eventual marriage took place secretly.

Sympathizing with the unrest of the mass of Italians and the popular uprising then brewing, Margaret and Ossoli devoted themselves to the cause of the Italian Revolution and its leader, the liberal patriot, Guiseppi Mazzini. Then when Margaret found she was expecting a child, she withdrew to the less turbulent scene of Rieti, fifty miles north of Rome, in May, 1848. Her son, Angelo, was born in September, and she returned to her husband in Rome, leaving the baby in safety with a nurse.

After the Roman Republic was proclaimed in February, 1849, and the French besieged the city in April, Margaret Fuller became director of an emergency hospital and helped to carry supplies to Ossoli's defense post. The Italian Revolution produced some of Margaret's most moving journalistic writing. Her *Tribune* "Letter XXXIII" printed on July 6, 1849, provides one example. "An inland city cannot long sustain a siege when there is no hope of aid," she wrote, describing the bombardment in which "the French were not ashamed to use bombs also, to kill women and children in their beds." When the Republic was overthrown later that very month, the Ossolis escaped to Rieti and claimed their child.

Next the family located for a time in Florence, where she worked on writing a history of the Roman Revolution, convinced it was her finest work to date. The Ossolis seemed a happy and congenial couple to friends like the poets, Robert and Elizabeth Browning, who knew them in this period.

For various reasons, however, Margaret determined to return to America. In part she needed to earn money to help support the three of them, and also she wanted to arrange publication of her new manuscript. Despite strange forebodings about the proposed voyage, the Ossolis borrowed $300 on a 100-day note and booked cheap passage on the *Elizabeth*, a merchantman. They sailed from Leghorn on May 17, 1850. The voyage was relatively uneventful, except that the captain died of smallpox and son Angelo, after being infected with the same disease, survived; Margaret worked on her manuscript, and passed her 40th birthday.

On the last night of the voyage, sometime in the early hours of July 19th after the passengers had retired, a raging gale blew up, and the *Elizabeth* was driven onto a sandbar off Fire Island. The heavy cargo of marble caved through the ship's bottom, and the boat lurched, water pouring in. The boat broke into pieces on the rocks and was swept away, with only a few survivors. The fierce winds and enormous waves had made any real rescue attempt impossible.

Only dead little Angelo was washed ashore. Margaret and Ossoli were never seen again. Her prized last manuscript was never found. The child's body was buried at Mount Auburn Cemetery in Cambridge and a monument erected there to the three of them. The portion of lines on Margaret read:

> *"Margaret Fuller*
> *In Riper Years*
> *Teacher, Writer, Critic of Literature, and Art.*
> *In Maturer Age*
> *Companion and Helper of Many*
> *Earnest Reformer in America and Europe"*

Distinguished friends mourned her untimely passing and immediately began to write in memorial praise of both her and her work. Succeeding generations of critics have not yet ceased adding laurels to the reputation of Margaret Fuller.

M. G. S.

# 6

## CORNELIA WALTER
### *Editor of the Boston Transcript*
### [1813–1898]

><><

Edgar Allen Poe called her a "pretty little witch." A fellow
Boston editor called her "the brilliant lady editor of the
*Transcript*," and her paper eulogized her as being "in all
things fearless, and with no thought save the public good."
Somewhere in between stood Cornelia Wells Walter, at age
twenty-nine the first woman to edit a daily newspaper in
America. Holding the editorship of the *Boston Transcript*
for five years, she supported cultural and literary developments in Boston, urged consideration of abolition of slavery, worked for civic improvements, and took stands
which, though not always popular, she believed in.

Cornelia Walter was born June 7, 1813, to Boston merchant Lynde Walter and his English wife Ann Minshull.
The seeds of her journalistic career were initially sown on
July 24, 1830, when her older brother, Lynde M. Walter,
established the *Transcript*. An evening daily, it was published by Henry Dutton and James Wentworth and, like its
contemporaries, was very important to the mercantile interests of the port of Boston. When Lynde Walter developed
cancer in 1840 his twenty-seven-year-old sister took her
place in the family home on Belknap Street as companion,
nurse, secretary, and unacknowledged assistant editor,
working at his side and quietly submitting items from her
home.[1] She would continue working mostly from her home
when she formally assumed the editorship.

At Lynde's death July 24, 1842, exactly twelve years
after the first issue of the *Transcript*, the publishers approached Cornelia's father with the proposal that she

become editor. The idea of a woman editor was unheard of at that time. To be editor was to be associated with office work, to become involved in a world that was "supposed to belong to men by divine right."[2] Consequently, when she accepted the position, she requested anonymity. She was destined not to remain anonymous long; and though she initially experienced "no little antagonism," she succeeded "to the satisfaction of all concerned, to the advantage of the people, and to her own credit."[3]

A woman of "unusual beauty, warmth, and dignity," Miss Walter was also a retiring individual and chose to work from her home during her five-year editorship. A biographer describes her "remarkable powers of mind, a keen perception, a great force and vigor of expression, and, withal, a peculiar womanliness which gives a light and graceful touch to her trenchant and fearless pen."[4]

She early showed her courage. Despite her great respect for her dead brother and for the way he had conducted the *Transcript,* she began moving away from his weak, noncommital attitude toward abolition and slavery. On August 3, 1842, she ran a report from Philadelphia on a race riot there and concluded, "The *Gazette* says that the ferocity of the white mobbists was beyond all precedent." The next day she described the aftermath of the riots and the plight of black citizens who had been victimized, terrorized, and left homeless.

A year later she excerpted from the weekly abolitionist paper, the *Northern Picayune* of New York, a visiting reporter's anecdotes on cruel treatment of blacks in Boston by white people of that city. And in the same issue she carried a letter from the Lexington (Kentucky) *Intelligencer,* under the headline "Slavery Denounced by the Son of a Slaveholder."[5] A few days later, her courage and her quick wit caused her to append the following comment to an article titled "Negroes Rising," by the *Richmond Enquirer's* New Orleans correspondent. The reporter wrote, in that July 4 issue, that the cost of slaves would certainly be rising, "as the demand will be unusually great," and quoted expected prices. Miss Walter's comment: "rather a queer day for writing about *such* an article."[6] But she was not a firm abolitionist, however keen her perception of the unfairness and general cruelty of the slave system. In early 1844, for example, she dismissed the possibility of immediate emancipation, which had been urged in a New York representative's proposal to the United States House a few days earlier. Her reasoning: "There is no danger that the North ever would be in favor of an immediate abolition of slavery—nine hundred ninety-nine out of a thousand of Northern people would go against it. It must, if done at all, be done gradually, discreetly, so as not to be injurious to our interests."[7]

Yet she kept edging toward support of abolition. Writing in May, 1844, about John Greenleaf Whittier, she called him a poet and a friend of abolitionists, and said of his work or his works collectively that they were "true *then*—and they are true *now*." In June she carried in full the minutes of a meeting of the Colored Citizens of Boston, including a resolution for abolition of separate schools for colored children. Unlike several of her contemporaries in the American press, she did not exclude news of black citizens.

A striking contrast can be made between the editor of the *Transcript* and the editor of the now famous New York *Sun*. The latter gentleman, when approached by Willis Hodges with a reply to an editorial proposing curbing black suffrage in New York state, responded through an underling, "The *Sun* shines for all white men and not for colored men," and said that if Hodges wanted the black cause advocated, he could start his own paper.[8] Hodges did just that, and the *Ram's Horn* was the outlet in New York, just as Walter's paper was an outlet in Boston.

Other letters and commentary were to follow. For instance, a May 29, 1845, notice of an antislavery convention, with this comment appended: "We insert the above by particular request, and think with the writer that reform is advisable in what he alludes to." The editor was moving slowly toward greater awareness of slavery as a cruel institution and the following day published her strongest statement on the institution. Having completed a reading of the autobiography of Frederick Douglass, a distinguished black writer and orator for the abolitionist cause, she predicted the imminent dawn of the "sun of liberty" upon black citizens. And she took her stand:

> The time is past when men can fold their hands and say with truth, we are neutral in the matter. A course, high and holy in its purpose, the merits of which have been presented a thousand times to the minds of all classes . . . now renders this state of things impossible, and the excuse of ignorance or neutrality can no longer be presented.[9]

She saw selfishness at "open war" with "charity and generosity" and espoused Douglass' arguments for freedom for the black race. Finally, as a professional writer and hence a critic of the literary works she discussed, she called the autobiography a "well written history," and, from someone self-educated at peril of the overseer's lash, "an extraordinary performance."

Readers got an additional dose of information on the slavery issue that same day. Without any comment, she cited a report from the New Orleans *Picayune*. A mulatto boy, accused of stealing a watch, had been imprisoned and lashed twenty-five times daily, until he was a mass of "raw, trembling skinless, putrid lacerated flesh." He lay in the police jail until an old black man, owned by the same master as the child, came to carry him home. Finally a doctor examined the little prisoner and had him sent to a hospital.

No comment was affixed. But served up in juxtaposition with the Douglass piece, it left readers no doubt as to where the editor stood on the matter. Her stand on this and other issues motivated a later *Transcript* editor, writing a eulogy in 1898, to say of her: "Careful to consider deliberately, to look at all sides of a question before forming an opinion, she burned her bridges once a conclusion had been reached. To use her own words, she had "nothing but contempt for an editor who was careful to leave a loophole for retreat.' "[10]

Cornelia Walter took on other issues with the same

determination. In her first month as editor she wrote of physicians, some good, to be sure, but some "vile quacks who impose on the ignorant and credulous," tampering with the lives and well-being of the populace. She expressed a hope that the "ablest talent" would aspire to the medical profession, thus counteracting "those famous homocides."[11] Three days later, perhaps not intentionally related, she editorialized that an honest man is "firm as a rock, bold as a lion, mild as a lamb, wise as a serpent, harmless as a dove, *and as rare as a phoenix.*" Other issues and concerns on which she took editorial stands included what she saw as the exhorbitant prices charged for fruit and the resultant waste when fruits, too costly to purchase, were thrown away rotten; the dust on Charles Street, and the discomfort and embarrassment caused to Boston's citizens and visitors by the condition of its main thoroughfare; and the need for artesian wells, "which would enhance the health, comfort, and convenience" of Bostonians.[12]

Though she espoused causes which she was convinced were right and justified, Miss Walters was, overall, a conservative editor. Herself a well-read person, she strongly opposed much of the "cheap literature" flooding the market at the time, produced by entrepreneurs more interested in profit than in quality of content or appearance. She said that much of the cheap literature was "engendering a love of ephemeral, light and superficial reading," but acknowledged the value of the availability of inexpensive works of history, science, and philosophy. The cheap literature question had several sides, she acknowledged, and if people could be served and publishers remunerated through mass distribution of good materials, all well and good. A few months later, quoting the New York *Express* on the same topic, she concluded with her own remark: "Cheap literature is desirable, but not so cheap as we have had it of late." Because she was a book lover, and she felt that "No book is worth reading that is not worth keeping," she wanted books printed and bound with some thought to posterity.[13]

On a related note, Miss Walter read a wide collection of exchange newspapers and, in accordance with the practice of the day, quoted generously from them. Upon occasion she commented on the performance of fellow editors. Thus in 1842, she warned that editors "are in danger of converting their Journals into mere puffing machines," mere promoters of products and causes. She called attention to a humorous and, perhaps, extreme example: in a marriage announcement for the eleventh of fourteen daughters, the long-suffering father had evidently prevailed upon the editor to include the fact that he had three more unmarried daughters, "all of whom might bid fair to ... make good companions." Her observation: "We never before saw the marriage list converted into a medium for puffing the single daughters."[14]

But on a more serious note, she agreed with the sentiments expressed by the King of Prussia in an address to the Presidents of the Provinces, from which she quoted extensively in early January, 1843. The king called for punishments against journals that published falsehoods, sanctions that would somehow force journalists to rectify the injuries their falsehoods caused. While not pressing for censorship per se, Miss Walter wrote, "*Something* of the kind would not, we think, be amiss in this country."

A day earlier, in her new-year statement, traditional for editors of the time, she had made her first formal statement of editorial policy, and had promised: "It will sometimes be our misfortune to offend; but we shall be studiously observant of our phraseology, and especially cautious that the offense is in the opinion, and not in terms of its conveyance." Her conservatism was reflected in her opposition to the abolition of capital punishment. "We like reform," she wrote in May, 1845, "but whilst we acknowledge this, we believe the reforming spirit may be carried *much* too far." Besides, she reasoned, a sentence to life-in-prison might harden the heart, making it callous to repentance, negating any opportunity for reconciliation with one's Maker.[15]

Yet despite her conservatism, she included continued and sympathetic coverage of the Irish cause. She carried frequent letters from and reports about Irish rebel leader

Daniel O'Connell, a controversial policy for Boston in the 1840s with its large Irish and British populations. The Mormons, however, a controversial and often persecuted group, were given continued coverage, though without any of the sympathy or acceptance accorded other groups. But the Mormons for her were clearly a religious aberration and their practice of polygamy an odious departure from the norm. In quoting from a correspondent's private journal of a summer, 1843, tour of Mormon settlements at Montrose and Nauvoo, Illinois, she labeled the towns "One of the most dangerous communities that ever sprang up in this country." She also included the journal writer's sentiments against allowing the settlements to exist unmolested.[16]

Her religious sentiments and loyalties also made the editor unsympathetic to woman's rights as a political position. In 1843, however, she openly espoused female colleges and seminaries, which, she wrote regretfully, "are scarcely known in the Eastern States."

Regardless of her position on women's suffrage and activism, she was not opposed to inserting items by female writers. Poetry and essays appeared with regularity, as did letters. One by "Senex" decried the fact that though "the lords of creation, in a most disproportionate ratio, have departed for the promising West," and thus were not available as escorts, restrictions against women going out alone were tighter than ever. "To wait upon a lady, is now voted a decided bore," she complained. Yet women were still prisoners to silly conventions. A few days later, one "Jasper" countered with the complaint that ladies were "so reserved and ceremonious that I had supposed they did not wish young men to *intrude* by offering their services."[17]

Cornelia Walter apparently had the companionship necessary to participate in Boston's cultural and intellectual life. Her first-hand accounts of literary and artistic events were rich with enthusiasm—and, at times, caustic. In fact, her review of the works and performances of Edgar Allen Poe were often biting. A much-publicized appearance at the Boston Lyceum October 16, 1845, was followed next day by a *Transcript* article which called his appearance "a failure," and "The Raven" which he read "a composition probably better appreciated by its author than by his auditory." A further comment October 18 criticized Poe for reading before the Lyceum a poem which he had, she said, composed before the age of twelve, the editor having gleaned that bit of erroneous information about "The Raven" from "those who know."

Responding to frequent jibes thereafter, Poe attacked Miss Walter in early November, 1845, in his *Broadway Journal*, calling her "that most beguiling of all little divinities," and a "pretty little witch." He also lampooned Boston, called its inhabitants "Frogpondians," and said he was ashamed to admit he had been born in Boston.

The verbal battle enjoined, the two writers kept at each other. On January 7, 1846, Miss Walter ridiculed the poet upon the failure of his paper:

> *The Broadway Journal's proved no go—*
> *Friends would not pay the pen of Poe.*

Later, she called the poet "a wandering specimen of the Literary Snob," and ventured that: "Whenever seen in print his falsehoods are ever met by the reader with the simple explanation—poh!—Poe!" Her opinion of Poe echoed that of the New England literary establishment, and she published in the *Transcript* on May 25, 1846, news that the trustees of the Boston Lyceum had publicly denounced Poe and his work in their annual report. From then on, Miss Walter dropped the subject and did not mention the poet's name until December 31 of that year, when she wrote that several eastern newspapers had reported his grave illness. The *Bostonian*, the New York *Home Journal*, and other papers launched fund drives to support his treatment and recovery. Such, she commented, was as it should be. But then she cited New York *Tribune* accounts of his steady recovery and his return to writing, and urged that he get a grip on himself and avoid the circumstances which had led to his ill health, remembering "his *duty to himself*, as a man and as a *writer*."

It was not only to Poe that she turned her critical

literary eye. Ralph Waldo Emerson also came in for his share of barbs in early February, 1844. After a full account of an Emerson lecture on "Young American: or the Peculiar Social Aspect and Destiny of America," Walter wrote that she was disappointed. The lecture, she said, needed a "more strict adherence to his theme, and a more positively *practical* bearing." She further attacked the "insupportable theories" of "original thinkers," who were not always "practical men," a generally accepted criticsm.

Yet, three months later, she cited Emerson in support of the Lyceum movement as a catalyst for the discussion of ideas, a place "where he who had anything to utter might utter it freely; where almost any topic was in place."[18]

The theme of innovation and fresh ideas had been considered earlier that year in a comment on poetry by James Russell Lowell. Miss Walter applauded "reform and improvement made where they are needed, and this thoroughly and carefully." But she disapproved of having the world "torn to pieces," and saw Lowell doing that. Unlike his colleagues in the literary establishment, she criticized Lowell. "He pours out his rhymes too fast; he does not condense enough," she wrote. To her, he embodied a greater danger: "We have the fear that our American literature is growing a little *too* fast."[19]

Despite her literary conservatism and even snobbery, Miss Walter was an American, the daughter of pioneers. In a comment on a registry of the wealthy in Philadelphia she reflected her pride in an ancestry that had meant the hard work of development and colonization. Called *A Curious Book*, the registry listed and offered biographies of all Philadelphia residents and properties worth $50,000 and more. Noting the spread of such directories, the editor remarked that, though in natural history small chestnuts might grow into mighty oaks, yet the wealthy "blush to see their parents registered as the offspring of honest tradesmen, butchers, tailors, grocers and the like." As a result, she lamented, young people did not learn to honor "a virtuous though ignoble ancestry."[20]

In addition to the many issues and potential controversies with which she involved herself as editor of the *Transcript*, Miss Walter also made the paper a faithful record of the times. To meet the mercantile needs of Boston merchants, she carried the front page full of advertisements, arrival and departure schedules of steamships and freighters serving Boston harbor, minutes of meetings of the Massachusetts legislature, the agricultural export report, extensive advice on gardening, and such consumer items as the availability of fresh strawberries. The *Transcript* also did regular coverage of fashion, though the editor at times questioned the wisdom of some of the fashions touted.

The *Transcript* reported fires and alarms, railroad and mill accidents, murders, robberies and arrests, and, particularly in winter, reports of weather in various parts of the state. Herself a writer, she also included frequent treatises on writing and writers, as much to indulge her own interest as to promote a love for writing among her readers.

At times her columns contained humor and wit. Shortly after she became editor, she quoted a seasick Englishman who, on a choppy sea, was overheard saying, "If Britannia rules the waves, I wish she'd rule 'em straighter." The captions for one-paragraph items, which appeared in almost every issue, usually signaled Miss Walter's reaction to them. Thus a story about an unnamed gentleman who bought twenty dozen spelling books to distribute to the children of his country was labeled "Commendable." Headed "Painful" was an account from New York of a young woman whose hand was crushed in a steam-powered printing press. Under the title "Another Warning" was run the story of how a three-year-old was shot accidentally by an older playmate. And labeled "A Heroine" was a story that told of a serving girl who, with quick wit, lured a would-be silver thief into a pantry and locked him there till help could be called.[21]

Like other newspapers of the period, the *Transcript* also carried extensive correspondence from and about other countries. The young nation had not yet forgotten that other important worlds lay outside its boundaries, and so Walter reported on developments at the British and French courts as well as on issues being considered in Sweden, Prussia, China, and Japan. She also used generous amounts of news from states outside Massachusetts, and at times used columns from traveling correspondents in Rome and London. In July, 1846, a correspondent wrote extensively from northern Wisconsin, Michigan, Minnesota, Oswego (New York), and Montreal. Another communicated "street scenes from New York City." She herself spent an extended period one summer in Ipswich and reported from there via letters "To Him Who Sits in the Elbow Chair," the chair her brother had occupied in his days at the *Transcript* and now used by the newspaper's publisher.

Though she was conservative in ideas and philosophy, she was not afraid to write about and use innovations. She offered detailed descriptions of such inventions as the piano, daguerreotype, and telegraphy. In fact, she used dispatches sent via "Magnetic Telegraph" in reporting an election in Delaware and stock prices in New York. She was, in short, interested in the world around her and was keenly aware of her role as editor in informing her readers about the ideas and happenings which concerned them.

In September, 1847, less than five years after she had assumed editorship of the *Transcript*, she resigned that position to marry William Boardman Richards, a Boston iron and steel merchant. When news of her resignation was made known, she received several offers from other newspapers, putting to rest any question of her recognized value and effectiveness as a journalist and as an editor. Indeed, Dutton and Wentworth, the publishers and owners of two-thirds of the paper, issued a statement September 1, 1847, saying in part: "It was a great experiment to place a lady as the responsible editor of a daily newspaper. She made the trial with fear and trembling, and her success has been triumphant .... As an editor, she was a woman of great resolution and high determination and when she took ground, no flattering tongue could dissuade her from her purpose."

Cornelia Walter Richards and her husband had five children; the retired editor devoted most of her time and

interest to raising these children. She contributed occasional articles to the *Transcript,* and involved herself in the
civic and cultural life of Boston. At her death January 31,
1898, twenty-one years after that of her husband, the *Transcript* praised her for her sense of honor: "the kind of honor
that leads men to accept defeat when victory may be had
by following paths which their consciences tell them are
devious." It was high praise for one's successors to offer.
Yet she, herself, probably wrote the most fitting and complimentary line in the inscription she requested for the
marker on her grave in Jamaica Plain, outside of Boston.
The simple legend reads, "Here lies one who tried to do her
duty."[22]

S. M.

# 7
## JANE GREY SWISSHELM
### *Abolitionist, Feminist, Journalist*
### [1815–1884]

"To live is to contend, and life is finished when contentions end," is how Jane Grey Swisshelm summarized her life and what it meant. The daughter of Scottish-Irish parents, left fatherless at the age of seven, threatened with tuberculosis in her early teens, and powerfully committed to Presbyterianism, she became a pioneer and crusader whose voice and pen were felt across the United States.

Jane Grey Cannon was born December 6, 1815, in the then frontier town of Pittsburgh, Pennsylvania. When her father died she was taught lace making and subsequently added to the family income by teaching the art, seated on the laps of her more mature pupils. When she was fourteen she took a position as a public school teacher in Wilkinsburg, a small town just outside of Pittsburgh. She also began painting for profit, once selling a piece for the then grand sum of five dollars. Her love of painting continued throughout her life, though she put it aside in the early years of her marriage because it interfered with her responsibilities as a housewife—the soups and breads were neglected too often.

The mismatched marriage, which began in 1836 and ended in 1857, was in trouble almost from the start. Hardy, handsome James Swisshelm was a Methodist, dominated by his widowed mother, and convinced that a wife's job was to put aside her preferences and strive to make him happy by doing what he wished. While he admired his wife's brains and abilities, he and his mother worked diligently to reform Jane, to convince her to use her talents in preaching Methodism and salvation. On the other hand, he encouraged her antislavery sentiments and the abolitionist writing she did and was the inspiration for her first serious journalistic efforts.

But in spite of his support, Jane Swisshelm felt trapped by a domineering mother-in-law and a religious incompatibility between herself and her husband. The frustration born of this unhappy marriage found an outlet in at least some of her many crusades. In her sixty-nine-year lifetime she was to become an abolitionist editor, one of the first female journalists to write for Horace Greeley's *New York Tribune*, the first woman to sit in the Senate press gallery in Washington, an enemy of alcoholism, a nurse in civil war hospitals, a fiercely anti-Indian crusader, and a feared and respected lecturer on women's rights, abolition, and temperance.

How would a woman born into religion and subjugation become the pace-setter Jane Swisshelm became? Even in later life she herself seemed amazed that "one who, in 1837, could not break the seal of silence" which her religion set upon woman "even to pray with a man dying of intemperance," could address the Minnesota Senate in session in 1862 "with no more embarrassment than as though talking with a friend in a chimney corner."[1] Some glimpse of the cause may be seen in Swisshelm's retrospective comment on her sublimated desires to be a painter:

> Where are the pictures I should have given to the world? Where are my records of the wrongs and outrages of my age; of the sorrows and joys; the trials and triumphs, that should have been written ... in the eloquent faces and speaking forms which everywhere presented themselves... ? Why have I never put on CANVAS one pair of those pleading eyes, which has garnered the woes of centuries?[2]

The woes and the pleadings of victims of slavery, learned in abstract terms in her childhood, became real to Jane Swisshelm in 1838 when she and her husband moved to Louisville, Kentucky. During the two years they remained in Louisville, she observed slavery firsthand. Here, also, she seems to have become committed to abolitionism. Though she continued to avoid public statements, she recognized the power of the press. But, as she wrote in her memoirs, "Even this was dreadful, as I must use my own name, for my articles would certainly be libelous. If I wrote at all, I must throw myself headlong into the great political maelstrom ... no woman had ever done such a thing, and I could never again hold up my head under the burden of shame and disgrace which would be heaped upon me."

Yet throw herself in she did and for well over three decades used the press to further every cause she believed in, from abolition to dress, from dietary improvements to women's rights. In the summer of 1842, when she was twenty-seven, her stories and rhymes began appearing in *The Dollar Newspaper* and *Neal's Saturday Gazette*, both of Philadelphia. Using the pen name Jennie Deans, she also wrote on abolition and women's rights for Pittsburgh's *The Spirit of Liberty*, published by Reece C. Fleeson. "My productions were praised," she wrote later, "and my husband was provoked that I did not use my own name. If I were not ashamed of my articles, why not sign them?"[3] Her own byline first appeared in 1844, over an antislavery piece in *The Spirit of Liberty*. When that paper was discontinued, she began writing for the *Pittsburgh Commercial Journal*.

The short-lived *Spirit of Liberty* was replaced in 1847 by the *Albatross*. Editor Charles Shiras asked Mrs. Swisshelm to become a regular contributor, but she reckoned that she could reach 500 readers in the *Journal* for every one in the *Albatross*. Besides, she reasoned, "In the one I reached the ninety and nine unconverted, while in the other I must talk principally with those who were rooted and grounded in the faith." She stayed with the *Journal*, regularly submitting work from her home.

The *Albatross*, however, ceased publication after a few months, leaving no abolitionist paper in Pittsburgh. With her husband's assent, she established the *Pittsburgh Satur-*

*day Visiter.*[4] The decision was not made lightly because editing a paper meant working in an office, a prospect she considered "remarkable and very painful." And, owing to the limited funds available for the abolitionist publication, it also meant using whatever facilities were offered, including office space with the handsome editor of the *Commercial Journal.* She knew the potential for gossip that arrangement could offer. She took the challenge, with her husband's approval however, and brought out the first edition of the *Visiter* on January 20, 1848.

The paper attacked slave catchers and the Fugitive Slave Law. It was adamant in its stance, and responded to one proslavery critic with the following poem:

> *Perhaps you have been busy*
> *Horsewhipping Sal or Lizzie,*
> *Stealing some poor man's baby,*
> *Selling its mother, may-be.*
> *You say—and you are witty—*
> *That I—and, 'tis a pity—*
> *Of manhood lack but dress;*
> *But you lack manliness,*
> *A body clean and new,*
> *A soul within it too.*
> *Nature must change her plan*
> *Ere you can be a man.*[5]

The *Visiter* was also a vehicle for occasional women's rights crusades. The editor's strategy, however, was moderate, almost elitist: education, legislation, suffrage for property holders. "Say nothing about suffrage elsewhere until it proved successful here," she advised in later years. Women should "make no claim which could not be won in a reasonable time. Take one step at a time."[6]

At the same time, the editor wrote, women should be wary of current fashions foisted on women. Only ninnies and consummate fools would wish to imitate the "fashion plate mongers" in their ridiculous and unhealthy garb, she said. Corsets interfered with proper breathing. Metal-rimmed hoop skirts injured children. Long voluminous skirts collected filth, and caught fire. The editor broadened her arena of advice in 1849 and 1850 in a weekly series of "Letters to Country Girls," on reading, diet, makeup, gardening apparel, cooking, laundering, dress, and a host of other topics. In a column titled "The Heart and Lungs," she wrote: "It provokes me to look at the pale-faced, hollow-eyed, hour-glass-shaped concerns that might have been women if they had been brought up to it; and nursed their granddaughter's baby . . . instead of sliding into a suicide's grave at twenty."[7] The series, widely reprinted, was edited and published in book form in 1853, an early effort at freeing women from many of the superstitions and ignorances which she perceived to be part of female existence.

In another innovation with wider consequences, Mrs. Swisshelm asked then Vice President Millard Fillmore for a seat in the Senate press gallery while she was in Washington to cover the vote on slavery for the Mexican territory. He agreed, not without trying to dissuade her, and on April 21 and 22, 1850, she joined the press corps in the gallery. She was then representing both the *Visiter* and Horace Greeley's *New York Tribune,* and she sold her "Washington Letters" to Greeley for five dollars a column.

Her days there were numbered, however. In keeping with her tendency to inaccuracy and sensationalism when these suited her crusading purposes, she gossiped in a *Tribune* column that Daniel Webster had fathered a family of mulattoes. She knew the furor it would raise and that publication might endanger her position as a correspondent for the *New York Tribune.* Because it was good antislavery copy, which could influence the outcome of the upcoming presidential nominations, she printed it in a *Visiter* column. Two weeks later she retracted and the *Tribune* apologized in print. But observers have credited that story with Webster's defeat for the 1852 Whig nomination.[8]

Her early impression of Washington was of a dirty, snobbish place populated by slave catchers and woman oppressors, "the very worst place in the country in which to make any great pioneer movement in reference to women's social position."[9] And yet she was later to spend the best part of two and a half years there in humanitarian and journalistic work.

Meanwhile she did not neglect the Pittsburgh paper. It was merged, for financial reasons, in 1852 into the *Family Journal and Visiter* and she became associate editor, continuing her crusade for the abolition of Negro and women slavery. The latter reality was becoming painfully real to her because her husband considered her his property and had become embittered over her mother's will, which left property to her and not to her husband. His position was supported by law, so Swisshelm began a crusade in the press for women's property rights. She found support from a young attorney, Edwin M. Stanton, who admired her writing and told her so. Much later, as Secretary of War, he was to come to her aid in Washington.

But she could not escape the growing unhappiness in her marriage and, in 1857, she resigned from the *Visiter* and left her husband in Swissvale, Pennsylvania. Taking her six-year-old daughter, Mary Henrietta, the freedom-loving journalist moved to Minnesota with dreams of building a cabin in the wilderness outside of St. Cloud. Dissuaded by relatives who feared reprisals from Indians forced off their long-held tribal lands, she settled in town and was soon back in the newspaper business.

In soliciting advertising support for the new St. Cloud *Visiter*, she was offered the backing of General Sylvanus B. Lowry, a southern Democrat, who supported slavery. She quickly accepted, but used his financial backing to oppose slavery. In an ironically written endorsement of Lowry's presidential candidate, James Buchanan, she predicted on February 18, 1858, that under Buchanan's leadership, "the Democratic party is likely to succeed in reducing all the poor and friendless of this country to a state of slavery." And the fight was on.

Lowry supporter James C. Shepley, a Democratic lawyer in Minnesota, was asked to give a public lecture attacking "strong-minded women." His remarks were clearly aimed at the abolitionist editor, and she retaliated on March 18, commenting that Shepley had failed to mention one kind of strong-minded woman, "frontier belles who sat up all night playing poker with men." Shepley, enraged at this undisguised attack on his wife, responded with vigilante-style action. The *Visiter* press was wrecked, and some of the type was thrown into the river. Mrs. Swisshelm then printed an account of the attack, blaming Lowry for instigating and participating in it.

Though public support was in her favor, a lawsuit put her newly repaired press out of business—but only temporarily. August 5, 1858, saw the first issue of the St. Cloud *Democrat*, in which she pledged that "the paper we edit will discuss any subject we have a mind. . . . If these fellows destroy our office again, as they now threaten to do, we will go down to Hennepin County and publish the St. Cloud *Democrat* there."

Slavery was a major issue with the fiery journalist, but by no means the only one. Her unhappy marriage and the inequities facing married women by law led her to agitate for reform of laws unfair to wives and widows. Life on the frontier had made obvious to her the need for railroads, and she promoted them, while arguing that landowners should not be paid exhorbitant prices for properties bought for rail lines.[10] Learning of a disastrous Penn Central wreck shortly after the line was opened, she editorialized that the way to keep one train from running into another was to have a red light at the rear of each train. "The suggestion was accepted immediately," she wrote in her memoirs, "and this is the origin of the red light signal."

Her fears for her safety in Minnesota influenced her opinion of Indians and prompted her angry and often sensational reports about "those red-jawed tigers whose fangs are dripping with the blood of the innocents."[11] Her anti-Indian campaign was slowed somewhat in the war years. Sent to Washington to urge Abraham Lincoln to order speedy executions of thirty-four Sioux Indians captured while avenging white incursions on their lands, she visited the wounded Union troops and wrote about their deplorable conditions.

While she traveled to and fro, she filed frequent columns, editorial letters in which she portrayed the country through which she journeyed and the people she met. These letters included current gossip, strong emphasis on antislavery sentiments, and frequent references to the Scriptures. Her letters also reveal that she perceived herself as terribly frail but terribly courageous, virtuous to a fault, and happy to realize it.

In addition, her columns were filled with advice on how people should live and think. She liked fenced towns, tidy appearances: "Mantorville (Minn.) has fences and looks as if the people intended to stay there," she wrote April 12, 1860. She prefered simplicity in table settings, objecting to the Minnesota penchant for "sauce plates: half a dozen plates, one for oysters, one for fowl and potato, one for cabbage. . . ." Put them all on one plate, she preached, as is done in Pennsylvania.[12] And as to what should be on the plates, she called for "well-baked bread," as opposed to "hot soda dough" as served in New England.

The combat with Lowry, Shepley, and company had led to her first public speech, and from then on she lectured frequently around the country on such topics as "Women and Politics," "Slavery as I Have Seen It in a Slave State," "Women in the War of Rebellion," and "The Indian Massacres of Minnesota; The Wrongs of the Poor Indian and What Should be Done with Him." According to one critic, her self-confidence grew with her publicity.

"She seems never to have been conscious of a mistake,"[13] one biographer wrote, and held opinions, once formed, in the face of strong counter arguments. It took her a long time to support Lincoln, and even what support she gave was grudging. She originally considered him inept and unworthy, a man bent on using the war to his benefit and emanicaption as a tool in his own aggrandizement.

But even a determined Jane Swisshelm was gradually won over by Lincoln and his wife. In her commentary immediately after his assassination, she wrote that she had feared his leniency and magnanimity: "Honest, upright, single-minded and living in a community where crime is the exception, he was utterly unable to realize the total depravity and vindictive barbarism of slaveholders as a class, and I have always feared that his long-suffering with these irreclaimable sinners would prolong the war until the patience of the North would be exhausted and a disgraceful peace made."[14]

Beyond the ideologies and politics surrounding the war, Mrs. Swisshelm kept before her readers the day-to-day realities of the conflict. She told of human foibles and magnanimous courage. And she seemed to be trying to make a Union victory everybody's business. During the early days of the war, she urged in her columns that the state's womenfolk use their handiwork to provide the Minnesota regiment with clothing, blankets, soap, and simple sewing kits. She criticized the bright red caps some wore as making them easy targets. She advised on their raingear and diet, and shared farewell scenes as witnessed at the Minnesota camps.

In June, 1863, she visited Washington hospitals and wrote, "I want whiskey . . . to wash feet, and thus keep up circulation . . . pickles . . . lemons . . oranges. No well man or woman has a right to a glass of lemonade. We want it all in the hospitals to prevent gangrene."[15] Not only did she urge public contributions to the war hospitals but she also published criticism of them. A *Tribune* article on lice in the beds of a self-proclaimed model hospital led to her dismissal there from her post as volunteer nurse. Reflecting later on the incident, Swisshelm wrote: "Nobody denied the truth of my statements about Douglas Hospital, and I never learned that any one objected to the facts or their continuance. It was only their exposure which gave offense."[16]

While in Washington, Swisshelm secured a job in the War Department, partly owing to her earlier acquaintance with Secretary of War Edwin M. Stanton. There she had the opportunity to view at first hand a good many females who had little preparation or aptitude for office work. She wrote disdainfully of women who used their feminine attractiveness to aid their advancement and said that the serious woman should leave her feminine charms at home.

This is not to suggest that she was an envious plain Jane, jealously downplaying other women's good looks. Indeed, the *Minnesota Pioneer* described her, in 1850, as "quite a Jenny Lind in appearance ... with an unusual expanse of forehead, dark brown hair, combed over her temples, light blue eyes, nose rather prominent, mouth small disclosing very fine teeth ... countenance pleasing, and smile truly enchanting."

Although she was attractive, the hard-working editor did what she could to look plain. She expected the same of the women she hired. In addition, she expected and demanded competence, and once refused to hire a woman whose vest-making business was failing and who wanted to start a new career.

"I want the women whom the work wants, not those who want the work," she insisted. "Do not let your generosity run away with your judgment," she advised, in helping women find jobs.[17]

At the same time, her pioneer spirit fought traditional constraints and what she saw as unfair practices. So when she could not afford to pay printers union wages, she learned the trade and trained her female assistants as typesetters. From 1858 to early 1863 she was both editor and practical printer, issued a paper a week, did a large amount of job work, was city and county printer for half a dozen counties, and published legal notices, tax lists, and Extras.

Though she sold the *Democrat* to her nephew in June, 1863, she continued to write for it. Following the war, she agreed to edit a new paper, the *Reconstructionist*, which first appeared in Washington in December, 1865. Her strong criticism of President Andrew Johnson was so severe, however, that she soon lost her job in the War Department and with it her income. The *Reconstructionist* folded, too, and she returned to her early family home in Swissvale, Pennsylvania, claiming ill health and fatigue.

But the last had not been seen and heard of Jane Grey Swisshelm. A biographer noted that whenever she became aware of incidents which fit her "anti-Catholic, anti-Indian, or pro-woman rights campaigns,"[18] she took up her pen and fired off columns, usually to the New York *Independent*. In 1880 she published her recollections and reminiscences of *Half a Century*, as much an ode to life as she wished it were as a report on a life as she felt she had lived it. She died July 22, 1884, at the age of sixty-eight, a crusader and an innovator whom the Pittsburgh *Commercial Gazette* eulogized as "one of the leading characters of the century."[19]

S. M.

# 8

## JANE CUNNINGHAM CROLY
### *Jennie June, Women's Advocate*
### [1829–1901]

><><

Her brother observed that "Thousands of gifted women are now making themselves heard in poetry, dissertation, fiction and journalism because Jennie June opened the path for them."[1] The New York *Times* labeled her the "best known" woman journalist in America. Mid-nineteenth century women found in her a champion for their concerns. For over four decades her articles in metropolitan newspapers and magazines attracted wide readership, ranging as they did from diet to dress to working women's experiences.

An innovator and reformer, Jennie June[2] established both the first women's club and the New York Women's Press Club, was among the first women to syndicate her material, campaigned in print for sensible fashions and better eating habits, wrote several important books, and taught journalism and literature.

Jennie was born Jane Cunningham on December 19, 1829, in Market Harborough, Leicestershire, England, the daughter of an unpopular Unitarian minister. Reverend Joseph H. Cunningham's strict views were not taken too kindly and, following the stoning of the family home in 1841, he moved his wife Jane and four children to the United States.

Jane's early education was received at home in her father's extensive library in Wappinger's Falls, New York. Later she attended school at Southbridge, Massachusetts, where she edited the school paper, wrote plays, and acted as stage manager. Following her formal schooling she

85

taught district school and then was housekeeper for her brother John, a Congregational minister in Worcester County, Massachusetts. There she learned much about cooking, which was compiled in her popular 1866 cookbook. In Worcester she also helped write a semimonthly publication that she read aloud for the members of the congregation, "an audience that crowded the church" for each reading.[3]

Her father's death left twenty-five-year-old Jane Cunningham almost penniless. Undaunted, she decided to take on the journalism world and went to New York City to pursue a career as a journalist. Because journalism was not then acknowledged as a profession suitable for women, she used a pen name, borrowed from a poem from Benjamin Taylor's volume, *January and June*. A clergyman, an occasional visitor to the Cunningham home, had applied it to twelve-year-old Jane, in an inscription in a book of poetry. Taylor's poem, "The Beautiful River" is introduced with the line: "On such a night, in such a June, who has not sat side by side with somebody for all the world like Jenny June." And in the margin beside the poem, her admirer had written, "You are the Juniest Jenny I know." That line so impressed her that she chose as her professional name "Jennie June,"[4] and with that name became a forerunner of the trained newspaper women of today. In her approximately forty-year career she was reporter, drama critic, assistant editor, correspondent, editor, syndicated writer, fashion reporter and critic, and pioneering women's-section editor.

Her first article was accepted by Charles A. Dana, then assistant editor of the *New York Tribune*. Jennie June's by-line also appeared soon after in the *Sunday Times and Noah's Weekly Messenger*, and the *New York Herald*. Her career blossomed as a fashion writer even as she satirized current trends and criticized women's designers. She was especially critical of long skirts which collected dirt as they literally swept the sidewalks and thoroughfares, and of hoops and crinolines, which were dangerous as well as awkward. In 1873 she introduced a campaign for standard evening dress for women. And she made frequent com-

ments on dress, manners, and feminine pastimes in her
*Sunday Times* column, "Parlor and Side-walk Gossip,"
which attracted a growing female readership.

Her popularity and literary flair enabled the enterprising young writer to sell her material simultaneously to
several papers. Indeed, her work made up for the lack, at the
time, of women's departments and regular home and fashion beats. She found her way around, wrote lively and interesting copy, and prompted at least one admiring male editor to make the backhanded compliment, "Why you go on
so naturally and make so little fuss about your work that
I sometimes forget you are a woman."[5]

The *New York Herald* brought more to Jennie June
than just money or literary recognition. It also introduced
her to a handsome, self-educated Irish immigrant, David
Croly. His shorthand—not his knowledge of classics, writing, and debating—had landed him a reporting job, after a
brief apprenticeship to a silversmith. His extreme original-
ity and individuality were to enliven his work, intensify his
efforts, and, eventually, cost him his career. That latter
development was far in the future, however, and the two
young journalists were married on Valentine's Day, 1856.
That same year Jennie called the First Women's Parliament
to meet in New York, a move which presaged four and a
half decades of effort to unite women for their own education and advancement.

In 1857 she broadened her circle of literary outlets,
contributing to the political monthly, *Democratic Review*.[6] She also pioneered syndicated features, selling her
hand-copied material to the New Orleans *Picayune*, the
Baltimore *American*, the New Orleans *Delta*, the Richmond *Enquirer*, and the Louisville *Journal*. She interviewed such notables as Louisa May Alcott, Phoebe Cary,
Robert G. Ingersoll, and Oscar Wilde, and moved familiarly
in high social and intellectual circles.

In 1859 the Crolys fled the everyday sameness of a
New York newsroom for "The West," heading for Rock-
ford, Illinois. David became the editor and publisher of the
Rockford *Daily News*, then owned by William Gore King,

husband of Jennie's sister Mary. But while Jennie worked on the *Daily News*, she wanted bigger journalistic game, so the Crolys returned to New York in 1860,[7] this time with an infant, Minnie, in tow. David joined the New York *Daily World* and Jennie began her long relationship with the popular women's fashion magazines published by William Jennings Demorest and his wife, Ellen Curtis Demorest, two highly influential individuals whose tastes and values were then setting the tone for dress and behavior for hundreds of thousands of readers.

Jennie was editor, for a time, of *Demorest's Quarterly Mirror of Fashion* and in 1860, when the journal and the *New York Weekly Illustrated News* were incorporated into the *Demorest Illustrated Monthly*, she became editor and chief staff writer, a position she held for twenty-seven years. She wrote regular advice columns and conducted the "Ladies' Club" department, consisting chiefly of questions and answers. One reader wrote, "I would like Jennie June to know that we think her ideas about boys excellent. I have a little brother only six years old, and I intend to preserve her lectures until he is old enough to comprehend them, that he may be profited by their teachings."[8]

Jennie June directed a good deal of her editorial attention to middle-class girls seeking employment. She featured various new jobs for their consideration, including bookkeeping, secretarial work, department store management, opportunities in art, teaching, nursing, storekeeping, and horticulture. It is somewhat ironic that she used her influence to promote as careers for women the very types of work in which many modern-day women now find themselves trapped. But at the time she was writing, she was pressing for horizons then unfamiliar to many of her readers.

In addition to her editorial position at *Demorest's*, this prolific journalist also managed the women's department of the *World* from 1862 to 1872. During the same time she wrote women's news, drama, and literary criticism for the *Weekly Times*, *Graphic Daily Times*, and the *Messenger*.

The Crolys had four more children, three born during

the 1860s: a son who died in infancy; a daughter, Vida; a son, Herbert David; and daughter, Alice Cary Croly. But Jennie June, despite her cookbooks and lengthy columns of advice to homemakers, did not spend much time on household tasks, which she turned over to hired help. A rather strictly adhered-to schedule allowed morning hours for her family. Then she left for her office each noon where she "always worked up to midnight and seldom put down my pen until two o'clock," she later reminisced.[9]

Social and professional responsibilities usually superseded home interest, except during the morning. Indeed, she was later to be criticized by her son Herbert, first publisher of the *New Republic*, for what he perceived to be his mother's neglect of maternal and housekeeping duties.[10] And, in reflections toward the end of her life, she said that professional involvements by a married woman could be justified only by the "failure or inadequacy" of her spouse, a situation which justified her own situation: large household, inadequate income, sickly husband.[11] David Croly had ended his journalistic career by age forty-eight, unable to reconcile with his idealistic views of the world the compromises he was called upon to make as editor.

Yet she insisted in print that woman's finest work was to be a caretaker, homemaker, and educator of children.[12] And while she acknowledged the benefits brought to middle-class women by new labor-saving devices, she urged that women who could afford such innovations should spend their newly found leisure profitably, using their time to learn more about nutrition and health. Books she collected and used to expand her columns illustrated her concern. In 1866 she published *Jennie June's American Cookery Book* for young inexperienced housekeepers. A best-seller in its day, it was directed at young middle-class women who couldn't afford maids and found cooking and house keeping unfamiliar and threatening responsibilities.

Three years later she published an anthology of selected columns, *Jennie Juneiana: Talks on Women's Topics.* The pieces discussed and commented on dress and fashion, as well as current fads in food and home decorations. She called for independence and skills for self-sufficiency, as well as for simplicity in decor, simplicity in housekeeping, simplicity in diet. In 1885 and 1886 Jennie was to publish two other homemaker volumes, *Knitters and Crochet* and *Letters and Monograms*. And an 1891 volume, *Thrown On Her Own Resources*, was full of advice for working girls.

In 1868 an event at the New York Press Club, and Jennie June's response to it, led to a profound change in the way American women looked at themselves and each other. Jennie was by then one of America's most quoted and most prolific women writers. Yet she, along with other well-known women of letters, was refused a ticket to a banquet sponsored at Delmonico's by the New York Press Club in honor of the visiting Charles Dickens. She was eligible to attend as a journalist, but ineligible because she was a woman.

Unwilling to smile sweetly and accept the affront to herself and her fellow female journalists, Jennie renewed her request, drawing support from *New York Tribune* editor Horace Greeley and other prominent male journalists, as well as from her husband David. When a grudging reply required that enough ladies buy tickets so they could keep each other company, Jennie retaliated. The women would not attend. But their boycott did not end the matter. Jennie, her publisher Nell Demorest, Fannie Fern, Kate Field, and other literary figures established a women's club. They called it "Sorosis," a gathering of sisters.

The club was ridiculed. The male Press Club invited Sorosis members to a breakfast, feeding them but not allowing any conversation nor participation by its female guests. In response, Sorosis, a few weeks later, returned the courtesy: a tea for the Press Club, which reversed the discrimination. The women gave speeches and the men were consigned to silence. They were, however, allowed to laugh. Not until the third meeting between the two groups, where the men and women paid their own way into a party, did the women experience any degree of equal treatment by fellow professionals.[13] Though journalists were proud to point to the work they did in exposing injustices, it took

Sorosis to bring about the right of women journalists to join their male counterparts at something as simple as a public dinner.

But being invited to public dinners was only a minor achievement. The founders of Sorosis recognized that more important goals needed to be set—and achieved. The organization provided an incentive for women and the women's-club movement in America. Jennie felt that it would create a bond of fellowship among women and stressed that "a well-rounded club was an epitome of the world."[13] What was needed, she said, was a unity among women from all classes and occupations who would cooperate in finding answers to the many problems and challenges facing humankind. She was president in 1868, 1870, 1886, 1887, and 1888. She wrote in 1877 of the organization: "It considers its work principally social and educational. It demolishes caste at one blow. Its members represent all classes, from those who earn their daily bread by teaching, or writing, or cutting in wood, to the wives and daughters of millionaires."[15]

Sorosis was not the first women's club, but was the first of any endurance, a forerunner of the women's-club movement. By 1889 the nationwide General Foundation of Women's Clubs was founded. Jennie's involvement in Sorosis and the women's club movement had grown out of her professional development and helped support progress for many other women.

Her innovations in social movements did not detract from her journalistic accomplishments, however. In 1873 she introduced a shopping column, "Returning to Town." It described merchants in both small shops and large department stores. It told which shops offered the best quality, which carried bargains, and which sold the cheapest items. During the autumn of that year she investigated working conditions for low-income female workers on New York's East Side. Her experiences as she prepared the article, "What a Lady Saw," led to her fight for women's rights. And while she admired Susan B. Anthony, leader in the women's-suffrage movement, she preferred to campaign for women's right to work and to leave suffrage to someone else. Financial independence and economic equality were more important, she believed, than the right to vote, and women needed to earn their rights. She wrote that to attain equal rights in their homes, women must take their share in home duties: "For equal pay they must give equal work—equal in quality as in quantity; for equal education they must show equal energy and aptitude and for equal political rights, an intelligence beyond the eternal discussion of the trimming of a dress or bonnet."[16]

Though she was an innovator, Jennie was also a traditionalist who seemed driven to protect women from their own independence. Her columns during 1875 carried such headings as "Maidenhood," "Boy and Girl Love," "Qualifications for Marriage," "Engaged," "The Honeymoon," and "Duty of a Wife." That same year, her book, *For Better or Worse: A Book for Some Men and All Women*, urged women to take more responsible roles in their marriages.

During this time Jennie's husband David was chief editor at the New York *Daily Graphic*, where he published an avant-garde magazine. Unresolved differences with the publishers in 1877 caused him to leave newspaper work and to immerse himself in reading and philosophizing. The Crolys had for some time been active disciples of the Positivist Movement, French philosopher Auguste Comte's religion of science. Idealists that they were, the Crolys found strong appeal in the altruistic goal of a religion, purified of what they saw as superstition, and united by reason instead of standing opposed to it. They opened their home to the new religion, and were soon recognized as among its chief promoters.

Espousal of and involvement in the Positivist cause seems to have been part of a pattern in Jennie June's life, and she often emerged as the spokesperson for many of the ideas and movements she admired. Indeed, one acquaintance described the regular Sunday evening receptions in the Croly house near Washington Square "as near to a salon after the traditional Parisian standards as any that America has known."[17] Yet social success does not seem to have been the major motivating force in Jennie June's life. She might well have been responding simply to her many personal experiences and to what she saw in the course of her varied journalistic assignments.

In her long career, she wrote countless columns about current fashions. But she also wrote about education, justice, compassion for the less fortunate, and the need to press for social and civic reforms. Among improvements she promoted were closer inspection of health standards in stores and restaurants, responsible management of and protection for New York's state forests, and the cleaning of New York's cluttered and often garbage-strewn streets.

*Demorest's Monthly* was very much a crusading magazine, and Jennie June's pen put most of the crusading tendencies of the publishers into words. The team was dissolved when the Demorests left the magazine. She bought half-interest in a dying competitor, *Godey's Lady's Book*, and tried to revive it. Two years later she abandoned the attempt and established a new magazine, *The Women's Circle*, as an organ for the General Federation of Women's Clubs.

Jennie June believed that the glamour of a successful career came through training, hard work, and perseverance. "There is no sex in labor," she once said, "and I want my work taken as the achievement of an individual with no qualifications, no indulgence, no extenuations simply because I happen to be a woman, working along the same line with men."[18]

In her later years, the irrepressible journalist received an honorary doctorate from Rutgers Women's College and was appointed to a new chair of journalism and literature there.[19] She was the first woman to teach journalism at the college level in a time when there were no schools of journalism. In 1898 depression hit the magazines she edited and they were all either abandoned or absorbed by others. Though financial difficulties and a badly healed hip injury forced her to curtail her physical activities, she continued writing and completed the voluminous *History of the Woman's Club Movement in America*, a testament to early leaders of the women's movement. But with completion of that work, she retired from journalism and sought relief from the pain and weakness which plagued her.

Shortly after her seventieth birthday and ten years after her husband's death, she left for London to live with her daughter, Vida Croly Sidney. She took treatments in London and Switzerland, with only limited success,[20] and, shortly after returning to New York, died there December 23, 1901.

On the eve of her departure for England, *Harper's Bazaar* had given her a typical male compliment, calling her a model of fashion and deportment, with "handsome features—strong and stern yet rather pretty."[21] The irony of the comment is all the more apparent when compared with the reality of her life: she stressed usefulness rather than prettiness, and her work served more as a model for action than as a panderer of appearances.

The more fitting commendation came in a testimonial by the Rev. Phoebe A. Hanaford, vice-president of the Women's Press Club of New York City. Rev. Hanaford praised Jane Croly, who had founded the organization in 1889 and served as its president until she died, and pointed to her "ability as an organizer, and her social qualities which could attract and hold women together in strong bonds of mutual esteem and fellowship."[22]

S. M.

# 9

## ELIZA NICHOLSON
### *Pearl Rivers, Publisher of the Picayune*
### [1849–1896]

Eliza Jane Poitevent Holbrook was a 27-year-old widow when in 1876 she assumed the leadership of the New Orleans *Picayune*, then the largest daily in the South. She followed a 100-year history of courageous women in journalism who, as widows, had picked up where their dead husbands had left off. But hers was to be a succession with a difference. In her 20 years as editor/publisher she was to help open journalism as a viable career for women and to awaken a staid and stodgy giant into a newspaper of innovative leadership.

Born March 11, 1849, in Hancock County, Mississippi, on the banks of the Pearl River, Eliza was prepared for gentility from her early days. Her happy childhood was spent amid the nature and wildlife of southern Mississippi, which inspired much of her poetry. An 1888 essay of hers recalled: "I am kin to the birds. I was raised up in the woods with them and I lived with them until I was twenty years old. They were my first music teachers and they never sang a note that I could not translate into human language."[1]

Eliza's late teens were genteelly Southern. Between 1864 and 1867 she attended, with little joy, the Amite Female Seminary in Louisiana, to be "finished." Her graduation released her into a short-lived career as a poet, but left her, as she was later to lament, like too many other young girls: "among the most helpless and most pathetic class of people in the world—young girls who have been gently reared, who have been given the ordinary useless education women get, and who are thrown on their own resources without one solitary qualification."[2]

Yet she had her writing and, using the pen name Pearl Rivers, harking back to fond childhood memories, soon became a recognized poet. Her poems appeared in John W. Overall's *The South*, the New York *Journal*, the New Orleans *Times*, and the *Picayune*. During a visit in 1869 to her grandfather in New Orleans, she won a post as a twenty-five-dollar-a-week literary editor for the *Picayune*. To take a job in an office was to fly in the face of genteel Southern convention, but it opened a whole new world to twenty-year-old Eliza. She was the first newspaperwoman in conservative New Orleans and among the first in the South. Her work immediately brightened the pages of the *Picayune* during those early Reconstruction years.

Pearl Rivers' apprenticeship included selecting poetry and prose and preparing the Sunday edition. She expanded the literary features of the morning paper, including fiction, essays, and sketches by no less a literary light than Mark Twain. Her editing showed careful attention to detail and the rare discrimination which was later to leave a lasting impression on journalism. As might be expected, much of her own creative work found its way onto the pages she edited. She also began more conventional reporting, and her first signed article as a staff member appeared February 19, 1871, about a trip she took to Pascagoula, Mississippi, via Mobile and Chattanooga.

The apprenticeship blossomed into marriage in 1872 to the sixty-four-year-old *Picayune* publisher, Colonel Alva Morris Holbrook. When, in 1872, Holbrook sold the newspaper to a group of businessmen, Pearl Rivers' involvement also declined, giving her added time to write poetry and edit *Lyrics*, a volume of her works that was published the following year.[3]

She retired temporarily to homemaking and writing and did not resume her work in the *Picayune* office when Holbrook bought back the morning paper the following year, after it had been financially mismanaged. Four years later, with the carpetbag blight hanging over the South,

Holbrook's death left her $80,000 in debt. The law at the time allowed the widow $1,000 if she would leave the paper and declare bankruptcy. But 3½ months after Holbrook's death, she assembled the *Picayune* staff and committed herself to stay. She was aware of masculine sensitivities and made her position clear: "I am a woman. Some of you may not wish to work for a woman. If so, you are free to go, and no hard feelings. But if you stay—will you give me your undivided loyalty, and will you advise me truly and honestly?"[4] Some staffers quit, a few were dismissed, but most remained. The new editor showed, from the first day, that she had learned well in her apprenticeship and short marriage to the dedicated newspaperman.

But her first day as editor left the young widow wondering why she had chosen to enter the male-dominated world of newspapers instead of working a s a women's fashion writer, a dream of her early childhood:

> I never felt so lonely and little and weak in my life as on the first day when I took my seat in Mr. Holbrook's big editorial chair, and for months afterward my lack of confidence was so great that I used to wonder why the staid old *Picayune,* accustomed to being managed by such wise old fellows as Kendall, Holbrook, Bullett and Wilson, didn't just roll over and split its sides laughing at me.[5]

In addition, however, there was loneliness for her in her uniqueness: "As the proprietor of a newspaper my position is, in a way lonesome and peculiar. Under the disadvantage of being a woman, the work of a man is mine with its wear and responsibilities. I miss the pleasure and encouragement men of our profession have in friendly association."[6]

And in an 1895 paper before the Atlanta gathering of the International League of Press Clubs, she advised women not to aspire to manage and edit newspapers: "It is serious and hard work, carrying with it a care that cannot be entirely lifted by a devoted husband [she had by then remarried] and faithful and willing workers who aid me in the *Picayune* management."[7]

It is little wonder, then, that she sought and accepted the support of other women journalists. In 1886, when the Women's National Press Association met in New Orleans, she was elected president.[8] Later she was made the first honorary member of the New York Women's Press Club founded in 1889 by Jennie June, editor and syndicated columnist otherwise known as Jane Cunningham Croly.

She also recognized and encouraged journalistic talent in women, hiring Elizabeth Gilmer and introducing her to the world as a columnist, Dorothy Dix, who became famous for her advice to the lovelorn. And she made Martha Field, as Catherine Cole, a special correspondent for the *Picayune*, covering such events as the Columbian Exposition. Miss Cole also corresponded from Europe and covered Washington.

As might be expected, predictions of imminent failure met the new editor upon her accession. But they were quickly disproved. In her first years with the paper, before becoming editor, she had introduced fashion, arts, and kindred subjects through her columns and sections. She had expanded the book reviews and had introduced living and deceased writers and essayists. Now, under her editorial leadership, the *Picayune* would undergo even greater changes.

Pearl Rivers, as she had become most widely known, believed firmly that a newspaper should and could be an instrument for social change and civic improvement. She therefore recognized the need to broaden her paper's appeal beyond violence and such primarily masculine interests as politics, and the markets. She established a society column, "Society Bee," which began on March 16, 1879. She added separate fashion columns for men and women, frequently using Jennie June's syndicated correspondence. She introduced the "Green Room Gossip," in which former Yankee Major Nathaniel Burbank discussed entertainment and entertainers. Her literary interests and talent shone in the young people's section, "In Lilliput Land." It featured fiction, poetry, illustrations, advice, and subtle admonitions to proper conduct.

There were also columns for homemakers, "Women's World and Work," later renamed "Household Hints"; a medical column, "The *Picayune's* Family Physician"; scientific and agricultural columns; a humor column written by Burbank, "The *Picayune's*"; and "The *Picayune's* Telephone," which commented on such public concerns as the shabby condition of certain streets, minor and not so minor mismanagement by city officials.

An 1894 stroke of creative genius introduced cartoonist L. A. Winterhalder's weather frog in a daily column, "The *Picayune's* Weather Prophet." A forerunner of forecasters' pets of today, the frog became a logo, a mascot, and a widely popular public relations device. Two years earlier, a sports column had captured reader interest, as the *Picayune* covered the newly discovered pastime of football and other athletic diversions.

The whole range of interests exhibited by the paper that Pearl Rivers edited reflected her editorial ambitions. Granted, there had been precedents, as in the popularizing done in New York by James Gordon Bennett sixty years earlier. But she was the genius who brought the winning combination to the South. A promotional ad in July, 1876, shortly after she assumed leadership, promised to give the latest news, cultivate and promote good literature, and to be in every sense a Southern family newspaper. In addition, it would be independent of party, while not neutral on principle. In keeping with this promise, she kept tight control over the paper. No scandals, affairs, divorces, pregnancies, or oddities of behavior were allowed. An August 3, 1879 editorial, in fact, denounced sensationalism and scandal-mongering: "Where no good can come from dragging private scandal into general notoriety the press should follow the practice of the discreet and philanthropic citizen and draw the veil of silence over what had best be forgotten."[9]

In addition, coverage of cruelty and violence was restricted. Indeed, cruelty to animals upset her greatly. Having spent most of her early childhood with animals, she felt their plight almost personally, and by 1884, the *Picayune* took a strong editorial stand asserting that there was more "cruelty practiced toward animals in New Orleans than in any other city in the U.S."[10] It was time for the people of New Orleans to do more than feel sorry for animals, the editor insisted. She organized the Louisiana Band of Mercy to teach children to be kind to animals and to practice protection for them. One of the first members enrolled was her three-year-old son Leonard. In November, 1884, she opened a department on the paper entitled "Nature's Dumb Nobility." The *Picayune* aroused public opinion, and by 1888 the state branch of the Society for the Prevention of Cruelty to Animals was founded in New Orleans.

Because the literary impact of a well-edited newspaper was important to her, Pearl Rivers included the very best. She hired and bought freelance from H. G. Wells, Rudyard Kipling, Emile Zola, Mark Twain, Bret Harte, Joel Chandler Harris, and Arthur Conan Doyle. She made the Sunday newspaper, said one historian "the library of the masses,"[11] all the while developing and expanding its news coverage.

Though she eschewed violence and scandals, she did not hesitate to place her paper squarely in the middle of the burning issues. Though she herself wrote few of the editorials, under her leadership the paper urged calm and courage during the recurring yellow fever plagues of the late 1870s. It supported the development of the New Orleans harbor and the draining of the swamps to prevent epidemics. It urged development of an artesian water system and the electrification of the city's lighting system. She herself turned the switch to light electrically the newspaper plant in 1886. When the hazards from downed electrical lines became apparent, the paper led a public safety campaign.

Believing that the total prohibition of alcohol sought by the Women's Christian Temperance Union would be self-defeating, the *Picayune* nonetheless campaigned in support of Sunday closing laws for saloons in 1884 and the years following.[12]

Other causes which Pearl Rivers and her newspaper championed included the plight of the colorful organ grinders who were facing banishment from New Orleans streets.

It campaigned for railroad service into and out of the city;
for better, isolated hospitalization for leprosy victims;
against prostitution and political corruption. An 1890 murder of an Irish policeman and the subsequent acquittal of
the accused Sicilian Mafia assassins threatened to disrupt
the city. The *Picayune* urged calm in the face of apparent
jury tampering. The words were apparently lost on the
readers, however. Mobs stormed the jail and killed eleven
of the accused in their cells.

At the height of her productive journalistic career,
Pearl Rivers was not alone. She had, in 1878, married
George Nicholson, a loyal ally from her first days as editor.
Thirty years her senior, Nicholson ran the paper's business
side and she the editorial. The team was a good one. In the
next eighteen years steady growth and improvement took
place. The *Picayune* developed a wider selection of departments than its contemporaries, and its society news appeared in one of the largest Sunday sections then published.

Advertising volume increased, too, as new developments in ad sizes and shapes started appearing. The *Picayune's* job printing operation was, in 1885, the largest in
the city. Circulation was also on the rise, jumping from
6,000 combined daily and Sunday circulation in 1878 to
40,000 for the annual business review issue in 1880. By
1891 the combined daily and Sunday figures topped 49,000,
and the Carnival editions at Mardi Gras time claimed a
circulation of 100,000.[13]

Headlines took on a new look as well, taking advantage
of practices being developed across the country. The display was usually conservative, in one-column form with
many banks. But sometimes the news and the headlines
spread across several columns, even the full page.

By 1892, the *Picayune* was taking 14,000 words of telegraph a day, twice the volume of five years previous. Presidential messages ran in full, giving heavy emphasis to national and international developments.

The Nicholsons had two sons, Leonard and Yorke,
born 1881 and 1883 respectively. For them was written
much of the prose and poetry the publisher was able to

create in the midst of everything else. Two long dramatic poems, "Hagar" and "Leah" the former written in 1893, the latter in 1894, were printed in *Cosmopolitan.*

She also began, in 1895, to compile a second volume of verse. It was never completed because of one of the repeated influenza epidemics that struck the Gulf Coast in the 1800s. Eliza Jane Nicholson died of influenza on February 15, 1896, ten days after her husband died of the same disease.

In a tribute, the *Times-Democrat,* strongest competitor of the *Picayune,* said of its deceased publisher:

> Hardly a philanthropic institution in the city, hardly one of the many benevolent schemes constantly set up in New Orleans to benefit the deserving poor or the helpless but found in Mrs. Nicholson an ardent sympathizer, a powerful helper with voice, money, labor, time and pen.[14]

S. M.

# 10

# IDA MINERVA TARBELL
*Muckraker*
[1857–1944]

><■><

The fearless investigative reporter whose sharp documentary reporting took to task the giant Rockefeller oil trust in the early twentieth century was Ida Minerva Tarbell. She was a soft-spoken, ladylike, middle-aged woman.

The powerful executives of Standard Oil, whose sordid business practices she so candidly revealed, could hardly believe this searing exposé came from the same genteel Miss Tarbell who had spent several years interviewing them. They were astonished that her pen could be so mighty a sword.

But her famous nineteen articles of 1902, which ran in the popular crusading dime periodical, *McClure's Magazine,* and were published as a book in 1904, stand even today as a classic work. And she remains the only woman recognized equally among the famous male journalists of America's muckraking era from 1902–1912. Historian Frank Luther Mott praised Miss Tarbell along with Lincoln Steffens and Ray Stannard Baker as "the undisputed leaders" in the distinguished "literature of exposure" in the *History of American Magazines.*

She was one of the era's group of reform journalists earnestly bent on searching out corruption in government, politics, and all phases of American life. Their sensational work built circulation for magazines such as *McClure's, Cosmopolitan,* and *Munsey's.*

In a scornful speech before the Gridiron Club in Washington, D.C., in 1906, President Theodore Roosevelt coined the smear word *muckrakers* for these reform journalists.

He compared the group to the "Man with the Muckrake" in John Bunyan's *Pilgrim's Progress*, too busy dredging up filth to consider even a celestial crown.[1]

Ida Minerva Tarbell was born Nov. 5, 1857, on a farm in Erie County, Pennsylvania, in a pioneer log house built by her grandfather, Walter Raleigh McCullough. Her mother was Esther Ann McCullough, a native of Pennsylvania and former schoolteacher, a descendant of Sir Walter Raleigh and Samuel Seabury, the first American Episcopal Bishop.[2] Ida's father, Franklin Sumner Tarbell, also a native Pennsylvanian, had educated himself at Jamestown Academy in New York, by working as a carpenter and a riverboat captain.

The year Ida was born he had gone West to the Iowa prairies, planning to buy a farm for his young family. But he was caught in the financial panic of 1857, went broke, and was forced to teach school until he had enough money to return home to Pennsylvania. That proved to be 1859, when a new opportunity in life awaited him with the discovery of oil near Titusville. Immediately he foresaw the need for storage containers for this new liquid gold, and using his carpentry skills, he designed and built wooden oil tanks. He soon had a profitable business along Oil Creek, with a shop at Cherry Run in 1860, and shortly thereafter moved to the prosperous oiltown of Rouseville.

Young Ida, who had at first resented losing her peaceful loghouse, grew up in the boisterous shadow of oil pits, derricks, dance halls, brothels, and saloons. But her parents had cushioned her in a loving atmosphere in the midst of this hectic new world, and she learned to submerge herself in avid reading.

When now and then she stormed out of the house in anger for a few hours, she recalled that her mother wisely "always let me carry out my revolts and return when I would, no questions asked." From this she got, she later wrote, a lifelong feeling of self-esteem, with no fear of being "punished or laughed at."[3]

After five rewarding years in Rouseville, Tarbell moved his family to a more prestigious home in Titusville, when Ida was thirteen in 1870. In adolescence, because of her growing interest in science, she began rejecting Biblical literalism and orthodox religion, although her parents were devout Methodists. She did keep a profound faith in God, however, to the end of her days.

As a girl she also reflected on the Women's Rights Movement then current and on the ideas of such feminists as Elizabeth Cady Stanton, Susan B. Anthony, Frances Willard, and others. As a result she began doubting the values of marriage, which would "fetter my freedom," as opposed to the independent life of a career.[4]

In 1876 Ida Tarbell entered Allegheny College in nearby Meadville, Pennsylvania, planning to become a science teacher. Only ten women had graduated there since the doors were opened to them, and in her class she was the only woman among forty men. She graduated with a B.A. degree in 1880. For the next two years she taught at Poland Union Seminary in Poland, Ohio, but soon found that teaching was not her element. Since few jobs in science were open to women in laboratories or research in those days, the frustrated young woman went back home to mull over her future.

Through her parents she met Dr. Theodore L. Flood, editor of *The Chautauquan,* a religious magazine published in Meadville, and he invited her to join his staff in 1883. Thus as a second choice, she embarked on her remarkable career in journalism. The magazine was an influential monthly, a supplement for home study courses of the popular Chautauqua Movement. Her assignment was both to write and edit articles ranging from Bible topics to contemporary social problems.

From the start she was fascinated by journalism, and her talent for research, interviewing, and writing was evident. She stayed eight years with her job and rose to be managing editor. Then, in her early thirties, Ida Tarbell felt restless. She set her sights on being a free-lance correspondent in Europe and a graduate student abroad.

Although she was warned she was "not a writer . . . you'll starve," (by one of her bosses), she felt supported for this determined venture by her habit of "steady, painstaking work," and her knowledge of French. With encouragement from her parents, she headed for Paris in 1891.[5]

From 1891 to 1894 she attended the Sorbonne and College de France in Paris, largely supporting herself by writing articles for American newspapers and magazines. Meanwhile, she had decided to study the role of women during the French Revolution, especially the life of Madame Roland. She was concerned with the rightful place of women in society, realizing how often her American contemporaries were "a doormat, toy, and tool." What were women like who played an important role in French history she wondered? That would be her research.[6]

Miss Tarbell landed in Paris with $150 and settled on the Left Bank, happy under the spell of the legendary city. Like millions of young people before and since, she had little money but had a wonderful time exploring Paris. She was especially proud when she sold a piece to *Scribner's Magazine* for $100.

Another source of her sales was *McClure's Syndicate*, and by the summer of 1892, publisher S. S. McClure called on his new writer, enroute to Switzerland. Climbing the four flights to her thrifty walkup, he promised her ten minutes of his time—and stayed for two hours. (In fact, he had to borrow forty dollars because the banks closed while the two became mutually enchanted with one another's talents. McClure was "much impressed with her ability and character," reported Mott in his *History of American Magazines*.) McClure also assigned Miss Tarbell to write about the achievements of great French scientists, such as Louis Pasteur.

Not only was the idea of her future work exciting, but she was "electrified" and "captivated" by McClure's "vibrant, eager, indomitable personality."[7] For years they were to remain close friends, this gifted writer and the man Mott called "an editorial genius."

By 1894 he had persuaded her to return home to America and join the staff of his brash new dime periodical, *McClure's Magazine*, where her real fame beckoned. It was the young publisher's "endless searching after something new, alive and startling" that appealed to her. In time he was to publish many "first" articles on subjects such as radium, the x-ray, Marconi's wireless, gliders, and flying machines.[8]

Although it was hard for her to pull away from her beloved Paris, she was finally lured to settle in New York, to cast her lot with this promising magazine whose authors eventually were to be such as Conan Doyle, Robert Louis Stevenson, Rudyard Kipling, and many others.

Her first major assignment resulted from the fascination with Napoleon Bonaparte sweeping America in the late nineteenth century. Editor McClure wanted to publish a notable collection of Napoleon prints owned by Gardiner Green Hubbard of Washington, D.C. Miss Tarbell's job was to research and write the text. This celebrated series not only brought an enormous boost in circulation, but recognition for its author. (In praising Miss Tarbell in his *History of American Magazines*, Mott quoted the quip: "Tarbell discovered Napoleon, but McClure discovered Tarbell.")

In 1895 she published the renowned articles as a book, *A Short Life of Napoleon Bonaparte*, a best-seller that soon sold 100,000 copies. The very next year Scribner's published her second book, *The Life of Madame Roland*.

Next S. S. McClure assigned his famous journalist to study the life of Abraham Lincoln. He was convinced that there must be a wealth of fresh unpublished material about the martyred president who had been dead only thirty years. There must be, he said, people who remembered Lincoln, as well as stories never before told and records never yet examined. For the next four years, she undertook her great study that was to result not only in a circulation-winning series for *McClure's* but in her two-volume book, *The Life of Abraham Lincoln*, published in 1900. Mott, in his *History of American Magazines*, has observed that Miss Tarbell's remarkable work in reporting and writing on Lincoln "helped to put *McClure's* in the forefront of American magazines in circulation," advertising patronage, and prestige.

In her search she not only turned up new facts about Lincoln, but punctured some old legends, such as Lincoln's failing to show at the first planned wedding with Mary Todd.[9] Eventually she came to be regarded in later years, as a pioneer investigator whose research had pointed toward the real Lincoln.

Ida Tarbell travelled to the places where Lincoln had lived, in Kentucky, Illinois, and Washington. She talked to unknown people, as well as such important figures as Joseph Medill of the *Chicago Tribune*, Charles A. Dana of the *New York Sun*, and Robert Todd Lincoln, who was so impressed by this reporter that he gave her an unpublished daguerreotype of his father. She used this later for her book.

Early in her Lincoln research she was severely discouraged by John Nicolay, one of the President's former secretaries who had published his own "documentary study." He told her that he himself, together with coauthor John Hay, had already "written all there was worth telling about Lincoln's life." And then later, after she persisted and her book was completed and winning respect, he told her jealously that she was "invading my field ... to decrease the value of my property."[10] (Indeed, hundreds of scholars have invaded and are still invading Nicolay's "field.")

Immediately after the Lincoln study came her most challenging assignment. In an era of monopolistic trusts, it was inevitable that the crusading publisher would investigate the Standard Oil Company. In 1900 Ida Tarbell was his natural choice for the task, because of her firsthand knowledge of the Pennsylvania oil country. (The creative idea for this story was also hers.)

For the next two years she painstakingly interviewed various oil captains and studied documents, especially the secret railroad oil transportation agreements of John D. Rockefeller. As she doggedly pursued her subject, she was warned that she would anger powerful people. But during her girlhood she had experienced the hatred of small independent oil producers around Titusville for the unfair competition of Standard Oil; her own father's business finally failed because of the giant monopoly. She could not be shaken in her work now. Indeed, her extensive research left her with a sense of moral outrage. "The more intimately I went into my subject, the more hateful it became to me," she said afterwards. "No achievement on earth could justify those methods."[11]

Her articles first ran serially in *McClure's*, then appeared as a two-volume work, *The History of Standard Oil*, in 1904. The results of her first-class investigative reporting were sensational at the time, and even today her fame still rests primarily on this work.

Miss Tarbell was outspoken in her concluding chapter. She wrote: "As for the ethical side, there is no cure but in an increasing scorn of unfair play—an increasing sense that a thing won by breaking the rules of the game is not worth winning. When the business man who fights to secure special privileges, to crowd his competitor off the track by other than fair competitive methods, receives the same summary disdainful ostracism by his fellows that the doctor or lawyer who is 'unprofessional,' the athlete who abuses the rules, receives, we shall have gone a long way toward making commerce a fit pursuit for our young men."

About the same time Ida Tarbell's trustbusting exposé of Standard Oil was published, other celebrated writers were also specializing in unearthing corruption in American society. They included Lincoln Steffens, Upton Sinclair, Ray Stannard Baker, Mark Sullivan, David Graham Phillips, and others. While some of these writers wore the Roosevelt label of "muckraker" like a badge of honor, Miss Tarbell considered it a term of "chagrin,.' and preferred to be called a "fact-finder" or "historian."[12]

In 1906 Ida Tarbell, along with several other muckrakers, purchased their own journal, *The American Magazine*, formerly *Frank Leslie's Illustrated Monthly*, which they began editing together. During this period her major contributions were articles on the high protective tariff as another means whereby trusts gained monopolistic control.

With the sale of the magazine in 1915 to the Crowell Publishing Company, Ida Tarbell turned her interests to lecturing on the Chautauqua Circuit. So knowledgeable and popular was she as a speaker that her new career continued for the next seventeen years. Until 1932, in fact, she usually travelled the wide United States for several months out of each year. Her lectures deal with a variety of topics, especially the need for social responsibility in business. She also talked on the problems of peace, the Versailles Treaty, the League of Nations, and disarmament.

After her early career as a muckraker, her later articles and books seemed somewhat mild and conservative. In 1916 she published her *New Ideals in Business*, after touring a number of factories and talking with executives and employers. And after that came two biographies of business leaders, the lives of Elbert H. Gary in 1925 and Owen D. Young in 1932. One critic complained of "the taming of Miss Tarbell," and said she had become a "eulogist" of the kind of men once her "sworn enemy."[13]

She was an active citizen. During World War I President Woodrow Wilson appointed her to the Women's Committee of the Council on National Defense. After the war she attended the Paris Peace Conference as a correspondent for *Red Cross Magazine*. In 1919 she was a delegate to President Wilson's Industrial Conference and in 1921 to President Harding's Conference on Unemployment.

At a spry sixty-nine in 1925 she went to Italy to observe the radical new fascist government there and interviewed the young dictator, Benito Mussolini, whom she found "gallant," even if a "fearful despot."[14]

Where was this great journalist while the women of America marched toward the nineteenth amendment in 1920? Surprisingly she was only "lukewarm" on the subject of suffrage, and disliked "militant" feminists, despite her own unusual and independent life. As she grew middle-aged she came to resent her youthful enthusiasm for women's rights and her opposition to marriage. In a series of articles published in *American Magazine*, and later as a book, *The Business of Being a Woman*, she argued that "woman had a business assigned by nature and society . . . of more importance than public life."[15]

When she was eighty-two Ida Tarbell published her

autobiography, probably one of the best accounts of any early American career woman.

During the last years of her life she had lived on a farm in Connecticut. At eighty-six she died of pneumonia in a hospital near Bridgeport. The *New York Times* obituary called her "the dean of American women authors," noted her outstanding research on Lincoln, and said she "won her fame for her fearless exposé of the Standard Oil trust."[16] Miss Tarbell belonged, said historian Mott, to "a golden age in our periodical literature."

M. G. S.

# 11

# ELIZABETH MERIWETHER GILMER
*Dorothy Dix, Personal Advice Columnist*
[1861–1951]

><><

Dorothy Dix, America's first important personal advice columnist, was a national figure as "mother confessor to millions" for more than half a century from 1896 to 1951.[1] The venerable real-life Elizabeth Meriwether Gilmer attained a worldwide popularity equalled by no other American newspaperwoman until Ann Landers took up several years later where the pioneering Dorothy Dix had left off.

Mrs. Gilmer's column, "Dorothy Dix Talks," began in the Victorian 1890s and continued without interruption past World War II, indeed a phenomenon. Hers was the oldest newspaper feature to survive under the same authorship generation after generation. Dorothy Dix even predated the Katzenjammer Kids and all other comics.[2]

Her germinal column of readers' personal questions, accompanied by short, snappy, and sage answers became a classic. Early in her career at the turn of the century, Mrs. Gilmer's work in the *New Orleans Picayune* had caught the attention of William Randolph Hearst, who whisked her away to his *New York Journal.*

By the time of the first World War "practically every group in the country seemed to be writing to her" for advice.[3] "Her byline became more well-known than almost any woman writing," said the *New York Times* in her obituary.

Dorothy Dix became increasingly "an American byword" as the years rolled on, celebrated in books, magazines, cartoons, theatre plays, movies, even in the skits of vaudeville comedian Will Rogers, and Burma Shave's roadside poetry: "Love and whiskers do not mix, Don't take our word, ask Dorothy Dix'" Her biographer later quipped that she became "Whistler's Mother—with a typewriter;" not to know her would be like not knowing the president of the United States.[4]

By the time she died at 90 she was a millionaire, reputed to have 60 million readers around the world. Her daily deluge of fan letters numbered from several hundred up to 1,000. Few persons who read an English-language newspaper anywhere on earth were unfamiliar with the photograph of the silver-haired, owlish-eyed Dowager Dix. Everywhere her column was acknowledged as an influence shaping morals and customs of her readers.

This girl who became Dorothy Dix was born Elizabeth Meriwether on a 1500-acre Tennessee plantation in Woodstock, Montgomery County, near the Kentucky border, on November 18, 1861. The Meriwethers were distinguished Southern gentry and well-to-do before the Civil War. Her aristocratic father, William Douglas Meriwether, descended from a family who had moved to Tennessee from Virginia and was kin to Meriwether Lewis, the explorer. In addition to inheriting wealth, Meriwether made some money horse-breeding.

Her mother, Maria Winston, died when ELizabeth was small, and a strict stepmother, Martha Gilmer Chase, took over.

Although the Meriwethers, like so many other Confederate families, were among the South's "new poor" after the war, young Elizabeth was taught the refinements of being a lady and also was encouraged to use the family's fine private library. By the age of twelve she was a confirmed bookworm. "I cut my teeth on the solid meat of good literature," she was to say later.[5]

After the family moved to Clarksville, Tennessee, she attended the Female Academy there and Later Hollins Institute in Virginia. Already in grammar school she found that her favorite occupation was writing compositions.

In 1882 when she was just twenty-one, Elizabeth Meriwether married George O. Gilmer, her stepmother's brother. This stepuncle, a suave, good-looking man ten years her senior, Gilmer impressed the tiny, shy Elizabeth, who weighed scarcely ninety pounds and stood hardly five feet tall, with his airy talk about investments, travels, and dreams of becoming an inventor.

They were married only a short while, however, when he showed clear signs of strange moodiness and an inability to get along with others or to keep a job. His case was only to grow worse during the forty-seven years that his wife steadfastly refused to retreat from their tragic marriage.

In the early years, Mrs. Gilmer tried to cope at home with this husband, who eventually was recognized to have an incurable mental disease. As a result of this stress, she herself had a nervous breakdown in the early 1890s. To recuperate she went to the peaceful resort of Bay Saint Louis on the Mississippi Gulf Coast. She needed time to come to terms with earning a living in an era when it was really considered humiliating for respectable women to work outside the home.

As fate decreed, she there met the South's newly-successful woman publisher, Eliza Nicholson, owner of the *New Orleans Picayune*. Mrs. Gilmer showed her some clippings of newspaper features she had recently free-lanced and sold her a story for three dollars.

To the wise Mrs. Nicholson goes the credit for quick perception of the talents still locked away inside Mrs. Gilmer at age thirty-three. In 1894, the future millionairess was hired as "Girl Friday" for the *Picayune's* ace editor, Major Nathaniel Burbank, for five dollars a week. Although Burbank's first grudging reaction was that Publisher Nicholson had foisted "a little canary" on him when instead he needed "a roustabout," he soon realized that she was a first rate newspaperwoman.[6]

In her shabby room on Camp Street, Elizabeth Gilmer, who had been assigned the usual cub reporter's drudgery of gathering the vital statistics, set herself the chore of studying America's finest newspapers for their writing style. And shortly she graduated from obituaries, birth notices, and short items to her own column of advice to women,

"Sunday Salad." The style of her "sermonettes," in contrast to that of most women writers of the 1890s, was crisp, breezy, even colloquial. She wrote common sense in plain words and avoided "highfalutin', flowery language."[7] She chose the pen name of Dorothy Dix—alliterative pseudonyms being voguish in those days for gentlewomen concealing their real names from the stigma of the sordid newspaper world. And she was an overnight star. This new Dorothy Dix got an avalanche of fan mail from folks who sensed that somehow she could give trustworthy advice. The *Picayune* capitalized on its promising property by changing the title of her column to "Dorothy Dix Talks," the name it was to bear for fifty-five years.

It was not long before scouts of publisher William Randolph Hearst made note of Dorothy Dix. Hearst, in his cutthroat competition with Joseph Pulitzer and the New York *World*, was in the market for the kind of feature writing that boosted circulation. Initially, however, Mrs. Gilmer rejected Hearst's flattering offer to join the New York *Journal*.

With the kind of loyalty to family and friends that characterized her life, she would not desert the ailing and aging editor Burbank, who had trained her in journalism. Besides, the *Picayune* already had lost its publisher, her benefactor, Eliza Nicholson, who died at only forty-seven. It was not until Burbank also died in 1901 that Mrs. Gilmer felt free to leave.

Her first big assignment from Hearst, during a six-months-trial period, was covering the front-page story of Carry Nation, the temperance leader, on her saloon-smashing tour of Kansas. Dorothy Dix's account of Carry's fanatical crusade, in which she and her followers were literally smashing bottles of booze all over the abashed sunflower state, won respect from *Journal* editors and readers.

"What a waste of good liquor," wrote Mrs. Gilmer, a true Southern belle, with a twinkle in her pen. She shook her head humorously at the "business-like looking hatchets" of the Nation crowd who called themselves "joint-smashers." This, declared Dorothy Dix, had to be "the strangest and most intemperate temperance movement."[8] Letters from all parts of the country applauded her work," according to her biographer.[9]

Although she was already forty in 1901, reporter Gilmer had arrived in New York with a youthful, adventurous spirit. On sight she was a gem in the eyes of the brilliant Hearst editor, Arthur Brisbane. While he was a sharp-spoken coach, he helped polish her writing with short, well-chosen words and warned that most newspaper readers were either too tired, busy, or uneducated "to hunt a dictionary to find out what a word means."[10]

By 1902, Coach Brisbane, proudly proclaiming that Dorothy Dix was "good stuff," had said: "Did any man ever make a quicker success in the newspaper business than Dorothy Dix?"[11]

To the shrewd Hearst editors of the yellow journalism era, however, Mrs. Gilmer's uncanny ability to interview people and win confidence had a lot more cash potential than could be realized through advice columns and ordinary feature writing.

Indeed this woman's charismatic personality was to make her a famous reporter for murder trials—those read-all-about-it entertaining courtroom dramas that were America's real-life soap operas before the advent of television. An avid public devoured the lurid details told in the press about the nation's love triangles by the "sob sisters" —women writers who could wring tears. The bigger the society names involved in the trials, the gorier the facts, the better the circulation. A skillful sob sister had not only to be a keen observer in court, but able to wangle sidebar interviews from involved family and friends of the victims and/or accused, in the days before "fair trial" was taken so seriously. Dorothy Dix was a stellar sob sister.

She covered numerous cases, including that of Harry K. Thaw, the playboy heir accused of killing architect Stanford White after a quarrel over pretty Evelyn Nesbit; of Nan Patterson, of Floradora Sextette fame, for murdering her book-maker boyfriend; and Albert Patrick, for killing Texas millionaire William Rice.

By 1917, however, Mrs. Gilmer was weary of this legal circus and relieved when the Wheeler Syndicate offered her the chance to write only her column six days a week, three columns of sermonettes and three columns of questions and answers. Besides, she had long been adamant that her advice really did some good for people, whereas she doubted the value of crime reporting. Always she treasured readers' appreciative letters like the one that said: "In my dark hour I read your answer and it gave me the will to hold on and try again."[12]

Thus Elizabeth Meriwether Gilmer returned to New Orleans, free of office time clocks and writing assignments, and began writing "Dorothy Dix Talks" from a spacious home overlooking Audubon Park in the elite Garden District. Received as a celebrity, she plunged into the city's civic and social life. In 1927 Tulane University awarded her an honorary degree. In 1928 the city of New Orleans held "Dorothy Dix Day" in a public park, and thousands turned out to celebrate the great lady and hear admiring orations.

Only once did Mrs. Gilmer break her rule of no-more-murders. In 1926, at the age of sixty-five, she was persuaded to cover the front page Hall-Mills case when a wife was accused of killing her preacher-husband and his alleged girlfriend, a choir singer. Dorothy Dix, as her advocacy reporting of the courtroom drama showed, felt very sympathetic towards the "wronged" widow—who indeed went free.

Meanwhile, people "from every rank and condition of society, every degree and culture and education," continued to write Miss Dix about "everything under the sun."[13]

To sample her columns over the years is to read about perennial human problems as old as the Bible and as fresh as today. People wrote to her about extravagant wives, cruel husbands, interfering mothers-in-law, passionate teenage lovers, abused and runaway children, old and forgotten parents, and sought her opinion on health, wealth, beauty, recipes, romance, marriage, suicide, religion, etiquette.

Girls wrote about how to "get dates and acquire husbands." Boys wondered how to be "lady-killers," and both "pop the question" and "wriggle out" of affairs. Wives agonized over "philandering husbands," and men over "nagging wives." Parents "craved information about how to deal with adolescent kids," and "keep them from making mistakes that will wreck their lives."[14]

A fair share of humor kept high reader interest in her column. There was the man in love with a married woman who asked, "What is the quickest and most humane way of getting rid of her husband?" Likewise, the wife who wanted Miss Dix's advice on "doing away with his (her husband's) current glamour girl?" A girl sought a magic potion for "the makings of a peaches-and-cream complexion and sex appeal." An older reader wanted an explanation "on what becomes of the soul after death."[15]

And there was the eight-year-old boy who appealed to Miss Dix for help in persuading his parents to allow him a dog. She agreed: "Yes, Bobby," she wrote, "I do think that a boy without a dog is as forlorn as a dog without a boy." And also the bride who wondered if she should tell her prospective groom about her false teeth. "Marry him," advised Miss Dix, "and keep your mouth shut."[16]

Mrs. Gilmer preached the gospel of common sense. By and large she advised marital partners to work out their difficulties and avert divorce; children to obey reasonable parents; lonely older folks to take charge of their own lives and even remarry when possible; and young men and women to play life straight with high ideals. She firmly believed that "our lives are just what we make of them, and we are architects of our own fate."[17]

Regarding women's suffrage, she was an early advocate of the proposed nineteenth amendment. And from the turn of the century, she campaigned in her column for women's education and the right to employment. While she believed that mothers of young children should seek jobs only out of necessity, she said that all women should be trained at least in some vocation. She argued that some women would not find husbands, and married women could lose their male support through illness, death, or divorce.

Mrs. Gilmer's long life spanned vast social changes. On her column's fiftieth anniversary in 1946 she reflected that when she began her column, girls would write about the propriety of having "gentlemen callers in their parlors, without the mothers present." She observed: "Now they want to know about taking vacations with boys or going off on trips with them." Girls used to save their "first kiss" for their husbands, she continued, but "now petting parties are the vogue." By 1946 women could wear beach costumes so brief that "police would have run them in back in their grandmothers' time." And now "swapping husbands is of no more moment than returning a hat to the bargain counter . . . after she has lost her taste for it."[18]

In 1923 "Dorothy Dix Talks" had gone to the Ledger Syndicate, and by 1942 it was with the Bell Syndicate. Eventually Mrs. Gilmer earned upwards of $90,000 a year, according to her biographer.

In 1929 her husband, George Gilmer, died in a mental hospital. He had been in and out of her home and institutions for most of their married life. He had some limited success as an inventor.

Mrs. Gilmer lived in gracious style during her latter days. Her stone mansion in New Orleans was furnished with antiques and objects of art. A butler opened the door to visitors for the plump, white-haired newspaper queen whose bright eyes still sparkled like the diamonds she wore. Until almost ninety she kept the habit of rising early to read her letters and write her column and riding afternoons in her chauffered car.

She lived on the mansion's upper floor, and her brother, Charles Edward Meriwether, and his family lived on the lower floor. His children and grandchildren, since she had none of her own, were her special delight.

Until the last months of her life, she was able to dictate her column, as always without ghost-writers, according to her confidential secretary of many years, Mrs. Ella Arthur, who did help answer the mail. Mrs. Gilmer died on Dec. 16, 1951, in Touro Infirmary, New Orleans. She had provided that no one could carry on under the name of Dorothy Dix.

An editorial tribute on her passing in the *Times-Picayune* said: "Few careers have been more useful than hers. Her splendid influence will long survive her passing."

Not long before her death she had written the final words on her own life: "My job has made me mother confessor to millions. I have given all that is in me trying to help them."[19]

M. G. S.

# 12

# IDA B. WELLS-BARNETT
*Crusader*
[1862–1931]

"God has raised up a modern Deborah . . . pleading as only she can plead for justice and fair treatment to be given her long-suffering and unhappy people," wrote Norman B. Wood in 1897.[1] Ida B. Wells-Barnett was "possibly the one black woman journalist of the nineteenth-century remembered in this century," said Professor Roland Wolseley in his classic history of the black press.[2] For despite the discrimination that has handicapped blacks in America, Mrs. Wells-Barnett was that sort of genius who in all times somehow rises above contemporary circumstances to greatness, like the Old Testament's prophetess who led the Israelites to victory over the Canaanites. Her life as a stirring orator and writer was an enduring crusade for racial justice, although journalism, she always said, was "my first love."[3]

Mrs. Wells-Barnett died in 1931, but it was years later, after the civil rights awakening in the United States, that she first came to be appreciated beyond those who knew black history. Most students of American journalism have given her a passing reference or slighted her altogether. None has treated her true stature.

Her fight against the brutality of lynching, in the reconstruction days of her youth and thirty years later with the revival of the Ku Klux Klan, established and sustained her reputation as a hard-hitting journalist. In 1892 angry white racists had ransacked and destroyed the newspaper she owned in Memphis, Tennessee, and might have killed her had she been in town. Her life threatened if she dared return, she could not be intimidated and did not relent in her outpouring of bold and dangerous words, but instead moved on to a new writing career in New York City.

Along with the celebrated black elder statesman, Frederick Douglass, who was then in his late seventies and had just returned from serving as United States Minister to Haiti, young Miss Wells in 1893 helped produce the pamphlet: *The Reason Why the Colored American is Not in the World's Columbian Exposition—The Afro-American's Contribution to Columbian Literature.*

Her widely-heralded lecture tours in Great Britain during the 1890s exposed the "land of the free" as being far from that for her own hunted and haunted black race and resulted in the formation of a British antilynching society that pointed an outraged finger of shame across the Atlantic Ocean. Even after she married the noted Chicago lawyer, Ferdinand Barnett, and was the mother of four children, she did not cease in organizing groups, talking, and writing for the betterment of blacks. For a period, she concentrated more energy at home and less in public, but she never ceased.

As she matured, her reportorial courage continued to take her to hazardous scenes of racial strife, including those seething with the dreadful aftermath of lynchings. She ventured into such caldrons as Cairo and East St. Louis in Illinois, before it was popular and acceptable, let alone safe, to cover such stories.

Through her organizational leadership, she sparked activism among black women and youths. Indeed, she was one of the first banner-carrying suffragettes in the nation, when many white women did not know what the campaign to vote was all about. Although she was one of the founders of the National Association for the Advancement of Colored People, a careful and slowly moving organization, there is evidence that Mrs. Wells-Barnett was less given to the drag of evolutionary change and compromise than were other leaders of her time. Notably, she differed with Booker T. Washington and his philosophy of accommodation.[4]

Her life started as Ida B. Wells, born to slave parents on July 16, 1862, in Tippah County, Mississippi. She was the eldest of eight children. Her father, James Wells, was the son of a white plantation master and one of his slaves. Acknowledged as a son, Wells was apprenticed to a carpenter. Later as a freedman, he was thus prepared, unlike many other former slaves, to earn a living.

Ida Wells' mother, Lizzie Bell, the daughter of a black slave and a father believed to be half American Indian, had a sadder, more typical story: at only seven years of age, she was sold away from her parents. The scars from beatings across her mother's back were to bring tears to young Ida. She never forgot those scars. After the Civil War, Ida's mother worked as a cook and attended school to learn reading and writing while mothering her large family.

Holly Springs, Mississippi, where the Wells family lived after their freedom, was about forty miles from Memphis. During the war the town had changed hands several times as a pawn of Confederate and Union forces. While no fighting took place there, some businesses and fine homes were wrecked or burned. Her father seldom lacked employment at carpentry during the time of reconstruction. A civic-minded man, he served on the first board of trustees of Rust College, which was originally founded as Shaw University in 1866. Young Ida received her early education at Rust, which in those days offered basic schooling as well. Apparently she was an apt pupil and passed a rather peaceful, happy childhood.

Years later, in her autobiography, Mrs. Wells-Barnett was to look back at her childhood and recall: "I had always been a voracious reader. I read all the fiction in the Sunday School library and Rust College." Oftentimes with no oil for lamps and no candles to spare, she would "sit for hours and read such authors as Charles Dickens, Louisa May Alcott, Charlotte Brontë, A. D. T. Whitney, and Oliver Optic," and largely as a result, "formed my ideals." She also read Shakespeare, and, above all, the Bible.

Then tragedy struck in 1878 when an epidemic of yellow fever claimed the lives of both her parents and their ten-month-old baby. Although Ida Wells was only sixteen at the time, she assumed the obligation to hold her surviving family of brothers and sisters together and prevent their dispersal into strange homes or orphanages. With the pittance from her parental inheritance and help from the local Masons, who were the children's guardians, the household survived until she took the district teaching examination. Her first job, with her hair tucked up and her skirts let down, was in a one-room rural school near Holly Springs.

By 1883 searching for a better life, Ida Wells risked the move to Memphis. An aunt there helped in caring for the younger children, and again she taught in a rural district school while studying for the teacher's examination for city schools.

It was during this period, in 1884, when she was just twenty-two, that she took on the historic action of challenging discrimination against black passengers on railroad trains. She had been travelling on the Chesapeake and Ohio Railroad enrounte to Woodstock, Tennessee, when the conductor tried to herd her into a dingy smoking car with the rest of the black passengers. Ida Wells refused to go and finally bit his hand. When the conductor then got the brute force of two more husky men, the three of them succeeded in ousting her. She got off at the next stop and returned to Memphis, resolved to file suit against the railroad for failing to provide "separate but equal" accommodations.[5] That same year she won her case before the circuit court and collected $500 in damages. But in 1887 the Supreme Court of Tennessee reversed that decision.

Miss Wells wrote in her diary, expressing the agony she felt then and was to feel often in years to come: "Oh God, is there no redress, no peace, no justice in this land for us?"[6]

She passed the qualifying examination in 1884 and taught in the Memphis schools for the next seven years. She was regarded not only as a capable teacher and professional colleague, but as a young woman who did not lack suitors for social affairs. She was described as "beautiful," "refined," and "ladylike," hardly expected to make a career of defying authorities and angry mobs in later life.[7]

During the summers she attended Fisk University and also wrote for the black church weekly, Living Way, beginning with stories about her suit against the railroad. Her clear and readable style, and the importance of her messages, brought Miss Wells other invitations to publish freelance work. Thus, early in her life, she came to realize her interest and gift in journalism. At first she used the pen name of "Iola," pseudonyms being popular, especially for ladies hiding their participation in the rowdy world of journalism.

During this period the Rev. William J. Simmons, of the American Baptist Home Missionary Society and an editor of the Negro Press Association, hired her as correspondent for his paper. This led to opportunities for travel, including a trip to Washington, D.C., in 1889, where she first met Frederick Douglass. "Dr. Simmons encouraged me to be a newspaperwoman," she wrote in her autobiography, and gave credit to "his influence." Ida B. Wells soon had the reputation of being "the brilliant Iola," "Princess of the Black Press," and a "writer of superb quality."

Soon thereafter, she was offered a share in the ownership, as well as the editorship, of a small black Memphis paper, *Free Speech and Headlight* and made a momentous decision to invest her savings. Already in 1891, however, she was embroiled in trouble with the Memphis Board of Education because of her articles lashing into the poor and neglected conditions of the black schools; she was dismissed from her teaching post. As usual unintimidated, she submerged herself in journalism. She abbreviated the name of her paper to *Free Speech* and steadfastly carried on with other investigations into racial discrimination.

Meanwhile, editor "Iola" travelled to most of the large towns throughout the Delta, into Arkansas and Tennessee, building up subscriptions. The popular *Free Speech* was soon "in demand all up and down the Delta spur of the Illinois Central Railroad," she recounted in her autobiographical chapter about those days. Circulation rose from fifteen hundred to four thousand under her able management. Then in 1892 her stories about the lynching of three black Memphis grocery store operators brought hostile responses from the white community.

The three men, Thomas Moss, Calvin McDowell, and Henry Stewart, had been jailed in connection with neighborhood disturbances. They were kidnapped from the Memphis jail, taken a mile out of town, where they were mutillated and shot to death. Expressing the "shock waves" among blacks, *Free Speech* asserted:

> "The city of Memphis has demonstrated that neither character nor standing avails the Negro, if he dares to protect himself against the white man or become his rival ... we are out-numbered and without arms.... There is therefore only one thing left that we can do; save our money and leave a town which will neither protect our lives and property, nor give us a fair trial in the courts, but takes us out and murders us in cold blood when accused by white persons."[8]

The whole incident, along with other problems of racial conflict at the time, brought Memphis to a festering situation between blacks and whites for weeks, she later related in *Crusade for Justice*, with the white press "fanning the flames of race prejudice," and *Free Speech* trying to tell the truth as blacks saw it. Meanwhile Ida Wells had obligations for assignments in Oklahoma and in the East. Upon arrival in New York she learned from an Associated Press story in the *New York Sun* that a wild angry mob had burst into the *Free Speech* offices, destroyed her type and furnishings, and warned that "anyone trying to publish the paper again would be punished with death." This happened on May 27, 1892. In addition, Miss Wells' Memphis home was under constant surveillance by white men, "determined to kill me on sight."

With friends both in Memphis and New York begging her not to return, Ida Wells, after some agonizing, faced the fact that any useful career from that point on must be carved in a new environment.

She took a job as writer with T. Thomas Fortune's respected black journal, *New York Age*. And she vowed not to retreat in using her pen as a powerful sword. In fact, she now had a lifetime cause "to fight against lynchers and lynching": "They had destroyed my paper, in which every dollar I had was invested. They had made me an exile and threatened my life for telling the truth. I felt that I owed it to myself and my race to tell the whole truth," Mrs. Wells-Barnett wrote in her autobiography.

Before long she was a one-fourth owner of the *New York Age,* while she poured forth stories of all kinds on injustice toward blacks. Her former subscription lists from Memphis were turned over to the new paper so that readers who had lost their old paper now had a new one.

The reputation of "Iola" continued to grow, with front-page stories "to give the world the first inside story on Negro lynchings." Soon Ida Wells found herself on the lecture platform with a reputation as a speaker. Thus it was that, in 1893, the noted journalist was invited to tour England, Scotland, and Wales to tell her story of lynching in America.

Indeed her reception from the British press and pulpit was so enthusiastic that she was invited back for a second tour in 1894. This was when the famous British Anti-Lynching Committee was organized to crusade against the brutal treatment of blacks in America. During this second tour in Great Britain, the *Chicago Inter-Ocean* newspaper agreed to carry a weekly column, "Ida B. Wells Abroad." Her articles represented one of the rare occasions in those days that a white journal featured a black writer. Afterwards there was to be little doubt that 1894 had been the year "marked by a pronounced awakening of the public conscience to a system of anarchy and outlawry which had grown during a series of tens of years to be so common, that scenes of unusual brutality failed to have any visible effect upon the humane sentiments of the people of our land."[9]

When Miss Wells returned to America, her determination was heightened as a result of her international success. She continued her fight against lynching by more lecturing in the North and by organizing new committees wherever she went.

For her permanent residence she now decided on Chicago, where she had fought for the right of blacks to be represented at the World Columbian Exposition of 1893. And in 1894 she published her book, *A Red Report: Tabulated Statistics and Alleged Causes of Lynching in the United States, 1892–1893–1894*. Much of her data on lynching for the controversial new work came from that respected white newspaper, *The Chicago Tribune*, and to the dismay of her would-be challengers, was not readily disputable.[10] Her work was regarded as the only statistical and historical record of lynchings in the United States to be published since the Emancipation Proclamation.[11] Her story was offered for the whole world to use as an example of American inhumanity.

Her decision to live in Chicago was also influenced by her romance with Ferdinand Lee Barnett, a widower and widely-known lawyer and the founder of the *Conservator*, the first black newspaper in Chicago. Barnett had been among those who worked with Frederick Douglass and Miss Wells in producing their booklet on the Columbian Exposition. Married in 1895, the new Mr. and Mrs. Barnett were to become one of the most influential American black couples of their day. Barnett matched not only his wife's intelligence and drive, but also her dedication and courage. They had four children and until the youngest was in school, the devoted mother limited her public activities. After marriage, she had also developed the use of her name as Mrs. Wells-Barnett, accepting her husband's respected name and also keeping the famous maiden name she had established.

In 1901, the Barnetts were thought to be the first black family to buy a home east of State Street in Chicago, on Rhodes Avenue. At first they endured some hostility and humiliation from their white neighbors, who would turn their faces and slam their doors against the Barnetts. Once some jeering white youths outside the Barnetts' front door taxed the patience of Mrs. Wells-Barnett. Afterwards she let it be known that she now kept a pistol in her home, and if anyone threatened her or her family with harm, she was "prepared." She felt that "she had but one life to give, and if she must die by violence, she would take some of her persecutors with her."[12] This became a firm assertion that

Mrs. Wells-Barnett made famous during her antilynching crusades; if necessary, she would fight fire with fire.

After she had a family, Mrs. Wells-Barnett found time to teach a Sunday school class, and in 1910 to found the Negro Fellowship League in the heart of the crime area on South State Street in Chicago. In an old three-story building, the League provided counselling, job advice, recreation and meeting facilities, religious services, and even a temporary dormitory at twenty-five cents a night.

She became vexed at her middle-class friends who were unwilling to work among the poorer blacks.[13] She always regretted that she could not, like her friend, Jane Addams, the great social service contemporary at Hull House in Chicago, gain more support from persons of education, ability, and influence for their deprived brothers. Too many wealthy blacks, she declared in frustration, lacked compassion.[14] She often grew impatient of the lack of involvement in controversial concerns exhibited by both black and white clergymen. "She believed that they should assist them [the poor and troubled] with their improvement in this world as well as prepare them for the next."[15]

Enfranchisement was another lifelong cause with her. Everywhere she went she urged members of her race to register and vote. She understood well the power of politics in practical accomplishments. Early in the twentieth century, when many American women were dimly aware of the suffrage movement, she was busy organizing the first black women's group, the Alpha Suffrage Club. At least twice she marched in suffrage parades, in Washington, D.C. in 1913 on the eve of Woodrow Wilson's inauguration, and in Chicago's famous parade of 1916 when 5,000 women surged during a drenching torrent toward the headquarters of the Republican National Convention.[16]

She did travel some after her marriage, but her adopted home of Chicago remained the center of her interest. During the second decade of the century she served as a probation officer for the Chicago Municipal Court.

For a time she worked with the black leader, W. E. B. DuBois, in the National Afro-American council, but she restricted her interests after Booker T. Washington's allies assumed leadership, because she disagreed with their soft-spoken approach. Similarly, although she helped to organize the NAACP in 1909, the centennial anniversary of the birth of Abraham Lincoln, she found this group also too compromising. .

As her children grew up and Mrs. Wells-Barnett grew older (she had not married until she was thirty-three), she continued to write for journals such as the *Chicago Defender, World, Broad Ax,* and the *Whip.* She also published pamphlets distributed by the Negro Fellowship League.

These pamphlets, which represented some of her most valuable writing, together with other documents and reports she had collected over the years, were later lost in a fire at her home. Alfreda Barnett Duster, the daughter who edited her mother's posthumous autobiography, was not able to find copies of most things for the University of Chicago's archives.[17] This includes materials on her plucky coverage of the nationally-publicized East St. Louis riot of 1918, when 150 black people were killed and almost a million dollars worth of property was destroyed. According to her autobiography, when she arrived there to undertake investigative reporting, she could find "no place to stay . . . all the colored people were in hiding."

Lost also were notes from her trip to Little Rock, Arkansas, in 1922, after the famous riot in Elaine, apparently brought on after blacks refused to sell white men their cotton at below market price. When she visited rioters imprisoned in Little Rock, it was her first return since her banishment from the South thirty years before. Although she found the Elaine story to be "a terrible indictment of white civilization and Christianity," she also promised the men she visited: "The God you serve is the God of Paul and Silas who opened their prison gates . . . He will open your prison doors." She wrote a pamphlet to help raise money to free the imprisoned blacks. Later a young man who came to her door in Chicago told her he was one of those who had heard her preach in the Little Rock prison about having faith in God.

One notable experience was a visit in 1909 to the

seething community of Cairo, Illinois, a North-South bor-
derline town, to investigate the flamboyant case of "Frog"
James, whose bloody body was dragged along a main street
with a mob, including women and children, shouting and
applauding. Then he was decapitated and his head stuck on
a fencepost for viewing, while the rest of his body was
publicly burned. After an exhaustive investigation, Mrs.
Wells-Barnett, a black reporter in a town where hatred was
raging like pestilence, escaped with her life and went to the
capital in Springfield to appeal for justice in the case. As a
result of her evidence, Governor Deneen issued a state paper proclaiming that the sheriff in Cairo at the time of the
lynching could not be reinstated because he had not pro-
tected his prisoner properly from mob violence. Later, on
January 1, 1910, the *Chicago Defender* recounted a speech
she gave on the Cairo case before a local club, praising it as
"commendable in every detail." "If we only had a few *men*
with the backbone of Mrs. Wells-Barnett, lynching would
come to a halt in America," declared the paper. Both stories
are told in detail in *Crusade for Justice.*

In another courageous fight, both Mr. and Mrs. Barnett
sought to save the life of "Chicken Joe" Campbell, a
"trusty" at the Joliet Penitentiary in Illinois. After a fire
broke out, in which the warden's wife burned to death,
"this poor devil" got the blame, although he was an innocent scapegoat in the Barnetts' eyes, according to her autobiography.

Ida Wells-Barnett undertook the initial investigation of
the case in Joliet after reading the story in the newspapers.
She wrote a moving editorial in his behalf in the black
*Record Herald.* Next her husband undertook Campbell's
defense in the Joliet court. After the local jury and judge
called for Campbell's hanging, Barnett took the case to the
state Supreme Court and won a commutation to life im-
prisonment. Mrs. Wells-Barnett was to die still hoping for
Campbell's freedom from Menard. She believed a "most
awful combination of circumstances" had allowed this
"crime to be fastened on a black man," in the face of the
real truth.

Despite poor health during 1920 and 1921, she continued her interest in the movement for black women's clubs. In Chicago women had founded the Ida B. Wells Women's Clubs, and she served for many years as their president, always urging her sisters not to be "do-nothings."[18]

In contrast with her husband who was active in Republican circles and was the first black in Chicago to be appointed assistant state's attorney, a position held for fourteen years, she was never deeply involved with formal politics. Yet the year before she died, Ida Wells-Barnett surprised some of her friends by becoming a Republican candidate for the state senate against two men. She came in third, but not until she gave her opponents a good race, including rousing speeches before large groups at the La Salle Hotel and Orchestra Hall. "Few women responded as I had hoped," she wrote with disappointment in her diary.[19]

After 1928, a senior citizen indeed, she had occupied much time writing her autobiography, which was not published until over forty years later. On March 25, 1931, during her sixty-ninth year, Ida B. Wells-Barnett died of uremic poisoning in Dailey Hospital, Chicago.

In her introduction to the posthumous autobiography, Mrs. Duster called her mother, "this fiery reformer, feminist, and race leader . . . ," and praised her "long and lonely fight." "The measure of success she achieved goes far beyond the credit she was given in the history of the country," the daughter observed.

In 1940, after a civic campaign, the Chicago Housing Authority changed the name of the South Parkway Garden Apartments to the Ida B. Wells Garden Homes. Their forty-seven acres of oasis among the blight of the area seemed symbolic of her life, often a flower alone in the desert of society.

In time historians of journalism must surely give Ida Wells-Barnett her rightful recognition.

M. G. S.

# 13
# ELIZABETH COCHRANE SEAMAN
## *Nellie Bly, Feature Writer*
### [1865–1922]

><====

Asked to name one woman journalist in history, chances are that most people remember Nellie Bly. She was, they vaguely recall, that pretty young girl reporter who raced across the globe, something like the hero in Jules Verne's celebrated novel, *Around the World in Eighty Days.* Indeed newspaper headlines did blaze about Nellie's dramatic journey by boat, train, rickshaw, and burro back in 1890 when her amazing feat was nearly as widely publicized as the first flight to the moon generations later.

Few people, however, seem to realize that publisher Joseph Pulitzer's circulation-building stunt for the New York *World* was not the only thing that created Nellie Bly's reputation as a great reporter. It was, in fact, her solid record in investigative journalism during the late nineteenth century, when few women would even contemplate hard on-the-street reportorial "leg work." Even before the world-circling spectacle was dreamed of, she was delving into taboo subjects of her contemporary Victorian society with the daring-do and thoroughness of a five-star reporter.

Nellie Bly was born Elizabeth Cochran, May 5, 1865, on a farm in Pennsylvania. The little town there was called Cochran's Mills after her father, Michael Cochran, a jolly Irish millowner, lawyer, and associate judge in Armstrong County. The flourish of a final "e" on her name was added later by the renowned journalist. Her mother, Mary Jane Kennedy, was a gentle, quiet woman, devoted to rearing the couple's ten children. Elizabeth early learned to fend for herself and hold her own.

Eventually the Cochran family moved to Apollo, Pennsylvania, where this adventurous daughter found excitement in slipping off to the railroad station to watch the daily train for Pittsburgh pass through. Elizabeth dreamed of travel, read voraciously, and wrote stories. Her childhood was sadly marred by the death of her revered father. Her only special education appears to have been a year at boarding school, at Indiana, Pennsylvania, in 1880–81. About the time she was twenty, she and her mother moved to Pittsburgh, apparently to find work in the city. Already Elizabeth was trying to sell free-lance articles. Their money soon ran out, and their boarding houses grew qualitatively worse, as Elizabeth noted how hard it was for women alone in the world.

Her first break in journalism came when she wrote an unsolicited piece and mailed it off to the *Pittsburgh Dispatch*—one that immediately impressed editor George Madden. It was a retort to another article which had appeared in his paper, "What Girls Are Good For." In true Victorian attitude, the editorial had declared that girls should stay home and not seek careers or suffrage. Elizabeth, an admirer of independent women like Susan B. Anthony and Elizabeth Cady Stanton, was insulted and angry. After all, she could sympathize with women who were working in the nation's offices and factories; some were middle-aged widows and fatherless girls. Moreover, wrote Elizabeth in her reply, women had a right to lead interesting lives.

Her unsigned contribution landed on Editor Madden's desk. He was sufficiently intrigued by the article's logic and style to advertise for its author. When a beautiful well-dressed and soft-spoken young girl appeared, Madden was amazed; however, her character and intelligence seemed evident. He found himself agreeing to try a further assignment from her—free-lance articles on divorce, a topic almost taboo in the nineteenth century. Using her own recent experiences among women, and her father's old law books and case notes, she produced work so commendable that Madden offered her a job as reporter for five dollars a week. It was 1885.

## Elizabeth Cochrane Seaman

For her byline she chose Nellie Bly, from the popular song by Stephen Collins Foster:

> *"Nelly Bly, Nelly Bly,*
> *Bring de broom along.*
> *We'll sweep de kitchen clean my lub.*
> *And have a little song."*[1]

Apparently Nellie altered the spelling from Nelly in the song for personal reasons, like the final "e" added to Cochrane. But choose a pen name she did, as was conventional in that era for those select women entering the boisterous profession of journalism and desiring to protect their real ladylike names.

As the first female staffer on the *Pittsburgh Dispatch,* the new Nellie Bly continued to demonstrate her creativity.[2] She was a reformer who wanted to go out among the poor, into the tenements and factories, firsthand, talking with people, especially immigrants. And she cheerfully took on her share of the run-of-the-mill assignments in a cityroom along with opportunities to interview the famous, like poet James Whitcomb Riley and the philanthropist Andrew Carnegie. Nellie was soon that rare female invited to join the Pittsburgh Press Club.[3]

All of her new career was exciting to the daring Nellie. But still she yearned, as years back in Apollo, to travel. Why not Mexico, she asked her editors? How were people getting along since Emperor Maximillian was executed? How much of a democracy was the land south of the border? At her very request for such an assignment, the *Pittsburgh Dispatch* was aghast. A young girl travel alone in Mexico! But as she argued, and finally promised her mother would be the chaperone, she won her way.

Her trip during the winter of 1886–7 proved fascinating —and later produced her book, *Six Months in Mexico.* From the moment she rode in, atop the train observation platform, her sensitive pen began to record the grinding poverty she found. She visited not only the cities but also the remote villages, and talked, in the Spanish she had learned so easily, with all manner of Mexicans. In contrast to the rich entrepreneurs and palaces she saw, she told of the destitute and uneducated masses and their hovels.

In one of her widely-publicized *World* stories, she declared that Mexicans are "worse off by the thousands of times than were the slaves in the United States." While her assertion seemed exaggerated, her details about impoverished lives were shocking. Then one night under her hotel door she found a note of warning: "Nellie Bly, one button is enough." Translated, this meant: "Get out of Mexico while you're still alive, because the officials don't like what you write."[4]

Nellie, having seen courts and prisons in Mexico, knew it was time to hide her reportorial notes in the suitcase and vanish. So she did, with the help of an admiring *caballero*, who put her safely on an outward-bound train, assuring the conductor she was really a niece of President Diaz! Nellie's mother had left the tour early, unable to adjust to Mexico. All the material for Nellie's book was camouflaged (from police inspectors) amidst her lingerie. Her long manuscript would take its theme from her newspaper exposé, which had concluded: "Mexico is a republic in name only. It is the worst monarchy in existence."[5] Back then few travellers had crossed the border, and Nellie's book was planned as a pioneering report for American readers.

In the summer of 1887, shortly after her return from Mexico, she felt ready to crash the gates of New York City. Intrepidly she headed for Park Row where the giants of journalism were producing the highly-competitive *Times, Herald, Tribune, Sun,* and *World.* Naturally she was attracted to the work of that dashing crusader from Hungary, Joseph Pulitzer. After the political shooting that had involved his managing editor, John Cockerill, Pulitzer had departed from the St. Louis *Post-Dispatch* and was trying his fortune with the *World.* He had turned Jay Gould's faltering paper into a lively, well-circulating one.

The story goes that Nellie Bly tried repeatedly to put in a job application there and was ignored or refused, and that finally, after waiting one day for three hours, she managed to barge through Pulitzer's office door. The publisher and Cockerill together were so impressed by Nellie that they yielded on their rule against hiring a woman as a reporter.[6]

According to this story, Nellie won their confidence by her unique proposal to feign insanity in order to enter a lunatic asylum, and thus expose firsthand the vile conditions rumored rampant in such places. Mental illness was another taboo subject in polite Victorian society. It would take courage for any reporter to be imprisoned on Blackwell's Island, where cure or escape was virtually impossible. It was only after much thought that Pulitzer and Cockerill agreed. And her rescue was pledged within a few days.

Next Nellie began putting on a theatrical performance that would have put Lillian Russell to shame. First she checked into a seedy women's hotel on Second Avenue. Soon thereafter, she appeared to be a deranged girl who spoke mostly Spanish, having just arrived from Cuba, and grew so irrational in her behavior and conversation that the hotel matron called the police. Summoned before a judge, Nellie was ordered to undergo a sanity test. Three separate medical experts at Bellevue Hospital studied her and found that she was definitely suffering from dementia with delusions of persecution! She was committed to the Blackwell Island madhouse. She was a mystery girl who was not certain of her name.

Meanwhile, the other New York papers had played handsomely into the hands of Pulitzer's publicity stunt. For example, the *Sun* carried a front page piece in its issue of September 25, 1887: "She is pretty, well-dressed, and speaks Spanish. She wandered into Matron Stanard's Home for Females—asked for a pistol to protect herself." The story continued: "Her voice was low and her dress was neat-fitting," but she didn't know if her name was Brown or Moreno or what; her memory was gone. Pulitzer must have chuckled.

Nellie, however, was appalled at what she was experiencing at the asylum ever since she landed in her dismal cell. She nearly caught pneumonia after three buckets of ice water were thrown on her for a bath; she could hardly eat the garbage she was fed; she cringed at the cold uncaring ways that patients were treated, and even teased. Although she abandoned her theatrics and begged to be reexamined, officials pushed aside her request and told her she would probably be there for life. After more than a week, as she was growing fearful of not being sprung from this hellhole, Pulitzer's lawyer appeared with arrangements for her freedom.

Then on Oct. 8, 1887, the *World* burst forth with a front page boxed story which promised to answer all questions, starting in the coming Sunday paper, about the "Mystery Girl." Thus to the chagrin of other New York papers, Nellie Bly's famous first person series on Blackwell's Island appeared. Written in her colorful, detailed, human style, the stories created a sensation, stirring the hearts of readers for the plight of the insane, whom Nellie called "the most helpless of God's creatures." She called Blackwell's Island a "human rat trap."

Nellie's career in New York City had a fantastic start. She was called before a grand jury who investigated the asylum; and she had the satisfaction, ultimately, of seeing sizable welfare funds voted for much-needed improvements. While as a result of the Bly series, controversy flew all over the nation about the inadequacies of mental institutions, Nellie was off on other reforms. She looked into dishonest employment bureaus, and sweatshops and factories, again by disguising herself, this time as a poor working girl. She posed as a patient to study the quality of medical care at the city's health care dispensaries. And wondering how "fallen" women were treated in jail, she "stole" fifty dollars from another woman's purse and languished for hours in the "hoosegow" herself. Amidst foul smells and fouler language, she made notes on what sort of troubles bring women before the law and how these women were handled. In a lighter moment she answered an ad for chorus girls and went on stage in a scanty costume. As for the mashers in Central Park, after Nellie got through telling her experiences with them, their numbers thinned out in panic for a while.[7]

Her inventive mind had few limits. When she fell on an icy street in the blizzard of 1888, she made a feature of that. Of course, she had to go behind the woolly scenes of Buffalo Bill's Wild West Show, and she drove her own horse and buggy through Oneida County, describing country life, from picking hops to reeling at barn dances.[8]

In one of her most serious assignments, she suggested tracking down the living wives of all former presidents of the United States. What became of first ladies, once they left the limelight? She talked with Mrs. John Tyler, still surviving, since she was many years her husband's junior, and found her spending time with her children and travelling; she talked with Mrs. James K. Polk, still bright-eyed in her old age, proud of seldom missing communion at the Presbyterian Church. She loved the cordial Mrs. Ulysses S. Grant, who spoke freely and told Nellie she would have been a penniless widow if her late husband had not worked hard to write his memoirs, just in order to provide lovingly for her. As for Mrs. Grover Cleveland, then current first lady, "President Cleveland did not believe it good policy for Mrs. Cleveland to be interviewed."[9]

With the controversy over the suffragettes mounting—were they hussies, as some thought, or leaders of new directions?—Nellie interviewed Belva Lockwood, an attorney and candidate for president of the United States, who had come from Washington, D.C. on a visit to New York. Despite the stern looks of the rimmed-glass, gray-haired Mrs. Lockwood, the young journalist admired her ideas about women's emancipation, and the two had a congenial meeting. She told Nellie how she worked her way through law school at a time when men scoffed at women for even trying to enter the profession, of her hopes for seeing American women better educated, and finally, of her dreams of an international court of arbitration between America and foreign countries.

On the eve of 1890, three years after crashing New

York City journalism, Nellie Bly was on the threshold of the assignment that etched her name into the mind of posterity. It was to be her fabulous trip around the world, emulating the fictitious hero in Jules Verne's popular fantasy, *Around the World in Eighty Days*, published in 1872.

When she first proposed the idea of a race around the globe, *World* editors chorused that only a seasoned male reporter should attempt any such spectacular feat. Not a lone girl! But as usual Nellie had iron determination behind her sweet face. This time Nellie was brought to the point of threat—she would find another paper to sponsor her if the *World* dared give that assignment to anyone else.

After much hesitation, *World* editors suddenly, two days before the historic date of November 14, 1889, notified Nellie of their decision to allow her to go. The deal was that she would race to beat the fictional record of Phineas Foggs' 80 days. But they were still concerned about the nuisance of her typically womanly baggage. Nellie settled that by reducing her necessities into one startlingly small satchel. She wore a practical blue broadcloth dress, a camel's hair coat, and her double-peaked ghillie cap. She looked darling, and her image was soon to capture the heart of America, along with her immense courage.

Carrying a pocketwatch with New York time, she wore a wristwatch for local times and a lucky talisman ring on her thumb. Off she sailed on the German steamer, the *Augusta Victoria*, for England. On the same Thursday of November 14, the *World's* page-one story broke, with stacked headlines: "Around the World, A Continuous Trip Which Will Circle the Spinning Globe, Nellie Bly to Make an Unequalled Rapid-Transit Record, Can Jules Verne's Great Dream be Reduced to Actual Fact? A Veritable Feminine Phineas Fogg!"

The lead on one of the great-life adventure stories of all time began: "The *World* today undertakes the task of turning a dream into a reality. Thousands upon thousands have read with interest the imaginary journey which Jules Verne, the prince of dreamers, sent his hero, Phineas Fogg, on, when he undertook to win a wager circumnavigating the globe within the limit of Eighty Days." And there was

Nellie, pictured in what later generations were to call the uniquely Nellie Bly Costume.

Pulitzer's *World* had scarcely dried the ink on its own bombshell story when the rest of the American journalism world joined in telling the true romance of Nellie Bly. Everybody loved that smart and pretty girl! They wanted her to win her race. Not even the dimpled, curly-headed movie star Shirley Temple would have any more adulation.

Overnight there were Nellie Bly games, Nellie Bly clothes, Nellie Bly dolls, Nellie Bly songs. The nation went Nellie Bly mad. And eventually half the rest of the world joined, too.

Her schedule called for her to make London by November 21st; Paris by the 23rd; Brindisi, Italy, the 25th; Suez, the 27th; Ceylon, December 10th; Singapore, December 19th; Hong Kong, Christmas; Yokohama, January 7, 1890; San Francisco, January 22nd; and the New York *World* office by January 27th. That would be seventy-five days. All of this was despite uncertainties of train and boat connections, not to mention all kinds of natural disasters of weather and wrecks that could happen.

But breathlessly the waiting world—which Nellie now held in the palm of her hand—began to hang on for the latest word. Was she alive so far? Was she somewhere near on schedule? She had not decided to find a beau and never come back? And would such a doll be safe amidst all those foreigners? There was no radio news twenty-four hours a day back then, but there was a newspaper telling all about it. The *World* circulation was not hurting.

She had set forth to "sample the present advanced state of invention in modes of travel and communication," the *World* had explained in that opening story, and she was looking "chic and pert . . . showing not an ounce of trepidation or fear." But it was twenty-four long days after she left before her own first dispatch reached the paper; it was days in the return mail after her nearly seven-day crossing. Her voyage, reported Nellie, was a delight despite stormy waters, with bracing sea air and lots of new friends among the passengers. Many of them got up at 2:30 A.M. to wave good luck as she boarded a tugboat for London. At South-hampton she was met by a *World* correspondent from London who had a cablegram from Jules Verne himself. Would this fabled Nellie Bly visit him in France? Immediately she began plotting how to detour 180 miles and still win the race! Out of Charing Cross station in London, she barely made her connection, jumping onto the rear of a mail train. But after crossing the English channel, and boarding another train, Nellie finally arrived in Amiens to meet the great Verne. "Is it possible that this child is traveling around the world alone? Why, she is a mere baby," he is said to have murmured as she stepped onto the platform.[10] In Verne's carriage she was escorted off to his magnificent estate where Nellie of the fairy tale sat amidst sumptuous surroundings, struggling to speak in French, aided by an interpreter. This, she well knew, would be one of her life's greatest moments. Upon request she got to see the writer's study, with his new manuscript, *Sans Dessus, Dessous,* (*Topsy-Turvy*) lying on his desk. This book predicted that people would one day sit in their homes and receive bulletins from planets! But the clock said the brief encounter must end, and with kisses on both cheeks, Nellie was off to Calais for the train to Brindisi.

By then the *World* was reporting that "the whole civilized world is watching Nellie Bly."[11] Fan mail was avalanching the paper, including proposals for marriage. She was a pioneer journalist. She was a pioneer of her sex. She was something.

Out of Brindisi she sailed into the Mediterranean on the Pacific and Oriental steamer, the *Victoria*. When the British ship anchored in Port Said on November 27th, she had her first sight of the East. The horde of pitiful beggars left her aghast, as did the people who whipped them away with canes. On shore she mounted a burro and set off sightseeing around the picturesque streets.

The grinding poverty appalled her, even after firsthand reporting of American tenements. As the ship plowed on, dropping anchor in the Bay of Suez and Aden, Nellie was first ashore, looking for local color.

When the *Victoria* at last reached Colombo, the storybook city of Ceylon, Nellie learned that it was being guessed that her next connection, the *Oriental* bound for China, might be delayed in leaving the harbor for a week or more. Undaunted and still optimistic, she checked into the Grand Oriental Hotel and ate a repast served by costumed Singhalese waiters. She splurged on a summer-weight dress for two dollars, bargained in the old street markets, sipped cool drinks, went bicycling, and even attended theater. Naturally she journeyed to Kandy to oggle venerated relics said to be the Buddha's true tooth and collarbone. Just when she feared she might be coming down with cholera, the *Oriental* was ready to sail.

During a six-hour stopover at Penang, Nellie rode ashore in a sampan and saw her first Hindu temple; however, she would not take off her shoes, as religious custom decreed, to enter. Reaching Singapore, she hired a rickshaw to thread her way through the crowded narrow streets. There she saw her first Chinese funeral, complete with trumpets, fifes, cymbals, roast pigs, and a scarlet-covered coffin. As she boarded her ship for Hong Kong, Nellie bought a little monkey—which was to be her joy and trouble the rest of the trip. Then the *Oriental* moved into a monsoon, with waves washing over the decks. Nellie, courage in hand, finally went to sleep in her flooded cabin. On December 22nd, two days ahead of its schedule, the ship made Hong Kong.

Back in the United States, everybody was playing the "Nellie Bly Guessing Game" sponsored by the *World*. "A Free Trip To Europe!" was promised on page one, "including first-class transatlantic passages, railroad fares, and hotel bills, to the person who first makes the nearest guess as to the exact time of Nellie Bly's Tour." Some thought she'd beat Phineas Fogg, and others thought she'd never come close. Others wrote asking if there really were a Nelly Bly or was she a figment of the *World's* imagination. [12]

By December 19th the *World* was bubbling with hope, yet page one cautioned: "Though the unswerving luck of this plucky Nell will no doubt prevail against dreadful monsoons and typhoons, the reading public is cautioned not to be overly optimistic." "Tune in tomorrow, when we will see if our heroine survives," is the way the radio soap operas were to entertain the broadcast public a couple of generations later.

Meanwhile, Nellie and Monkey celebrated Christmas in Canton, warmly welcomed by the American Consul. Again her wide eyes beheld all possible things. These included a leper village, the Temple of Horrors (with statues and pictures representing the gruesome tortures of the condemned in Buddhist hell), and the Temple of the Dead (with hundreds of bodies in caskets, some years dead) and opium-smoking judges and their nearby punishment room (complete with thumb screws and body pulleys, as well as the prisoners in jail). Christmas, 1889, for Nellie was far from jolly old St. Nick and mistletoe.

By December 28th she set sail on the steamer *Oceanic* and by January 3, 1890, was in Japan. From Yokohama she wired "Happy New Year," and was already reporting that Japan was a clean and beautiful land. And God willing, she would make San Francisco on January 25!

When she left the harbor on January 7th, the ship's band saluted Nellie Bly with "Hail Columbia" and "Home Sweet Home." The ship's engine mounted a slogan, too: "For Nellie Bly, We'll win or die!" Nevertheless, the ship's progress was slow, due to raging storms. As the *Oceanic* pitched, some sailors wanted Nellie to throw her monkey overboard—a jinx, according to superstition. Nellie prayed hard, but kept her pet.

Among the songs and jingles in the United States now there was optimism that the Nellie Bly saga would end happily. A typical one ran:

> "Oh Fogg, good-by," said Nellie Bly,
> "It takes a maiden to be spry,
> To span the space twixt thought and act
> And turn a fiction to a fact."[13]

At last the *Oceanic* steamed triumphantly into San Francisco Bay. While a furor broke on shipboard over a smallpox rumor, and possible quarantine, Nellie and her monkey jumped into a tugboat and headed for land. Never in her fondest fantasies could she have guessed the jubilation that awaited her. In that huge welcoming crowd, the Mayor of San Francisco was there. A band played, including new songs like "Nellie Blue Eyes." Flags waved, and everyone cheered. And Elizabeth Cochrane of Cochran's Mills was radiant.

As a special *World* train took her East, back to New York, the people—ranchers, farmers, children, Indians, cityfolks—were there at every whistlestop and between times, along the tracks. More applause for the great American miracle of 1890!

When Nellie pulled into Jersey City, where her round-the-world journey was to be formally timed, she waved her cap back at the hysterical throng of admirers, as officials called out: "Seventy-two days, six hours, ten minutes, and eleven seconds." And the mob rang out: "She's broken every record! She's a winner." The mayor could hardly shove his way through to clasp her hand. With a mob surging about her carriage, and people not only lining the streets but hanging from windows, she finally made it to the champagne reception at Astor House—after ten cannons boomed welcome from Brooklyn! With congratulations still pouring in from around the globe, Nellie, after a little rest, began a forty-week lecture tour of the country. First, however, she reluctantly passed her little monkey on to a zoo.

And then time passed. Nellie finished her tour and her extra free-lance articles, and with the front-page headlines fading away, she now had to decide what to do with "the best known face in America."[14] She went faithfully back to reporting for the *World*. While no assignment matched the extravaganza of the global trip, she did major stories, such as interviewing the young anarchist, Emma Goldman, in jail, and covering the Pullman Strike of 1894 in Chicago. After 1893 she had her own Sunday column. It was, however, coming back on the train from an assignment in froz-

en Nebraska in 1895 that she met the man she married—
and began her descent from fame, as abruptly as her star
had risen.

The dapper older stranger sitting in the next seat engaged her in conversation as a true admirer of the famous
Nellie Bly. And after that brief acquaintance during the
ride, the couple left the train together in Chicago and were
married at the Church of the Epiphany. Robert Seaman was
the millionaire president of a hardware company, senior
director of the Merchants' Exchange National Bank of New
York, owner of all kinds of real estate, an heir of a well-
established old American family.

But he was more than seventy, and Elizabeth Cochrane
was just thirty. While the *World* wrote well of the match,
and bragged of his wealth, pointing out that their Nellie
would now have "nearly everything that the good fairy of
the storybook always pictures," her enemies whispered:
Did she marry for money? Was she afraid of being an old
maid? Was it a rebound from her younger beaus, like the
handsome James Metcalfe, a founder and editor of *Life*
magazine, who had squired her about for many months?
Why would Nellie unite with a man more than forty years
older? Kinder gossips simply believed that she sought comfort and security, an end to her hard-driven career, with a
good, fatherly man.

At any rate, Mrs. Robert Seaman proceeded to completely take over Nellie Bly. Where there was once high
adventure, there was now unobtrusive society life. There
were no more bylines or brass bands. There were parties.
There was entertaining. There was luxurious travel. There
were vast business holdings to attend. And then suddenly,
in 1904, Seaman was dead.

Elizabeth Cochrane Seaman, as she came to be known
in the biographical reference books, studied the hardware
business with the same able mind that once plunged into
journalism. She tried to introduce innovations, expand the
company, and bolster workers' morale. But somehow, by
1913, she learned that dishonest employees had stolen
thousands of dollars and she was headed for bankruptcy.

## Elizabeth Cochrane Seaman

In 1914 she went away to Europe—perhaps to forget her sorrows for a time. At any rate she was caught up in World War I, and she was interned in Vienna. It was 1919 before she got home. And then, Mrs. Seaman, past fifty years old, in financial need, sought to return to her old newspaper work. Her friend, Arthur Brisbane, and editor for the New York *Evening Journal,* proposed she handle a column dealing with the problems of abandoned and neglected children. With characteristic commitment, she worked hard at the new assignment.

It was thirty years since America's sweetheart, the girl known as Nellie Bly, had made her trip around the world. The present Mrs. Seaman was a slight, graying figure, sitting unnoticed in a quiet corner. Around her were some of the young women now being hired in newspaper offices by the 1920s, following the lead of successful pioneers like Nellie Bly.

Then in the winter of 1922 Mrs. Seaman caught pneumonia and ten days later, January 22nd, died in St. Marks's Hospital. She was fifty-seven. There were no crowds to mourn her passing. In fact, there were no close relatives.

The New York *Times* noted in its obituary headline that "Nellie Bly" was "Famous for Rapid Trip Around the World and Other Daring Exploits." And the *Evening Journal* declared: "She was the best reporter in America." Elizabeth Cochrane Seaman would have cherished such praise. Generations later she remains the most famous of women stunt reporters.

M. G. S.

## 14
## WINIFRED BLACK BONFILS
*Annie Laurie, Reformist Reporter*
[1863–1936]

Winifred Black once described herself as a "practical, all-around newspaper woman. That's my profession, and that is my pride."[1] She was also the pride of William Randolph Hearst during the heyday of his San Francisco and New York newspapers. Dubbed a sob sister, she also might have been considered among the early muckrakers.

Following the prevailing convention for women journalists in the late nineteenth century, she frequently used a pen name, "Annie Laurie," taken from a lullaby dear to her half-Scottish mother.[2] Her mother died when the future journalist was fifteen years old, four years after the death of her father, a retired brigadier general in the Civil War who served as an internal revenue commissioner in the Grant administration.

As Annie Laurie, Winifred became beloved in San Francisco, helping reform hospital care and establish ambulance service in that city, saving San Francisco's flower vendors from being legislated off the streets, and keeping the city's Palace of Fine Arts from being consigned to the wrecker's ball. An inveterate prober, she investigated juvenile courts in Chicago; exposed charity racketeers in New York; and organized disaster relief following the Galveston, Texas, hurricane flood of 1900.

She also played more ordinary roles in the Hearst organization: society editor, drama critic, city editor, managing editor, foreign correspondent and syndicate writer, though, as one historian explains, she "never had the trivial things to do; only the cataclysmic,"[3]

## Winifred Black Bonfils

Born Martha Winifred Sweet on October 14, 1863, in Chilton, Wisconsin, the "statuesque, auburn-haired beauty,"[4] had been raised by an older sister. Ada Celeste Sweet, a federal pension agent in Chicago from 1874 to 1885, had provided well for Winifred and three younger siblings. A good private-school education preceded Winifred's early ambition for a stage career. Lured to New York, she didn't get beyond minor roles but she did meet several literary figures, including William Dean Howells, Edwin Booth, and Mary Mapes Dodge, whose encouragement influenced her literary career.

But the move to journalism came almost by happenstance. Her sister shared with the *Chicago Tribune* one of Winifred's letters in which the aspiring actress wrote of the trials and tribulations of stage life, describing her experiences on tour with an amateur theatrical company. The *Tribune* liked it, printed it under the name Winifred Sweet, and asked for more.[5]

Though this first chance to see her name in print as an author probably set the germ for her later career, a family crisis intervened before she made the change to journalism as a lifelong commitment. Having gone west in 1889 in search of a runaway brother, she found him safe on an Arizona ranch and, a few days later, found herself in San Francisco, in need of a job but only vaguely aware of how newspapers operated.

Her stage experiences had prepared her to act like an experienced reporter when she applied at the *San Francisco Examiner*. Managing editor Sam Chamberlin, though not completely taken in, gave her a chance: she was to cover a flower show. The story was accepted and she was hired, at $15 a week. Her first major story, however, was unacceptable, and Chamberlin gave her a lesson in journalism she was to internalize and exemplify: "There's a gripman on the Powell Street line—he takes his car out at three o'clock in the morning, and while he's waiting for the signals he opens the morning paper. It's still wet from the press and by the light of his grip he reads. . . . Don't write a single word he can't understand and wouldn't read."[6]

Her next major story, written in the lively, convincing style that she soon developed, was in the best of Hearst's "yellow journalism" tradition. As Annie Laurie, she was assigned to an investigation of the City Receiving Hospital in San Francisco, with special attention to the treatment of women there.

With the writer's eye to detail, she donned shabby shoes and a threadbare dress, tore out a "Plain Sewing Wanted" ad from the newspaper and put it into a worn handbag, and asked a doctor friend to drop belladonna into her eyes, so that the resulting glare would make her look of desperation all the more convincing.

After wandering up and down Kearny Street a few times she tumbled to the ground and waited for reactions. Her subsequent *Examiner* story told of being noticed and fretted over by passersby and gawkers, ignored by policemen and then tossed roughly into a prison horse cart. The supposed sick woman was bounced at full speed over cobblestoned streets, pulled from the wagon, and dragged into the hospital on Washington Street. Treated there with an emetic of mustard and hot water, she was then abruptly pushed back onto the streets.

As might be expected, the story of Annie Laurie's adventure brought furious reaction from the hospital's chief surgeon, who had treated her. It also brought a governor's inspection, firing of many on the hospital staff, initiation of ambulance service in San Francisco, and some improvement in the treatment of female patients.

Other exposés included the undercover stint in a Southern cotton mill; a job at a local fruit cannery for twenty-six cents a day; interviews with the proprietress of a brothel; and a role as a Salvation Army angel at the Barbary coast. These assignments called on her descriptive and melodramatic skills. They were intended to lure readers. But they were also aimed at improving people's lives, helping the unfortunate, nailing corruption.

In another crusade, she travelled to Molokai, the Hawaiian Island leper colony. Her vivid and heart-rending descriptions evoked sympathy and an outpouring of public support for the settlement whose famous and somewhat controversial chaplain and champion, Father Damien, had recently died of the disease, contracted during his work on the island. Her great feeling for people such as those she met on Molokai was life-long, as reflected in a *New York Times* comment the day after her death: "The poor, the oppressed and the helpless found in her a true friend and companion. The cause of the suffering and the helpless always elicited her sympathy and aid."[7]

Not content to champion only from afar or only for those far away, she also took up, in the best Hearstian sensational tradition, the cause of "Little Jim," and indigent children throughout San Francisco. The child, a cripple born to a prostitute in City Prison Hospital, was turned away from the Children's Hospital. Administrators cited overcrowding, and ignored the "little incurable."

In her role as Annie Laurie she pulled out all stops on the organ of public sympathy and played the public's sentiments. The *Examiner* used the series to launch a campaign for incurables at the hospital. Hearst put her in charge of major fund-raising efforts, and she organized a Christmas edition of the *Examiner*, written, edited, and published by society women of San Francisco. This special edition, which appeared December 21, 1895, sold 130,000 copies and raised $10,000 for the Little Jim Hospital Fund.[8] She eventually saw the opening of the wing; one of its first patients was Little Jim, who died there a few years later.

Yet it was not the public service aspects of her stories which brought Winifred Black minor notice in journalism histories. As Annie Laurie, she is most often acknowledged as a "sob sister" because of her sensational reporting during the 1907 trials of Harry Thaw, a railroad magnate accused of murdering his young wife's seducer, architect Stanford White. Three other women were also at the press table during this case. Dorothy Dix, Ada Patterson, and Nixola Greeley Smith all shared the "sob sister" title as a result of this trial and other sensational stories they covered. As one might expect, the men who also covered the trials and did similar kinds of writing all escaped being called "sob broth-ers," "weeping willies," or any such appellative.

Having begun early to develop her descriptive skills, Mrs. Black had, long before the Thaw trial, become an experienced crime reporter. So, for example, an April 13, 1895, *Examiner* headline read, "The Crime of the Cen-tury," and introduced part of the reporter's continuing cov-erage of the murders of two young women by the Sunday school superintendent at Emmanuel Baptist Church in San Francisco. Details of the murders, discovered on an Easter morning, of the appearances of the victims' bodies, and of the behavior of the superintendent prior to the murder had captured reader attention for several days. The Hearst ap-proach to law and morality found its way into her copy about the trial and about the eventual hanging of the con-victed killer.

She is also known for the ingenuity she used in getting stories, though less enlightened critics might simply say she used "feminine wiles." She used ploys then, not un-known or untried by highly paid males in the 1980s. To get aboard the cross-country campaign train chartered for President Benjamin Harrison in 1892, for example, she charmed the local host, California Governor Henry Mark-ham, reminding him of an earlier complimentary story she'd written. Once on board, she hid under a covered table in the presidential dining car until the train was well on its way. One of only four reporters on the train, she got inter-views with Harrison, his wife, and his son, partly because of the president's earlier friendship with her father, and partly because Harrison wanted to keep this tenacious re-porter in his corner.

Whether known as Winifred Black or as Annie Laurie, success "came to her immediately, because immediately she became uniquely invaluable," in the words of a con-temporary.[9] Her work for Hearst showed energy, en-thusiasm, and resourcefulness, and caught the imagination of that magnate's growing audience. Hearst had early seen the importance of women readers in the stimulation of retail advertising revenue, and she successfully brought this group to Hearst's *San Francisco Examiner* readership and later to that of his *New York Journal.*

A skilled reporter on the doings and misdoings of the famous and the infamous, she had herself come under the spell of the yellow journalism magnate. In a 1936 article in *Good Housekeeping,* she described Hearst as "simple-hearted," wise, understanding, "the most forgiving, most encouraging human being it has ever been my luck to know." He was, she concluded, "the strongest influence in my life."

Perhaps it was a case of mutual admiration. Perhaps her admiration drew his response. At any rate, she had Hearst's complete confidence. A biographer called her "the one woman on his staff with access to his inner councils."[10] This confidence made the Chief turn to her as the one person he would allow to write his mother's obituary, as well as a biography. In twelve days she churned out 54,000 words of history and eulogy, having been asked by the Chief for a memorial pamphlet. Much to her surprise and chagrin, however, *The Life and Personality of Phoebe Apperson Hearst* was hard bound, printed on vellum in Germany, and sold in 1928 for thirty-five dollars a copy. She protested that, had she known it was meant as such a formal production, she would have wanted more time to polish it.[11]

Caught up as she was in the adventure that was Hearst journalism, she once wrote: "I'd rather smell the printer's ink and hear the presses go around than go to any grand opera in the world."[12]

Her personal life did, indeed, take second place to her career. An 1892 marriage to fellow journalist Orlow Black ended in divorce five years later. An invalid son, Jeffrey, who died in 1926, was the subject of a book, *The Little Boy Who Lived on the Hill,* and provided the only occasion in which she reflected publicly on her own personal life and feelings.

A second marriage, in 1901, to Charles Alden Bonfils, a journalist with the *Denver Post,* lasted formally until her death, but was interrupted several times by the separate newspaper involvements of husband and wife. (The Bonfils name is used only infrequently in biographical treatment of Winifred Black.) Of two Bonfils children, a son, Eugene, died at the age of nine. A daughter, Winifred, stayed away from journalism altogether. Perhaps she was never intrigued by it. Perhaps she feared the addiction her mother wrote of: "Time—why that was made for slaves—not for newspaper men. . . . You took your day off at the shop because you were afraid somebody else would have the fun of the big story. . . . Your paper was your sweetheart and your wife and your children and your smart outfit—it was your life and your heart's blood and the very soul of you."[13]

Lured to New York briefly when Hearst moved there in 1895 to take on the Pulitzer monopoly, she toured with William Jennings Bryan in 1896 and covered over 600 of his presidential campaign speeches, writing the promotional sort of copy Hearst hoped would get his man elected.

But she loved the West and left the Chief's eastern venture in 1897 to join the *Denver Post*, a paper in the best crusading, "yellow journalism" mold. And in the name of public welfare, she investigated a new kind of immorality uncovered by Hearst reporters. In the winter of 1898–99, she was sent to Utah to expose polygamy as practiced among the growing Mormon communities there. Her accounts revealed her own indignation and that of her editor regarding a practice she perceived as perverse, unfair to women, and clearly ungodly. A typical headline in the series was "Crush the Harem: Protect the Home!"

Though she remained with the *Post* for many ensuing years, her loyalties remained with Hearst.[14] Ten years into her career she got, perhaps, her greatest scoop on a special assignment for him. A tidal wave crashed into Galveston, Texas, September 8, 1900. It left 7,000 of the city's 40,000 residents dead and countless thousands homeless, lost, and badly injured. Through the night many survivors huddled on the roofs of the buildings still standing amid the angry waters. In the next few days bayonet-wielding militiamen lined the Texas City wharves to keep sightseers, scavengers, and newsmen from invading the stricken city.

Donning a boy's cap and shoes, and shouldering a pick-axe, Hearst's ace reporter moved unnoticed through the guardsmen's lines and boarded the boat that met the relief trains from Houston. She spent twenty-four hours at the scene of the horror and filed exclusive front-page copy. Her stories for the Hearst syndicate told of courage, kindness, faith. She described the "terrible, sickening odor" of decaying bodies and the desperate need for disinfectant. She urged that her readers "in pity's name, in America's name, do not delay one single instant. Send this help quickly," she urged, "or it will be too late!"

Her copy September 14 told *New York Journal* readers of a man who had floated all night through the storm with his wife and mother on what was left of their roof. At midnight he had kissed them good-bye, thinking he could not hold on through the night. When day broke, he was alone on the raft. "He did not even know when the women that he loved had died," she lamented.

She described her emotions on realizing that vast fires she saw were licking the pyres of 1,000 bodies that day because burial at sea was not feasible. And she described the things that tore at her heart: "a baby's shoe, for instance, a little red shoe, with a jaunty, tassled lace; a bit of a woman's dress and letters."

The tireless reporter's work in Galveston was not, however, confined to reporting. Telegrams to her hotel from New York, Chicago, Los Angeles, and San Francisco indicated that the Hearst machine was sending massive amounts of help. Newspaper staffs were filling trains with food, medical supplies, and personnel, and she was to find hospital facilities and dispensary stations.

Hearst's sob sister showed she could manage more than tears. With the help of Galveston's police chief, she took over a school building that had survived the disaster, found blankets, cots, pillows, and cookstoves in other Texas cities, and hired two cooks. She organized the aid sent into the city and the over $350,000 in contributions sent by readers as a result of her stories.[15] She also helped find permanent homes for 48 orphans.

Six years later, April 18, 1906, when San Francisco was rocked by an earthquake, Hearst again hired her to cover the disaster for *Hearst International News Service*. She told the story of the 700 dead and the 300,000 homeless as a result of the fires that followed the quakes. Her copy included the personal, human stories, tear-jerking in the best journalism tradition, interpretive in the best 1980s model.

Her journalistic work also extended beyond the United States borders. She reported in 1910 on the suffragettes in England. She went to Europe in 1918 to study the effects of the war and the rumored armistice on American soldiers. Her ensuing copy warned families that their returning sons and lovers would probably be different people from those whom they had bid good-by several years earlier: "older, sadder, less trustful, less full of hope . . . stronger, more self-reliant . . . wiser." And she inveighed against what she saw as wretched treatment of American soldiers by ungrateful French citizenry and government. Once the saving is done, she wrote angrily, "his blood and his life is no longer needed," and he is cheated by merchants in the market piace, treated shamefully by people on the streets, and given shabby send-offs.

Closer to home, also in 1918, she was called to Washington by Secretary of the Interior Franklin Lane to chair the "U.S. Garden Army," which entailed a campaign to encourage American children to plant victory gardens at home so that more foodstuffs could be shipped to soldiers overseas.[16] She was to cover the Versailles peace conference that same year and the Washington naval disarmament conference in 1921 and 1922. At home she promoted San Francisco's first community Christmas tree, with generous backing from the Hearst coffers, and began her crusade for the building of what, only after her death, came to be the Golden Gate Bridge.

Retirement would have been unthinkable for this irrepressible woman. At the age of sixty-eight, in an extended assignment reflecting the best of crusading and reform journalism, she covered the International Narcotics Convention in 1931 in Geneva; she pressed in her copy for international treaties of cooperation in fighting and controlling narcotics traffic. She had earlier written a book, *Dope, the Story of the Living Dead*, partly in response to Hearst's suggestion. In it, she pointed to the growing problem of drug use in the United States, twice that in France, three times that in England, and eight times that in Italy. The book also urged the United States government to take serious and speedy action to meet the problem. Much of her writing, in fact, during the last ten years of her life, was in support of stronger drug control, and she headed Hearst's national campaign against drug traffic.

Despite increasing complication of diabetes and arteriosclerosis, she remained an active journalist until three months before her death. Her thrice weekly "Annie Laurie" columns for the *Examiner* and about 6 articles weekly for the Hearst syndicate were in her well-known, energetic style. Biographers tell of her continued zest for new adventures, including an airplane ride, her first, over 14,000-foot-high Mount Shasta, in northern California, just after her 72nd birthday.[17]

That she was respected in San Francisco is attested to by the fact that, on hearing of her death there on May 25, 1936, the city's board of supervisors, police commission, and board of education adjourned their meetings. An honor guard of police and firemen stood watch at her casket under the city hall rotunda. And city notaries acted as honorary pall bearers for her funeral.[18]

Hers was a style of journalism for its own age, and she won a place in history as well as in the hearts of her readers and fellow citizens. However much historians may dissect her work, and that of the yellow journalists with whom she worked, they must also look at the public interest which motivated much of that work and at the public service which it performed. They must also look at the enthusiasm and adventure, without which far fewer readers would have tried newspapers at all.

S. M.

## 15

# RHETA CHILDE DORR
*Freedom Fighter*
[1866–1948]

Rheta Childe Dorr spent her entire life fighting for freedom and opportunity for herself and for other women. No matter how young or old, she was convinced, women were entitled to equal pay for equal work, equal respect for their contributions, equal opportunities to use their talents. She fought for the illiterate young girls working in the factories and sweatshops of New York as well as for the suffragists in faraway countries. And as a war correspondent, she marched with a women's regiment in the Russian revolution. In her memoirs she explained, "I wanted all the freedom, all the opportunity there was in the world. I wanted to belong to the human race, not to a ladies' aid society to the human race."[1]

From the time she was twelve, Rheta Child[2] wanted to know everything about the women's movement. She and her sister disobeyed their father's wishes and crept out of their Nebraska home one night to hear Susan B. Anthony and Elizabeth Cady Stanton speak on women's suffrage. She joined the suffrage movement after the speech and, from then on, took it upon herself to stand up for women's rights.

Rheta was born November 2, 1866, in Omaha, Nebraska, the second of four daughters and two sons of Edward Payson Child, a neighborhood druggist. Her father, a native of Batavia, New York, had attended Rochester University, but had practiced medicine in Missouri and Arkansas without a degree. He married Lucie Mitchell of Ironton, Missouri, in 1861, and the couple moved to Lincoln, Nebraska, in 1862.

Rheta's early suffragist sympathies and her strong individualism apparently led her to reject formal education. After a year at the University of Nebraska, she dropped out, but not before she had immersed herself in history and literature, including Ibsen's *A Doll's House*. Though she longed to play Nora, she settled for working in a Lincoln post office and later at an insurance underwriting firm. In 1890 she moved East and discovered a new world and a new outlet as a resident member of New York's Art Student League. While in the city, she met John Pixley Dorr, a conservative Seattle businessman fourteen years her senior but charming and attractive. They married in 1892 and moved to Seattle to start a family.

But marriage didn't slow Rheta's growing concerns about women's rights. Inspired by the writings of Charlotte Perkins Gilman and other feminists, she persisted in her quest for a wider world of experience. For example, she interviewed Alaskan gold miners whom she encountered in Seattle and wrote about them for New York newspapers. Her husband had difficulty understanding Rheta's involvement with the women's movement, and she, in turn, could not understand his position. In 1898 they separated, and she left with little money and a two-year-old son, Julian, to support.

Determined to succeed as a journalist, she moved back to New York, where she spent two years free-lancing until she became editor of the *New York Evening Post's* women's section. She wrote fashions and housekeeping news to attract department store advertising, but also covered the burgeoning women's movement. A Wednesday column, "Women and Work," featured women prominent in politics, medicine, education, and philanthropy, and introduced her to "people worth knowing."[3] But an assignment to cover women's "invasion" of the gold-beating trade in New York influenced her profoundly. She was to examine the unrest created when women joined the ranks of semiskilled laborers whose task was to hammer small bars of the precious stuff into paper-thin sheets for use in delicate gold leaf work.

She moved with her son into an East-side, two-bedroom apartment to live among the toilers, to see for herself just what the women's invasion of the labor force was, and whom it affected. She would continue her past work minus the extra book reviews she wrote to supplement her meager salary. Her neighborhood, for two years, was an East-side ghetto, a "sea of pushcarts, peddlers, swarming children" and overworked, ill-paid Jewish immigrant males. And her occupations changed frequently as she moved from factory to factory, with more and more questions and fewer and fewer answers.

Paid even less were daughters and wives of her immigrant neighbors, women who worked for near nothing, never complained, and waited to get married. And while they waited, they were cruelly exploited. Mrs. Dorr did not understand their logic. How could women settle for slavery? she anguished. Was their acquiescence universal? Why did they accept injustice and ill-treatment? A partial answer came in an incident she experienced: a young factory girl, picketing during a women's shirtwaist makers' strike, was beaten by the shop foreman as a policeman looked on.

"Lifting her in my arms and wiping from her mouth several broken teeth, I made a loud demand for the man's arrest," she later reported. Summoned several days later, the foreman was summarily released by the judge who called the reporter's accusation "incredible," as the two women stood dumbfounded before him. The foreman awaited his accusers outside the courtroom, shouting, "Yah, you low-life yenty! See where you get off already. We knocks the teet' down yer t'roat an' you can't do nuttin." The slur was both sexist and ethnic, underscoring the fact that women were indeed powerless until they rose above race and class and joined forces. To reach such cooperation became a goal Rheta Childe Dorr set for herself, one to which she was to devote much of her life.[4]

As a result of a series of *Post* articles on Eastside working girls, she was appointed in 1904 chairman of the Committee on Industrial Conditions of Women and Children for the General Federation of Women's Clubs headed by Sarah Platt Decker. One year later her committee, backed by the Women's Trade Union League and the Association of Settlements, persuaded Congress to authorize the Bureau of Labor to spend $350,000 investigating conditions of working women in the United States.[5]

Her crusading work was beginning to bear fruit—but her editor still offered her no future. Indeed, when she asked for the raise which her popular features and columns seemed to warrant, *Post* managing editor, Hammond Lamont, told her: "Women are not paid the same salaries as men, nor can they ever expect to be. This may seem hard but after all there is a rough justice in it. Men are permanent industrial factors, women are mere accidents."[6]

The same managing editor had earlier assigned her "one funny piece" on the meeting of the New York Federation of Women's Clubs and had called the gathering "damned nonsense." His attitude had helped galvanize her stand as a fighter for women's causes. It also made her quit the ill-paying *Post* job and seek her future elsewhere. She was, after all, the only support for her little family of two, and her teenage son had constantly increasing shelter, schooling, and other needs.

The search took her, in 1906, on the first of nine trips to Europe, with enough commissions from newspapers and magazines to cover expenses for three months. She wrote on newly independent Norway, only one year separated from Sweden, and the coronation of its King Haakon. She attended a gathering of the International Women Suffrage Alliance, saw the vision, inventiveness and courage of its leaders, and became a staunch disciple of suffragist Christabel Pankhurst.

She visited Russia in the throes of social and political unrest and found there a torch that was to burn in her journalistic imagination for the rest of her life. The torch was being carried by male and female workers, by counterparts of the dispossessed immigrant laborers she had been writing about in America. But in Europe and Russia, the dispossessed seemed to have hope, seemed able to unite for better opportunities. She was buoyed by discovery, and took it as a harbinger of hope for women in America.

Though she was in those days capable of long hours and hard work, she was deceptively frail in appearance. One biographer describes her thus: "A small ambitious woman, slender and dark, with firm, arresting features and a vibrant personality . . . a rich contralto voice which had been molded by her need to maintain the respect of the editors on whom her career depended."[7]

Upon her return to New York, Mrs. Dorr helped organize and lead the Madison Square suffrage march. She wrote some suffrage copy to make money and sought a magazine interested in conditions facing women in industry. Her idea was accepted by *Everybody's Magazine*, and she was hired for thirty-five dollars a week to work in the sweatshops; there she gathered first-hand data for a series on "The Woman's Invasion." One major motivation was that a highly touted book, *The Woman Who Toils*, published in 1903, had purported to tell the working woman's story. Authors Marie and Bessie Van Voorst had gathered their materials in brief forays into assorted factories. But the book failed to portray factory workers as real people, to tell the laborers' stories in their own words, using their own examples. It had treated workers with little feeling and less respect.

In contrast, she wanted to understand the factory women—how they dressed, what they ate, what they talked about over their meager lunch breaks, what they aspired to. She also wanted her readers to understand these things, as well as what it was like, for example, to make iced tea cakes ten hours a day in a hot factory that reeked of sickeningly sweet odors of icing, flavoring extracts, and fresh cakes: "The women swayed and dipped, arms moving in arcs, to the cacophony of the brawling machine. In silence they worked, until I addressed a girl at the end of the line. 'Don't you get tired making that one gesture all day?' 'Sure. Me back's broke by noon,' was the laconic reply."[8]

And she wanted to demonstrate that women were permanent factors in the nation's industry and its wealth, and
that they ought, consequently, to be treated as independent
human beings instead of mere adjuncts to male-dominated
society.

So for the better part of a year, she visited and often
worked in factories in various parts of the country, among
immigrant groups and among native-born Americans. She
worked on corsets, men's coats and underwear, and in the
spinning room of a Fall River, Massachusetts, mill. She
made party cakes and tea biscuits, and saw soups, pickles,
and jellies produced. She watched young girls working
amid the stink of steaming blood and hot carcasses, stuffing
sausages and painting lard cans in Chicago packing houses,
and learned that their pittance was six dollars a week, far
below the amount paid male workers. Men held the skilled,
well-paid jobs. Yet, as in her own case, good numbers of
women were their families' major or only wage earners—
because of death, illness, divorce, unemployment, or any of
several reasons. Accidents? Nonpermanent? Hammond Lamont's smug answer simply didn't apply, in case after case.

Midway through her undercover investigation, she arranged to forward her copy to a collaborator at *Everybody's*,
William Hard. This would ensure progress toward the series while she continued data gathering. But the women's
slavery issue came home personally and cruelly to her
when, with much of the digging done, Hard informed her
that he no longer needed her, that the series was his.

She sought out a female lawyer friend, took Hard to
court, won, and saw her name put on the series. But when
she saw the series in print she realized it was, indeed, not
her work. She had found a race of dispossessed women
toiling as the slaves of industry. Hard had portrayed women
as a triumphant army of invaders, freed of household drudgery and gleefully snatching jobs from male workers. She
was appalled and angry.

But she soon found a new outlet for her crusading ener-
gies. *Hampton's Magazine*, a short-lived aggressive reform
magazine, had been established by Ben B. Hampton over
the skeleton of the dying *Broadway* magazine. Mrs. Dorr

sold him on the vast amount of her remaining material still undeveloped for the *Everybody's* project; she submitted between six and ten articles a year, along with regular coverage of fashion, education, women's suffrage, and other women's issues.

The first piece she submitted to *Hampton's* was really a series of isolated vignettes illustrating the double burden of factory mothers forced to work outside their homes all day and left to carry the mothering, washing, cooking burden all night. She described a birth on a factory floor, a pregnant woman's suicide, the life of a woman forced to work literally all night in her sweatshop-home.

She was driven by her firsthand experiences to tell the horrors to whomever would read, because she wanted to provoke awareness, concern, and change. She used many first-hand examples of the real women she had watched, worked with, and lived among. Most of the articles she wrote during her two and a half years with *Hampton's* reappeared in her first book, *What Eight Million Women Want*, published in 1910. In the introduction, the author apologized for the title but said it was impossible to determine with accuracy what one woman, much less what any number of women, wanted. Her caveat notwithstanding, the determined woman was telling her own hopes and desires in the stories of the women she interviewed and featured.

Her work on *Hampton's* went beyond women's issues. She covered the educational revolution introduced by John Dewey. She toured juvenile courts throughout the United States and questioned in a series the decisions that placed in detention children whose problems needed compassionate and enlightened attention.

She returned to Europe in 1912 to interview and write about suffragists and feminists. Partly because she focused on the plight of unwed mothers in Sweden, her stories from that country did not sell well. But suffrage copy from Paris and London, commissioned in advance, ran in *Good Housekeeping Magazine.* Two years later, as a result of this trip, she helped Emmeline Pankhurst, leader of the radical

British suffragists, write her autobiography, *My Own Story.* Her association with Mrs. Pankhurst and her daughter Christabel, whom she met earlier, as well as with other radical British feminists, aroused her discipleship, and she began pressing for militant action to achieve a women's suffrage amendment in the United States.

It was a logical outcome, then, that she should become, in 1914, the first editor of *Suffragist,* official organ of the Congressional Union for Women Suffrage. She organized publicity and used various approaches to bring the issue before the public. In a White House reception for about 500 women, she confronted President Woodrow Wilson on his nonsupport for the suffrage amendment. In a strategy planned in advance for its headline appeal, she pressed him so hard on the issue that he left the reception abruptly after snapping at her, "I think it is not proper for me to stand here and be cross-examined by you."[9] The strategy worked: the next day the story hit front page in many papers.

The abdication of the Czar of Russia in 1917 gave the enterprising fifty-six-year-old journalist the justification for a third trip to Russia as a reporter for the *New York Evening Mail.* She would denounce the Bolshevik program and write her second book, *Inside the Russian Revolution,* essentially a repudiation of the upheaval there which she saw as counterproductive.

She spent several weeks marching with the women's regiment, the Battalion of Death, one of several special regiments, male and female, organized by the government to inspire the rest of the army to a renewal of courage and loyalty. Led by Mareea Botchkareva, the battalion showed tremendous courage, suffered incredible losses, and provided Mrs. Dorr with a cause she could exult in. She wrote on the mismanagement of Russian industry under the Revolution; postrevolutionary needs in education, government, agriculture, leadership; and on what she believed should be the United States reponse to these needs. She interviewed at some length Anna Viroubova, a court regular and intimate friend of the czarina, and wrote a sympathetic account of life at the royal court. From Viroubova she got a picture of the insidious influence of the monk Rasputin on the czar and czarina, and called the sometime cleric a "wicked, deceitful, plotting creature, a monster of sensuality, an imposter, an all-around bad sort."[10]

Unable to bring notes out of the country, she secluded herself for over a month on her return and wrote from memory an extensive series of articles which were syndicated. Sometimes they ran simultaneously in as many as twenty newspapers.

She remained mobile, and traveled to Sweden, France, and England to cover American and Allied war efforts. A 1918 trip to the Western Front, where her son Julian was assigned in the American Expeditionary Force, led her to write the book, *A Soldier's Mother in France*, directed at the mothers of all United States servicemen. She sailed across the submarine-haunted Atlantic. She toured munitions factories in England and Scotland, where young women did the dangerous as well as highly skilled work, which they would have been considered too frail or incompetent to perform had the war not made their service indispensable.

Rheta Childe Dorr's active life came to an abrupt halt in 1919 when she was struck by a motorcycle in Washington. The accident affected her memory and her health, though she tried to stay involved in her work.

In 1920 she campaigned for Harding, joined the Woman's National Republican Club of Washington and developed an increasing scorn for pacifists and "do-gooders."[11] She made trips to Europe and England seeking a return to health, and wrote articles as a foreign correspondent for several papers.

In 1922 she met Anna Viroubova in Karlsruhe, in western Germany, to help her write her memoirs, *My Memories of the Russian Court*. Her own autobiography, *A Woman of Fifty*, was written in 1924. Documenting her highly personal crusade for women's rights, it is a notable record of the reform era, a pioneer effort to set down both the details of a career and the feelings and relationships of a woman who knew herself to be in a man's world and who felt constrained to fight for her rights.

In a similar vein, she undertook the difficult but re- warding task of writing a biography, in 1928, on Susan B. Anthony. A final work, *Drink: Coercion or Control*, dealt with the thorny issue of prohibition.

The death of her son while he was vice-consul in Mex- ico, and her deteriorating health ended her journalistic ac- tivities. She died August 8, 1948, having worked consis- tently for the rights of the forgotten and dispossessed. Her last days were spent in the home of her physician, Dr. Aileen Von Lohr in New Britain, Pennsylvania.[12]

S. M.

# 16

## DOROTHY THOMPSON
### *Political Columnist*
### [1893–1961]

In the early 1930s and 1940s Dorothy Thompson was a household word. She probably had more power and prestige than any woman in America, with the possible exception of Eleanor Roosevelt.[1]

During this period before World War II she was known to more than seven and a half million readers for her syndicated column, "On the Record." Her famous commentary had blossomed on the editorial page of the prestigious *New York Herald-Tribune* in March, 1936, running on alternate days with the column, "Today and Tomorrow," by one of America's favorite sages, Walter Lippmann.

Dorothy Thompson, an established foreign correspondent before she became a columnist, was the first woman to win respect as an important editorial-page figure. Almost overnight her column was being published in nearly 200 papers. Not only that, but she was featured as a weekly commentator by the National Broadcasting Company back in 1938–39 before television when Americans in droves listened to the radio.

A commanding woman, she was sought all over the United States for banquets, lecture engagements and commencements. She was the first woman ever invited to speak before meetings of such sacrosanct male groups as the Union League Club, the Harvard Club of New York, the National Association of Manufacturers, and the United States Chamber of Commerce; one year brought 7,000 invitations to speak.[2] She kept three secretaries busy around the clock while she telephoned up a trans-oceanic storm, talked to world leaders, or reigned over salons at home with distinguished visitors. She was the subject of a two-part profile in the *New Yorker* and a cover story in *Time,* both symbolic of her eminence. In 1938 her earnings were reported to be somewhere over $103,000—astonomical back then.[3] Fame and fortune were, for some years, the middle names of Dorothy Thompson, who became secondarily known as the wife of the first American to win a Nobel Prize in literature—Sinclair Lewis.

After World War II the bright candle of her unusual career began to flicker out. But no one who reads the history of journalism in America can ignore its brief radiance.

For one whose words were to stir the world, Dorothy Thompson had a modest beginning in life. She was born July 9, 1893, into a Methodist parsonage in Lancaster, upstate New York. Both her parents were English-born. Her father, a poor minister, was shifted about from town to town, including Tonawanda, Gowanda, and Hamburg, during her childhood. Her mother, Margaret Grierson Thompson, died when Dorothy was only seven, the eldest of three children, and soon after that she was left to feud with a stepmother, who was a church organist and spinster she had never liked.

Nor could the new Mrs. Thompson cope with a self-willed rambunctious tomboy like Dorothy. Finally in 1908 the Reverend Peter Thompson placed his teenage daughter with relatives in Chicago, where she studied at Lewis Institute. She was to remember her father in later years as a saintly gentleman who had considerable influence on her thinking—but who was unable to outwit or govern his second wife. At the private school, Dorothy developed some respectable scholarship, not only in English, but in French, German, and Latin.

In 1912 she entered Methodist-affiliated Syracuse College in New York, largely because the tuition was minimal for the children of Methodist ministers. Before she graduated *cum laude* in 1914 she made her name as an orator and conversationalist and as campus leader for women's suffrage. Later to be one of America's highest-salaried opinion molders, she worked as a waitress, sold books door to door, and labored in a candy factory, while earning her way through college.

It was her commitment to the suffrage movement, which had then gained high momentum, especially in the East, that provided Dorothy Thompson with her first job out of college. She began her career by addressing envelopes in the Buffalo office of the Women's Suffrage party and went about the state organizing meetings and stump-speaking; she soon had an admirable reputation.

In the next several years she lived in New York City's Greenwich Village and Cincinnati, Ohio, and worked at publicity, copywriting, and social service, while saving her money to go to Europe, hoping to become a foreign correspondent. Not a lot was accomplished in this early career period, unless it was that her experiences were later to help provide Sinclair Lewis with material for his novel, *Ann Vickers*.

With a few dollars finally in her pocket, six years out of college, Dorothy sailed for Europe in 1920, with a friend, Barbara De Porte, to embark on her dreamed-of career as a foreign correspondent. Two early stories carried by International News Service helped launch her journalistic work. They were articles on Terence MacSwiney, the Irish Independence leader, and on striking Fiat workers in Rome. After Barbara left for London, Dorothy lingered awhile in Paris and then went to Vienna in 1921 as a publicist for the American Red Cross; she also worked at space rates for Cyrus Curtis's *Philadelphia Public Ledger*.

Early in her Vienna days Miss Thompson's career received its upward push from Marcel Fodor, Hungarian-born correspondent for the Manchester *Guardian*, who became her journalistic mentor and friend; Fodor was at home not only in several languages but in Central European politics.

Shortly after their first meeting, he invited her to share a major news break—a scoop that further established the byline of Dorothy Thompson. The story dealt with the future of Austria's Hapsburg dynasty, a royal family still of decided interest even after World War I.

## Dorothy Thompson

In a cloak-and-dagger plot that read like something out of the popular comic strip, "Brenda Starr, Girl Reporter," the pretty, blonde Dorothy Thompson dashed off with Fodor in the dark of the night to overtake an unscheduled stop of the Orient Express near the Hungarian border. Their daring adventure was intended to trap the grandnephew of former Emperor Franz Josef, namely Charles, the discredited monarch who was traveling from exile in Switzerland in hope of recapturing the throne. As the drama turned out, Charles' attempted *coup* failed—but not before Dorothy had interviewed his entourage and filed an internationally important exclusive story for the *Ledger*.

Shortly after that, the free-lancing Miss Thompson trailed Fodor to Prague and, aided by credentials as a regular correspondent, she also gained interviews with Czechoslovakian President Thomas Masaryk and Foreign Minister Eduard Benes, which produced major articles.

Armed with successful clippings, the young journalist headed for Paris, accompanied by Fodor, and stormed the *Ledger* for the job as the regular Viennese correspondent. Thus Dorothy Thompson won her first journalism credentials as a fifty-dollar-a-week reporter; she was assigned to cover Austria, Hungary, and Czechoslovakia. In Vienna she bloomed as a respected writer, "blazing through Europe," as John Gunther said, "like a blue-eyed tornado."[4]

She was part of that circle of gifted writers, including Gunther, Clarence Streit, and Edna St. Vincent Millay, who gathered frequently at the posh Sacher's Hotel to argue about international affairs. Her Viennese apartment overflowed with interesting and distinguished persons; among the assortment she found her first husband, a dark handsome Hungarian Jew, Josef Bard, who had a reputation vaguely as a writer but also as a playboy. Their marriage in 1922 was difficult from the start, although the actual divorce did not come until 1927. Miss Thompson apparently outranked him by far, not only in talent but in marital loyalty.

Meanwhile Dorothy Thompson moved to Berlin as Central European Bureau Chief in 1924 for Curtis' Philadelphia *Ledger* and New York *Evening Post*, the first woman to head an important American overseas bureau. Amid the sophisticated atmosphere of the German cultural capital she relished her work and associates and gained a reputation for brilliance. In 1927 she met Sinclair Lewis at a press tea. The celebrated author of *Main Street* (1920), *Babbitt* (1922), and *Arrowsmith* (1925) was being lionized by almost everyone in Europe at the time; but when he met Dorothy, she intrigued him by refusing to be overwhelmed. During their much-publicized romance, the ardent Lewis pursued her all over Europe to press his courtship. He was then forty-two and she was thirty-four.

Before she was ready to settle down, however, Miss Thompson left him writing *Dodsworth* in Berlin and took off for the tenth anniversary festivities of the Bolshevik Revolution. Ensconced in Moscow's Grand Hotel, she wrote for periodicals and also produced a book, later published as *The New Russia*.

In 1928 she resigned from the Curtis papers and married Lewis in the chapel of the Savoy Hotel in London. After the wedding, one of the world's most famous couples started their honeymoon in a trailer—a "caravan" attached to their car, still something of a novelty in the British countryside. Not always sleeping in a rough camp style, they parked their trailer and slept instead in such mansions as that of her friend, Sir Harold Nicholson. Enchantment with the outdoor life ended one night during a heavy rain. The next day a team of horses had to pull the trailer out of the mud, and author Hugh Walpole offered the Lewises hospitality in his home. At summer's end they sailed for America.

They settled, especially in summers, near Barnard, Vermont, on a 300-acre showplace called "Twin Farms," with two houses and a sweeping view of the mountains and valleys. Famous guests were to pay them visits there, such as writer Vincent Sheean and Republican politician Wendell Willkie (with ample help from servants who maintained the rustic charms). There, too, passed some of the happiest days of Dorothy's life during her short marriage to Lewis. The couple also had a home in New York City.

Their only child, Michael, was born in 1930. That was also the year Lewis became the first American awarded the Nobel Prize in literature, and they went to Stockholm. Much of the next five years Dorothy Thompson continued to travel and write in Europe. Despite his growing problem with alcoholism, Lewis seemed devoted to promoting his wife's career. He not only read her manuscripts and helped polish her work, but made contracts with leading magazines. Once at a party he even went so far as threatening a fist-fight with Theodore Dreiser who had been accused of plagarizing several thousand words from Dorothy's newspaper articles for his book, *Dreiser Looks at Russia.* Lewis' pride in his wife's work, including his run-in with Dreiser, was told in a 1940 *New Yorker* profile.

At other times Lewis apparently resented his wife's limelight, which seemed to put him in the shadow. As his reputation tended to wane, hers continued to ascend. The *New Yorker* articles were entitled "The It Girl"—with double meaning: "it" in 1940 stood for "sex appeal"; "it" also had come to be the name that Lewis resentfully called "the international situation" which was Dorothy's main passion. She was always, declared Lewis, talking about "it." The profile also reported that a group of women talked of running Miss Thompson for president of the United States, and that Lewis had said ruefully: "Yes, and I'll write a column called 'My Day,' " a reference to the newspaper feature by Eleanor, the wife of President Roosevelt.

During the early years of her marriage to Lewis, Dorothy had won her famous interview with Adolf Hitler. She had tried for eight years to see the German dictator, pursuing him to various European inns, meetings, and secret hideouts, before he finally agreed to see her in 1931, at Berlin's Kaiserhof Hotel. In what proved to be probably the greatest error in judgment of her career, she had lightly dismissed the potential influence of the future world dictator, calling him "inconsequent and voluble, ill-poised, and insecure," and "a man of startling insignificance" who, she predicted, would not be able to seize power.[5]

Several years later when Miss Thompson's book, *I Saw Hitler*, appeared, she was expelled from Germany because of her by-then outspoken writing against Nazism. For years afterwards she kept the document of her expulsion proudly framed on her desk. Shortly after her interview in 1931, she changed her mind and began to live down her original underestimation of Hitler.

During the early thirties, Dorothy Thompson, extremely attractive, knowledgeable and articulate, was becoming a popular lecturer in the United States when she appeared on a New York *Herald-Tribune* forum; the wife of publisher Ogden Mills Reid, Helen, was so impressed that the paper's offer to Miss Thompson as a columnist came shortly thereafter. Her assignment from Mrs. Reid was to write a lively, readable column devoted to national and world commentary, one which would especially interest women. Miss Thompson made her debut on the editorial page March 17, 1936. "On the Record" was strong-minded, hard-hitting, emotional, fact-filled, and controversial. Overnight Dorothy Thompson was in the big league with Walter Lippmann, whose "Today and Tomorrow" ran on alternate days. And she was on record clearly for interventionism, and against the isolationism favored by many Americans before World War II.

Her emotional involvement with the campaign for intervention was symbolized in 1933 when she deliberately interrupted a German-American Bund Rally of 22,000 people in Madison Square Garden; she did this by loud guffawing and was escorted out by police. The incident sparked an international news story, of course, since she was Dorothy Thompson and Mrs. Sinclair Lewis, besides. By then most readers were viewing her either as a warmonger or patriot, depending upon their politics.

As the drift toward war mounted, magazine articles she published also added to her stature as a commentator. Her work appeared not only in popular magazines such as the *Saturday Evening Post* and *Cosmopolitan*, but in the select *Foreign Affairs*, including her piece, "Refugees, A World Problem," in the April, 1938, issue. This was influential in bringing about an international conference in Evian-les-Bains, called by Franklin D. Roosevelt; in fact her efforts in behalf of the subsequently created Intergovernmental Committee on the Refugees were honored at a dinner in 1941, with messages of praise read from both Roosevelt and Prime Minister Winston Churchill.

Some of her best columns, speeches, and broadcasts were collected in a book, *Let the Record Speak*, published in 1939. In this her voice rang out powerfully against Hitler and for American intervention. She wrote of her conviction that "the National Socialist Revolution in Germany would prove to be the most world-disturbing event of the century and perhaps of many centuries, that it would affect the whole of Europe and the political structure of that Continent, and eventually lead to a modification of the social order with serious repercussions on the whole world."[6] She also warned that there would be no more "free rides to freedom," and that it was "too late to hope that we shall preserve Democracy without effort, intelligence, responsibility, character, and great sacrifice."[7]

Another typical piece appeared on March 14, 1938, when she told America: "Perhaps the most contemptible phase of the rape of Austria is the German Nazi government's official explanation of it. The world has been treated to a display of brute force which is entirely in harmony with Nazi *Weltanschaunng*. Still, the leaders of the Third Reich evidently believe there is no limit to the credulity of the human race."

Her columns were generally sober, sometimes with faint humor as when she brought Lewis into them as her husband, "The Grouse." Her words and analogies were usually clear, as when she wrote her famous column on April 5, 1939, on Chamberlain, comparing his compromising actions with Nazism to those of the English classic, *Alice in Wonderland*. She declared that he was like Alice, who, even in a world of "unreasonable foreigners" continued politely, even blindly, to follow any directions given, such as "Drink Me" or "Eat Me," without considering that messages from unknown sources would be poisonous. Dorothy Thompson lashed into Chamberlain for his stupid policy of "muddling through," like the fairytale heroine, "without reasoning." She felt "reasonably sure" that Chamberlain had not even informed himself by reading *Mein Kampf,* Hitler's own book, which revealed his dangerous philosophy.

Dorothy Thompson's prominence in public life made her the subject of a *TIME* cover story on June 12, 1939. "She and Eleanor Roosevelt are probably the most influential women in the U.S.," said the article. She has had "one of the most phenomenally successful careers in U.S. journalism"; her readers were numbered at 7,545,000 from 196 newspapers. Assessing her work, including her 6 books up to that point, her various awards, honorary degrees from leading universities, her notable days as a foreign correspondent, and her current status as a "sensationally informative" editorial columnist, *Time* concluded that Miss Thompson had become to many women "the embodiment of an ideal, the typical modern American woman that they think they would like to be: emancipated, articulate, and successful, living in the thick of one of the most exciting periods of history and interpreting it to millions."

It was 1940 before Dorothy Thompson's stellar position as a world commentator was shaken. Although she was criticized as controversial and strident, Publisher Reid and his wife stood proudly behind her—until she switched her support from their Presidential candidate, Wendell Willkie, to President Roosevelt that year. Her main reason was that the international crisis required experienced leadership, but for a staunch Republican paper like the *Herald-Tribune,* her opposition stand was too much. In 1941 her contract with the paper was not renewed, and Dorothy Thompson's column went to the Bell Syndicate, whose main paper was the liberal, less-prestigious New York *Post.*

Once the isolationism controversy of the late 1930s was resolved and America entered the war, Dorothy

Thompson lost her eloquent cause. She continued to be a well-known lecturer and writer, but in essence, she was "like a great ship left stranded on the beach, after the tide has gone out."[8]

During the postwar years her syndicated column often focused on the Middle East, especially the creation of a Jewish state. She was frankly critical of the Zionist Movement, which, in her opinion, had grown too extreme to merit her earlier support. In her 1938 book, *Refugees, Anarchy or Organization?*, she asserted that Palestine, because of its Arab-Jewish conflict, was the wrong haven for the Jews. And in 1948, with the creation of Israel, she displayed sympathy for the uprooted Arabs.

By 1947 the *New York Post* had dropped her column, and subsequently so did other papers, because of offense to Jewish readers. As a result of her anti-Zionist position, she helped to found a group known as American Friends of the Middle East (AFME), which met with criticism as allegedly financed by Arab oil interests and the Central Intelligence Agency (CIA).[9] Although Dorothy Thompson's intentions were doubtlessly honorable, in hoping to create enlightened discussion about problems of the Middle East, her reputation was hurt.

Continually after World War II she moved toward a more conservative position. In 1952 she supported Eisenhower for president. The lustre of her commentary had dimmed. In a monthly column she wrote for the magazine *Ladies Home Journal,* she turned to mundane subjects beyond politics, such as morality, education, and even dieting.

Her marriage to Sinclair (Red) Lewis had finally ended in divorce, after some years of separation. In 1943 at the age of fifty she had entered into an apparently happy union with Maxim Kopf, a kindly, easy-going Austrian artist. His death fifteen years later was hard for her to bear, and "On the Record" was brought to an end the same year.

Just three years later at sixty-seven she died of a heart attack in Lisbon, Portugal, while visiting her grandchildren. Her body was brought to the Vermont village cemetery in Barnard for burial beside Kopf. Among the relatives and friends who gathered for graveside rites in May, 1961, was her old colleague, Vincent Sheean, who later was to tell his own version of that remarkable interlude in American history he called *Dorothy and Red*. Dorothy Thompson had truly been, as the title of another biography said, *A Legend in Her Time*.

M. G. S.

# 17

# MARGARET BOURKE-WHITE
*Pioneer Photojournalist*
[1904–1971]

"In a man's world," Carl Mydans once said, Margaret Bourke-White was "one of the greatest achievers of our time."[1]

This opinion from a distinguished male photojournalist was only one among the world's verbal wreaths on the occasion of her death in 1971. Although she had been away from the public spotlight for almost two decades, valiantly battling Parkinson's disease, she was widely regarded as one of the pioneering women photojournalists from the 1930s on.

During her lifetime this reporter-photographer received an accolade of honorary recognitions, including her selection as one of the "ten top living women of the twentieth century" for the New York World's Fair Hall of Fame.[2] *Life,* on whose staff she catapulted to overnight fame, along with the very first issue in 1936, called her the "world's pre-eminent woman photojournalist."[3]

Her life spanned from 1904, when the box camera with roll film was still a relatively new invention, to 1971, when the miracle of color television brought pictures via satellite from the moon.

Her career was simultaneous with the advent of photojournalism, a word coined in her youth, as the result of advances in photography and magazine production.[4] Her life cannot be considered apart from the heydey of picture magazines, when the great events of the 1930s, 1940s, and early 1950s entered homes through the print media and radio.

When she was a beautiful young woman still in her twenties, Margaret Bourke-White was already a celebrity, living in the Chrysler Tower penthouse above Manhattan, with a private secretary fending off an admiring public. "The world literally beat a path," to the studio of *Fortune's* golden girl who, a few short years before becoming rich and famous was unknown and near penniless.[5] Overnight the name of Margaret Bourke-White had ascended in the early thirties among professionals in journalism. "Maggie," as she came to be called by friends, was a "charming, brown-haired slip of a girl who had risen to her eminence as rapidly as the Chrysler Tower" itself and on "foundations quite as sure."[6]

Margaret Bourke-White, like the subjects of many success stories, was a person whose promise was suggested early in youth. She was the child of parents committed to both love and education in abundance for their daughter, and they were decidedly influential in shaping her character and career. This is clear throughout her autobiography, *Portrait of Myself*, dedicated "To My Mother and Father." She was born Margaret Bourke White (no hyphen) on June 14, 1904 in New York City. Her father, Joe White, was an engineer and inventor of modest means, much respected by his family and those who knew him. Her mother, Minnie Bourke, while limited in education, had a thirst for knowledge that kept her reading and attending school until she died past sixty. Margaret's parents inspired strong ideals, especially what she later called "the love of truth." Her father taught her "never to leave a job until you have done it to suit yourself and better than anyone else can do"; it was a self-set high ideal that gave Margaret unbounded persistence in accomplishing goals all her life.[7] As a girl, her curiosity was encouraged by both parents who spent time with her in studying nature and in collecting and caring for all kinds of pets, including snakes; in her approach to learning, she was taught to be fearless.

Before his early death when Margaret was only 17, Joe White had spent much of his career working with printing presses and in developing offset lithography; his main interest was the rotary press, and perfecting the processes of multicolor printing. Her father took Margaret on several business trips that influenced her early life; a trip to a plant in Dunellen, New Jersey, however, always stood out in her mind. It was here that her father's rotary press had been built. The child was fascinated by the spectacle of the foundry, viewed from its sooty balcony. "I can hardly describe my joy," she later wrote in her autobiography, "about the sudden magic of glowing metal and flying sparks." That memory of "beauty" was so vivid that later, as a photographer, she was to desire to show that magic world to others in pictures. Margaret also gave credit to her father for building World War I's first compact portable printing presses mounted on trucks, as well as the first printing press for Braille.

Photography was one of White's hobbies. He frequently tinkered with lenses and exposure settings, and ahead of the times even experimented with three-dimensional movies. It is therefore amazing that Margaret wrote she "hardly touched a camera and certainly never operated one until after he died."[8]

Margaret graduated from high school in Plainfied, New Jersey, where she was editor of the school paper and won first prize in a literary contest for fifteen dollars worth of books; she promptly chose works of science, since she planned to become a biologist. In 1922 she entered Columbia University for her freshman year. Almost by chance she took a course in photography, taught by Clarence White (no relative), who proved so exceptional a teacher that "a seed was planted."[9] Nevertheless, the following year, she was at the University of Michigan, where exceptional courses were available in herpetology. There at only nineteen she met and married Ernest Chapman, a graduate student in electrical engineering. Together they went on to Purdue University, but their youthful marriage lasted only two years, and Margaret returned to her mother in Cleveland, Ohio, where she worked in the Museum of Natural History. For her senior year she decided to finish at Cornell University in Ithaca, New York, both because of its science courses and its beautiful setting.

With family funds running low after her father's death,

she was faced with the need for a job. Suddenly she was inspired to try using her old second-hand camera from Columbia days, making and selling campus pictures to students and alumni. Although her old Ica Reflex had a crack straight through the lens, she photographed some of Cornell's landscapes and fine architecture; she claimed to know "so little about photography" that her undertaking was "impudent."[10] But recognition came at once when the *Alumni News* bought some of her pictures for covers. In this initial adventure in photography she belonged to the soft-focus school, with her photographs looking like "fuzzy Corots"—avant-garde in the 1920s.[11] More impressive yet, several architects wrote letters to this promising student, pointing to the job market for good architectural photographers. Just twenty-three years old, Maggie discovered that there was "a growing feeling of rightness with a camera in my hand," and that "being a photographer for a living was a tantalizing possibility."[12]

During spring break that year, still somewhat torn between biology and photography, she sought an opinion about her portfolio from members of a top-ranking architectural firm in New York City; they told her enthusiastically that she had a future, indeed, in photography.

After graduation she returned to Cleveland, her official place of residence, to obtain a divorce. She assumed her maiden name, and began using her middle name of Bourke with a hyphen on White, a new legal surname to launch her career. In 1927, she was a beginning free-lance photographer, grateful to earn five dollars for a finished photograph; by 1929 she would be sought by Publisher Henry R. Luce for his new magazine, *Fortune.*

Meanwhile, this novice photographer had an in-a-door bed apartment, and a kitchenette-sink-darkroom. While earning a living, mostly by free-lancing architectural and landscape photographs, she spent her time wandering about in Cleveland's backyard, making shots of derricks, smokestacks, bridges, locomotives, tugboats, and other industrial hallmarks. During the nation's big boom-before-the-depression, the young photographer found endless construction subjects. Most of all she felt an inner compulsion to make photographs inside the steel mills, this grown woman who had never forgotten her childhood impression of beauty inside a foundry.

Her first discreet inquiries about entering the mills brought the reply that women were not welcome inside this dangerous zone. Despite this, she was intrigued, as she recalled many years later: "The smokestacks ringing the horizon were the giants of the unexplored world, guarding the secrets and wonders of the steel mill"; and she knew this mission would be "close to my heart."[13]

In 1928 when Maggie first approached the president of Otis Steel Mills, he promptly expressed amazement that a "pretty young girl should want to take pictures in a dirty steel mill" and felt "flower gardens" would be more "artistic" for her; he cited dangers inside his mills, such as deadly fumes and acids, burning splashes from hot metal, and scorching radiation from intense heat.[14] Her persistence won him over, however, and at twenty-four, she began a spare-time study of the Otis Mills, mostly at night. The unhappy mill officials who were reluctantly forced to watch her were sure she would either be injured or driven away by the rigorous working conditions. Instead, she produced a portfolio of pictures so remarkable that the proud mill owners had them privately published as a small book, *The Otis Steel Company, Pioneer.* (Only a few copies were printed in 1929 and one of these is today in the special collection of the Cleveland Public Library.)

That same year Margaret Bourke-White received a telegram from the publisher of the then-new weekly news magazine called *Time,* inviting her to New York. She was to be hired for his proposed new venture, the expensive, dollar-an-issue *Fortune,* which promised to feature dramatic photographs of business and industry. Henry Luce and Margaret were friends from the start, with the publisher sometimes touring foundries and factories with her, lugging her equipment and sharing vending machine lunches.

When in 1929–30 the Chrysler Building was being constructed, with its phenomenal rise more than 1,000 feet above Manhattan, Margaret was there for the event. To get her photographs she perched on a high tower, swaying eight feet in the wind, sometimes in subfreezing temperatures. Eventually she moved into the building's penthouse apartment, together with two pet alligators and a few turtles.

When *Fortune* sent her to photograph industries in Germany, she felt herself intrigued by her nearness to Russia, which was then to journalists essentially a "closed country," she recalled in her autobiography. Despite the doubts of *Fortune* editors that she could wangle a visa, or see much inside the USSR even if she did, Miss Bourke-White persisted. Although the Soviet Embassy in Berlin at first rejected her day after day for six weeks, she finally managed to push by the bureaucratic red tape.

The Russians liked Maggie and allowed her considerable freedom of movement, not only in the big cities but in the villages. In one hut, she found Stalin's mother and made a fine photograph. And she rode with native guides over the Caucasus Mountains, sleeping in caves and eating raw mutton.

The result of her tour was her book, *Eyes on Russia,* published in 1931, which remains one of the first and most distinguished Western views of the USSR. In his preface, the critic, Maurice Hindus noted: "As an example of photography raised to the level of great art, it has to my knowledge no equal.... She writes with a clarity, a vigor, a warmth, which stamp her as a literary artist of real distinction." Thus early in her career Margaret Bourke-White was recognized to be nearly as fine a writer as a photographer; successive books were to continue as monuments to her writing talents.

Back in the United States, she continued with more daredevil assignments for *Fortune.* In 1934 she covered the great drought, barnstorming from the Dakotas to Texas in a rickety two-seater plane piloted by a stunt flyer from a country fair. The despair of people in the Dust Bowl made a deep impression on her and raised her social consciousness.

## Margaret Bourke-White

With the rise of photojournalism in the world and of
*Life* in America, Margaret Bourke-White became a popular
name after 1936. Publisher Luce was first to see that the
new European picture-magazines, growing from technical
advances in photography, were bound to come to America;
he purchased the waning, old humor magazine, *Life*, because he liked the name, and began mapping the high-
quality pioneer magazine that would proclaim world news
primarily in photographs. It was an instant success at ten
cents an issue. Margaret Bourke-White starred with the
cover story for the first issue on November 23, 1936, about
the construction of the world's largest earth-filled dam at
Fort Peck, Montana. Charter subscribers got what *Life's*
editors proudly proclaimed in their introductory editorial
to be "construction pictures as only Margaret Bourke-
White can take them," and "a human document of American Frontier life."[15] As usual she had gone beyond the assignment, searching out the truth, and found moving stories of plain people caught up in the New Deal's huge
work-relief project. The famous cover with her acclaimed
artistic study of the dam's immense concrete structure was
but one part of her photos and memoranda for the inside
photo-essay.

After that Miss Bourke-White was likely to be found
anywhere that *Life* felt something important was happening. She covered the flood of 1937 in Louisville, Kentucky;
that same year she toured the Arctic aboard a ship in a group
with the governor general of Canada, in the days when such
a trip was considered high adventure. On a sidetrip by plane
during her "top of the world" tour, she was on a small
chartered plane, which became trapped in treacherous fog.
The pilot made a forced landing on a tiny island, but had no
working radio or even rations; when the crew appeared
doomed, the fog finally lifted enough for the plane to escape
to Cambridge Bay, just as the gas was giving out.

Also in 1937 appeared her popular book, *You Have
Seen Their Faces*, which further established her reputation.
This story of the sharecropper South was a combined work

with Erskine Caldwell, celebrated author of *God's Little Acre* and *Tobacco Road*. Caldwell had sought out Miss Bourke-White to help "depict the ugly economic tragedy in a medium more vivid than language."[16] Travelling together most of one summer, the two gathered the bitter tales of poor Southerners. His realistic prose and her stark photos made a book still regarded today as a classic documentary against racial injustice.

In the late 1930s as Hitler mercilessly carved up Europe, *Life* shifted Maggie's focus essentially from home to abroad. On the eve of World War II she had a series of prime assignments which were to leave nobody surprised that Margaret Bourke-White later should be chosen the first woman accredited as war correspondent. One of her typically brilliant photo-essays, "Czechoslovakia: A Democracy Fighting for Its Life," appeared in *Life* on December 5, 1938. Through this, many Americans were made aware of the "valiant little democracy," "the tinder-box of Europe," and the "likely next objective of Adolf Hitler." Earlier, on September 5th, *Life* had carried her moving story on tiny, helpless Hungary, "about as big as Ohio," ready to be devoured.

Out of these and other experiences, Maggie, together with Caldwell, produced another well-received book, *North of the Danube*, a simple and dignified story that depicted the arrogance of the Nazis and the plight of everyday people.

During an interim in the United States in 1939, Maggie and Caldwell were married—a step over which she had long hesitated because of her deep involvements with her career. The marriage was to last for several years, and during this sojourn in the States they gathered material for a book, not published until 1941: *Say, Is this the USA?* As two creative artists, they had travelled coast to coast, interviewing persons from every imaginable walk of life, to "give the feel and impression of America." The book was another classic.

As the storm brewed urging American intervention, Maggie was swiftly off for assignments in England, Rumania, Turkey, Syria, and Egypt. It was 1941 that brought some of the spectacular work of her career. *Life's* editors foresaw that Germany's nonaggression pact with Russia would probably be violated, and they wanted their great journalist on the scene; as a result of her trip a decade earlier, she was one of the few Western journalists with such extensive knowledge of Russia. Caldwell was eager to join his wife. Reaching Moscow just a month before the Nazi attack, they found the American embassy already quietly preparing for evacuation of its citizens; in fact the Caldwells were urged to leave. But Maggie saw the situation at once as providing "the biggest scoop of my life." She wrote; "The biggest country in the world enters the biggest war in the world, and I was the only photographer on the spot, representing any publication and coming from any foreign country."[17]

For a time she had to evade a military ban on civilian cameras, sneaking photographs however she could, including from her hotel balcony above Red Square; she turned her bathroom into a darkroom filled with her paraphernalia, and hid-out under the bed when air-raid inspectors knocked on her door. When, finally, she was issued a pass as "the only foreigner with photographic privileges," she found the censorship of her movements made work almost impossible.[18] She was permitted to photograph Stalin inside the Kremlin, shooting photographs that include her famous cover shot with his almost-smile. In *Life* on September 8, 1941, she gave a lively first-person account of that experience.

Her never-to-be-forgotten shots, however, came from courageously climbing on top of the Embassy's roof one night to capture the panoramic spectacle of Nazi bombing. *Life* bragged of her "scoops" in its photo-essays, especially those of August 11, and September 1, of its luck, in having "a fine photographer at the scene of an historic news event."

Erskine and Maggie finally got permission to go for a few days to the Russian front. As the only woman correspondent, Maggie marched in the mud, trembled in the dugouts, shared the rations, and watched men die on the battlefield. Once she was only a half mile away on an exposed hilltop when Germans began wiping out a little village with incendiaries. The husband-and-wife team gathered the material which produced their final important book, before their divorce, *Shooting the Russian War*. Back in the United States, when war was declared, Maggie was eager to offer her talents in behalf of her country. In the spring of 1942 Margaret Bourke-White was named the first accredited woman correspondent in uniform.[19] Through a mutual arrangement between *Life* and the Pentagon, Lt. Bourke-White was to take assignments from both her magazine and the Air Force.

She flew first to England to a secret bomber base where B–17 squadrons were assembling for attacks on the Continent. For homebound patriots, she pictured life inside the "Flying Fortresses."

When the theater of war opened in North Africa, Maggie requested permission to go there and moreover, to fly on combat missions. Ironically, although she was sent by slow sea convoy for safety, her troopship was torpedoed. She spent eight anxious hours in a lifeboat before rescue. Once in Africa, she was flown in a cargo plane to a secret oasis in the Sahara desert to prepare for her bombing mission. There under the scorching sun, she practiced for her high-altitude flight, wearing heavy-weight gear of fleece-lined leather, overalls, leggings, and boots. On January 22, 1943, she rode in the B–17 lead of a formation of planes, destined for the airfield near Tunis, a chief air base used by the Germans in ferrying troops from Sicily. Nearing their target, her plane was shot twice in the wing; her crew, however, managed to surprise German troops and some recently landed planes. The mission was considered a key raid of the war and helped to push Germans out of North Africa. The proud story in *Life* (March 1, 1943) told how she had to "brace herself against a 200-mile-an-hour slipstream as she took pictures from the radio operator's window and the gunner's hatch." They reported that she was "too busy to be frightened"; she was the first woman to fly on a combat mission.[20]

During 1944–45, Maggie covered the ground war in Italy and the last stages of the war in Germany, assignments which brought two fine books from her own pen and camera: *They Call It Purple Heart Valley* and *Dear Fatherland, Rest Quietly*. Her trip to "the Forgotten Front" in the Cassino Valley was made at the frank request of the Pentagon to publicize the heroism of the foot soldiers. In Italy as in Russia, she was "one of the boys," bearing with fortitude the foxholes and shellings and all the hardships. She had some close calls while flying in unarmed Piper Cubs or artillery spotting planes. Despite the dangers, she also photographed heavy artillery action on the ground.

During the final days of the war, she journeyed along the Rhine River with the Third Army, documenting the collapse of Germany and the liberation of the concentration camps. She was there when the Americans marched into the infamous Buchenwald camp and recorded the tragedy for posterity. Of that terrible experience she reflected afterwards: "I saw and photographed the piles of naked, lifeless bodies, the human skeletons in the furnaces; the living skeletons who would die the next day because they had to wait too long for their deliverance; the pieces of tatooed skin for lampshades." One of her famous photographs was entitled "The Living dead;" standing beside the camp's barbed-wire fence were some of those for whom deliverance was probably coming too late—gaunt haunting, tattered people. (These accounts and photos appear in *Dear Fatherland, Rest Quietly*.)

After the war, Margaret Bourke-White was not long in the United States when another faraway adventure called. With India fighting for freedom from Great Britain, and civil strife between Muslims and Hindus rampant, *Life* wanted its ace journalist on the spot. She was to witness the anguish of partition, the birth of Pakistan along with free India, the riots and bloodshed. She talked with Mahatma Ghandi only hours before he was assassinated. Her book *Halfway to Freedom* was yet another triumph in both words and pictures.

Sent to South Africa in 1950 Maggie became the first woman to plunge more than a mile below the earth into the gold mines and publish the story of the abused black workers there.[21]

With the advent of the Korean conflict, she was once more a war correspondent, this time covering guerrilla warfare. It was on her way home from Korea in 1952 that she first noticed a dull ache in her left arm and leg. She was only 48.

In 1958 her mysterious malady, growing progressively worse, had finally been diagnosed as Parkinson's disease, a nervous disorder which slowly ravages the body's motor control. She did not surrender to the illness, but put up a gallant fight, one that included experimental brain surgery. After 1952 the prolific flow from her camera and typewriter gradually ceased, except for her remarkable autobiography, *Portrait of Myself*, published in 1963. She lived as actively as possible in the last days, taking pleasure in the natural surroundings of her estate in Darien, Connecticut. Death claimed her at age sixty-seven in 1971.

M. G. S.

# 18

## MARGUERITE HIGGINS
*War Correspondent*
[1920–1966]

Stamina and risk-taking characterized the reportorial style of Marguerite Higgins from her first assignment to her last. Her first journalistic prize, in fact, came as a result of her unwitting participation in the 1945 liberation of the prisoner compound in the Nazi concentration camp at Dachau. Her career would take her into Berlin as chief of the *Herald Tribune's* bureau, into the front lines in the Korean and Vietnam conflicts, and into the drawing rooms and antechambers of world leaders. She overcame the jealous sniping of male colleagues who complained that she took advantage of being a woman, but who were unable to offer any proofs of their accusations. She thought a great deal about the work she and her fellow journalists were doing and wrote movingly about her concerns: "First-rate war coverage, it seems to me, requires only two qualities that are not normally demanded of any first-rate reporter on a big story. They are a capacity for unusual physical endurance and the willingness to take unusual personal risk.[1]

By the age of thirty-six, Marguerite Higgins had received fifty journalism awards, including the 1951 Pulitzer Prize for Foreign Correspondence, the first woman ever to receive this award. She was also the 1950 recipient of the George Polk Memorial Award given by the Overseas Press Club for exceptional courage and enterprise in reporting. Other awards Miss Higgins received included the New York Newspaper Women's Club Award, the Long Island University Polk Award, the Veterans of Foreign Wars Gold Medal, the Distinguished Service Award given by the National Federation of Business and Professional Women, the Marine Corps' Reserve Office Award, and the 1951 Woman of the Year Award given by the Associated Press.[2]

Born in Hong Kong in 1920, Marguerite was the only child of Larry Daniel Higgins, a steamship company manager, and Marguerite Goddard, a French woman her father met during an overseas assignment with the United States Army Air Corps. Her early years abroad helped her become fluent in French, English, and Chinese. Her American schooling and eventual study of journalism at the University of California at Berkley prepared her for a career which was to be precedent-setting in many respects.

She began by reporting for the *Daily Californian*, the *Tahoe Tattler*, and the Vallejo *Times-Herald*, moved to New York to pursue graduate study in journalism, and found a job on the *New York Herald Tribune*. Her opportunity came partly because the draft was taking men away from jobs and more women were being hired at newspapers.[3]

To demonstrate that she was determined, thorough, and qualified for city room work, she got an exclusive interview with Madame Chiang Kai-shek, then a patient at New York City's Columbia Presbyterian Medical Center. Though the famous lady was refusing to see reporters or grant inverviews, Miss Higgins got into her room, held an interview, and sewed up the *Tribune* job.[4]

Her exclusive interview with Madame Chiang was just the beginning of a long succession of exclusives for which she became famous.

"Intensely competitive," with more "fire and zeal than most,"[5] she was not long satisfied with covering New Jersey fires, Connecticut circus disasters, and the women's war effort in New York. But her dissatisfaction had deep roots: "I had known since childhood that if there was to be a war I wanted to be there to know for myself what force cuts so deep into the hearts of men."[6] She asked the *Tribune* editors to send her to cover the war in Europe and, frustrated by their refusal, went to the newspaper's publisher, Helen Rogers Reid. Because Miss Higgins' reputation for tenacity and thoroughness had preceded her, the publisher consented. In August, 1944, Marguerite went to cover the war's closing days, first in the *Herald Tribune's* London bureau, then in Paris where she became, in her own words, a "cyclone of energy." She was determined to prove herself, determined to show that she could compete with and outstrip her colleagues. Each day she read every French newspaper, along with all dispatches from Agence France Presse, the French wire service, and personally checked the validity of all major news developments reported through her bureau. Of her work at that time she was later to reflect: "Because of the strict discipline of my city desk training, it never occurred to me to send out a story asserting, 'Such and such is happening according to the French Press.' I went to the ministry or individual involved, and probed until I found out to my satisfaction precisely what the facts were."[7]

Her copy on the Allied march across Europe dominated the front pages back home. Her work was of such quality that, at the age of twenty-five, she was named the *Herald Tribune's* Berlin bureau chief. But bureau chief or not, she personally went out on assignments to trouble spots, covered the capture of Dachau, Buchenwald, Munich, and Hitler's mountain-top hideaway at Berchtesgaden. In fact, as the long nightmare of the Second World War moved toward its end, Marguerite and a reporter for *Stars and Stripes*, the United States Army newspaper, entered Dachau in a jeep laden with captured German weapons. Far ahead of the liberating United States tanks, the two reporters had accepted the surrender of the Bavarian city of Augsburg and driven into the gunsights of the SS guards still in control of the Dachau camp. Using her command of German, she accepted the surrender, and the weapons, of twenty-two riflemen, and entered Dachau.

"I have never seen such wild joy and pandemonium," she wrote. Yet the tragedy was everywhere, as she later wrote from Buchenwald: "The dying, in their stench-filled barracks, whispered messages for their families and then proceeded to die before I could make sense of their wishes."[8]

Her stories won Marguerite the New York Newspaper Women's Club prize for the best foreign correspondence of 1945. Her participation in the bloodless surrender of two towns brought her and her companion, Sergeant Peter Furst, an Army citation for outstanding service with the Armed Forces under difficult conditions.

Marguerite also reported on the treason trial of Marshal Henri Petain, the Nuremburg war trials, and the Berlin Blockade. From there she went to head the *Herald Tribune's* Tokyo bureau in 1950. Convinced that the United States was locked in a death struggle with Communism, she frequently criticized, either in print or in personal interviews, United States presidents for not taking a firmer stand. In a *Saturday Evening Post* piece in mid-June, 1949, she urged that the Voice of America show its audience among European Allies "what the Communist states all over the world have meant in terms of deportations, incredible toil, terror, deplorable living standards and, in many cases, semi-starvation."[9]

For Marguerite, the enemy was Communism, and freedom was the issue. Toward the end of her career, the introduction to her book, *Our Vietnam Nightmare*, quotes a soldier's letter home: "It is maddening to see clippings from U.S. newspapers scorning our efforts. . . . If we do say 'to hell with Vietnam,' we might as well say to hell with Southeast Asia, then, maybe, to hell with Europe, South America, and then maybe, 'to hell with freedom.' "

So strong were her feelings that she once advocated use of the atomic bomb to counter any Chinese intervention in Korea. And so intense was her desire to see for herself the action she was reporting about that, immediately following the crossing of the border by the South Koreans, she headed to the front lines. The early months of battle saw her, the only woman of 131 correspondents in Korea, covering and involving herself in the conflict. A colleague later wrote of her:

## Marguerite Higgins

Miss Higgins was often as newsworthy as the event she was covering. She was both the paradox and the stuff of legends: the eye-batting blonde, in dusty fatigues, breaking the Army's ban on female combat correspondents in Korea ... she was a cross between Alice in Wonderland and Eleanor Roosevelt ... Maggie regarded the world with wide-eyed excitement and then rolled up her sleeves determined to do something about it.[10]

And her rolling-up of sleeves sometimes meant direct involvement in the combat zone. A *New York Times* writer, at the time of her death, told of the complaint an Army colonel had about one of her dispatches. It had, he wrote, failed to point out that Miss Higgins, "completely disregarding her own personal safety," assisted in administering blood plasma to the wounded as they were being carried to a temporary first aid station, all the while surrounded by small-arms fire. He called her action "heroic" and said her "selfless devotion" had helped save many lives.

*Herald Tribune* ace reporter Homer Bigart had also arrived to cover the war, kindling even more intense competition, which brought excellent coverage for the *Tribune* and Pulitzer prizes for both reporters. Bigart later admitted that "she made me work like hell."[11] Miss Higgins' daily front-line coverage made the front pages of the *Tribune*, bringing the sting and terror of war to readers:

As we lay there ... on our bellies ... in a rock-strewn dip in the seal wall ... a sudden rush of water came into the dip in the wall and we saw a huge Landing Ship Tank rushing at us with the great plank door half down. Six more yards and the ship would have crushed twenty men. Warning shouts sent everyone speeding from the sea wall, searching for escape from the L. S. T. and cover from the enemy gunfire.[12]

But a month after arriving at the front, she and all other newswomen were ordered to leave North Korea. Lieutenant General Walton H. Walker, who was convinced that women didn't belong in a combat zone subject to its primitive standards of dress, language, and sanitation, had her escorted to a waiting aircraft and shipped back to Tokyo. There the indignant reporter met with General Douglas MacArthur, the Pacific commander, who had earlier been impressed with the quality and accuracy of her work. She argued her case before the general; she was working in Korea, not as a woman but as a correspondent. MacArthur's subsequent telegram to the *Herald Tribune* read, "Ban on women correspondents in Korea has been lifted. Marguerite Higgins is held in highest professional esteem by everyone."[13] His simultaneous response to Walker reinstated her at the front, and suggested that Miss Higgins had proven a point, as much for other female war correspondents as for herself.

Part of this ground-breaking reporter's success had to be due to her ability to take things in stride and to enjoy the adventure in what she was doing. So, asked about front-line sanitation in Korea, she explained, "The Marines use the bushes on one side of the road, I use them on the other."[14] She asked no favors and expected to be taken seriously. But being an attractive, blonde female, she took some flak, not from enemy fire but from reportorial colleagues. A *Time* magazine article in 1951, for example, sniped that she was an expert on "The Foreign Correspondent and the Three-Hour Lunch" or "How to Write Out of Your Hat." Like other female reporters before and after her, she was accused of getting exclusive interviews merely by batting her eyelashes. Early in her career, she had noticed that there was a double standard for assessing the accomplishments of male reporters as opposed to those of female reporters. A woman would be called temperamental if she objected to five night assignments in a row. Her male colleague would be considered to be simply standing up for his rights if he reacted similarly. A woman who scooped the competition by waiting around when other reporters left the scene would be considered tricky and unfair, whereas a man would be called a go-getter. And in a disagreement between a woman reporter and a male colleague on the same paper, Miss Higgins wrote, "the woman is sure to be at fault because as every newspaperman knows 'women are hard to get along with.'"[15]

In the midst of the Korean conflict, Marguerite married Lieutenant General William E. Hall, who was working with the United States Intelligence in Berlin. At the close of the war in 1955 they settled in Washington, D.C., where she covered the State Department as a weekly columnist and diplomatic correspondent for the *Tribune*. The couple's first child, Sharon Lee, born in 1953, lived only five days. Two other children, Lawrence O'Higgins and Linda Marguerite, were born in 1958 and 1959.

But married life did not end her worldwide involvements. The 1950s and 1960s saw Miss Higgins travel along the edge of the Iron Curtain, interviewing Premier Nikita Kruschev. She also interviewed such leaders and officials as Generalissimo Francisco Franco of Spain, Queen Frederika of Greece, Marshal Josip Broz Tito of Yugoslavia, Prime Minister Jawaharlal Nehru of India, and Shah Reza Pahlavi of Iran. She called the latter "handsome," and "progressive" and said he "practices what he preaches."[16] She wrote and spoke as an opponent of Communism. In support of her position she wrote of the people of Hong Kong: "Their disillusionment with the Red regime has special significance because the Chinese intellectuals as a class had swallowed the stories that the Chinese Reds were reformers rather than doctrinaire Bolsheviks. They had to learn the hard way through personal experience, that Communists are about the same everywhere."[17]

After nineteen years in and out of war zones and in and out of the pressures of correspondence deadlines, she resigned from the *Herald Tribune* in late 1963, lured away to *Newsday's* Washington bureau by a highly paid position as columnist with an around-the-world expense account. She needed "more time to think," and a respite from those pressures. She wanted a chance to reflect on what was happening, to put together the larger picture. Her *Newsday* column, syndicated in over ninety newspapers, originated from world trouble spots, such as Havana, where she warned of Soviet involvement in Cuba.

Two trips to Vietnam in 1963 convinced her that Buddhist self-burnings were politically inspired, involving innocent dupes, and were planned to bring down the Diem regime. She portrayed Vietnamese President Ngo Denh Diem's overthrow and murder as a direct result of American pressure and policy, and criticized American policy in Vietnam. Her book, *Our Vietnam Nightmare,* opens with a statement of concern over what she perceived as ignorance and mishandling on the part of the United States: "Will Rogers said that everyone is ignorant—only on different subjects. Of Vietnam, more than most places, it can be said that there are no experts, only varying degrees of ignorance."

Careful, excruciatingly honest reporter that she was, Marguerite was troubled by what she saw as misinformation on the Vietnam war, propagated at least in part by poor reporting. She saw that, despite the facts which seemed plainly evident to the front-line observer, broadcasters and media personnel stateside relied upon second-hand accounts and press dispatches out of Saigon. Her information from first-hand told her one thing. American media, far removed from the reality, told American audiences something else. "It was the first time that I began to comprehend, in depth and in some sorrow, what was meant by the *power* of the press," she wrote, just months before her death.[18] And elsewhere, she commented: "Who knows? History might be perverse enough to decide that the men fighting the war in Vietnam know as much about the battle as the typewriter strategists."[19]

Her dispatches from Vietnam, as well as those from other trouble spots in earlier decades, spoke with passion and involvement. She reported on eyewitness accounts of Viet Cong terrorism in villages; disembowelments of infants in the sight of their parents, midnight massacres of whole villages, the cowardly and brutal murder of President Diem. She wrote of interviews with Buddhists, Communists, Montagnard villagers, turncoat Viet Cong. She philosophized and commented and was instrumental in getting the slain president's young children to asylum in

Rome. In her ten visits to Vietnam, as in her earlier work in Europe, she remained an outspoken crusader against Communism.

During a late 1965 tour of Vietnam, India, and Pakistan, the forty-five-year-old columnist contracted a rare tropical infection, leishmaniasis. Caused by protozoa which enter the blood stream through the bite of a sandfly, the disease hospitalized her in Washington, D.C., in November of that year. Treated first for malaria, then for cancer, she fought her last battle against an enemy more fearsome than tanks or artillery.

Despite the illness, her thrice-weekly column continued to appear in the Washington *Evening Star*, the Chicago *Daily News*, the Boston *Herald*, the Seattle *Times* and the Houston *Post*. Only two weeks before her death on January 3, 1966, was the column cut to once a week. In her last published column she criticized President Lyndon Johnson for treating the war in Vietnam as a "pesky but peripheral one in an atmosphere of business as usual." Always the realist, she wrote, "What now seems to have dawned on the President and his advisers is that Hanoi is in the south for keeps. An awareness of this within the Administration has led to the unhappy conclusion that priorities must be established and that many elaborate hopes of the Great Society have to be minimized."

The motivation that took her to Vietnam on this last tour and that eventually took her life is probably best described in her first book, written ten years before. Her own words are a fitting epitaph to a life lived to its fullest:

> As is often the case, the periods in my life which in retrospect seem the happiest were those in which I was working very hard for causes in which I believed and which symbolized purposes far beyond the range of personal self-interest.[20]

S. M.

Notes
Bibliography
Index

# NOTES

## 1. Elizabeth Timothy

1. The colony's name is spelled differently in different sources. Timothy's *Gazette* spells it Charles-Towne; elsewhere it is Charlestown and Charleston. The latter spelling, which the town's residents adopted in 1783, is used here for consistency.

2. Isaiah Thomas, *The History of Printing in America, with a Biography of Printers* (1874; reprint, New York: Burt Franklin, 1964), 1:42.

3. Frances Hamill, "Some Unconventional Women Before 1800: Printers, Booksellers, and Collectors," *Bibliographic Society of America Papers* 49 (1955), 300–314.

4. Elizabeth Dexter, *Colonial Women of Affairs: Women in Business and the Professions in America Before 1776*, 2d ed. (Boston: Houghton Mifflin, 1931), 173.

5. Aware of the popular sentiment, ironic as it may seem, against "foreigners," the printer had Anglicized his name from the French, Louis Timothee, says Leona Hudak, *Early American Women Printers and Publishers, 1639–1820* (Metuchen, N.J.: Scarecrow Press, 1978), 151.

6. *South-Carolina Gazette*, August 24, 1734; July 19, 1739.

7. Obituary, Lewis Timothy, *Gazette*, January 4, 1739.

8. *Gazette*, January 18, 1939.

9. *Gazette*, March 24, 1739; June 2, 1739.

10. *Gazette*, October 10, 1740; June 18, 1741; October 24, 1741.

11. *Gazette*, November 13, 1740.

12. *Gazette*, May 26, 1739; June 9, 1739.

13. *Gazette*, December 4, 1740.

14. *Gazette*, January 8, 1741; January 15, 1741; *General Magazine* 1 (March, 1741), 202–5. Cf. Hennig Cohen, *South-Carolina Gazette* (Columbia, S.C.: University of South Carolina Press, 1953), 222.

15. *Gazette,* August 27, 1744.

16. *Gazette,* March 21, 1743; March 28, 1743; April 4, 1743.

17. *Gazette,* April 11, 1743.

18. *Gazette,* April 11, 1743.

19. *Gazette,* August 15, 1743; August 22, 1743; November 21, 1743; November 28, 1743.

20. Peter Tomothy says, over his own signature, that he is buying new types and expects to provide better job printing and a better looking paper.

21. Edward T. James, ed., *Notable American Women, 1607–1950. A Bibliographical Dictionary* (Cambridge, Mass.; Harvard University Press, 1971), 3:465–66.

22. Two younger sons had died in 1739 during a smallpox outbreak.

23. Clarence S. Brigham, *History and Bibliography of American Newspapers, 1690–1820* (Hamden, Conn.: Archon Books, 1962), 2:1033, 1044.

24. Marion Marzolf, *Up From the Footnote: A History of Women Journalists,* (New York: Hastings House Publishers, 1977), 4.

## 2. MARY KATHERINE GODDARD

1. Ward L. Miner, *William Goddard, Newspaper man* (Durham, N.C.: Duke University Press, 1962), 11. Another daughter, born in 1736, and dead at age two months, had been named Catherine. This similarity in names probably accounts for Mary Katherine sometimes being listed as born in 1736.

2. Susan Henry, "Sarah Goddard, Gentlewoman Printer," *Journalism History* 57, no. 1 (Spring 1980), 24.

3. Titles of the Goddard newspapers appear with different punctuation in different histories. Copies examined use the titles as printed in Isaiah Thomas, *The History of Printing in America with a Biography of Printers* (1874; reprint, New York: Burt Franklin, 1964).

4. Miner, *William Goddard,* 21.

5. Lawrence Wroth, "First Press in Providence," *American Antequarian Society* 51 (October, 1941), 361.

6. Henry, "Sarah Goddard," 26.

7. Lawrence Wroth, *The Colonial Printer* (1931; reprint, Charlottesville, Va.: Dominion Books, 1964), 144.

8. Leona Hudak, *Early American Women Printers and Publishers, 1639–1820* (Metuchen, N.J.: Scarecrow Press, 1978), 231.

9. Thomas, *History of Printing in America*, 26.

10. Douglas C. McMurtrie, *A History of Printing in the United States: The Story of the Introduction of the Press and Its History and Influence During the Pioneer Period in Each State in the Union* (1936; reprint, New York: Burt Franklin, 1969), 2:125; cf. Joseph T. Wheeler, *The Maryland Press, 1770–90* (Baltimore: Waverly Press, 1938), 11.

11. Miner, *William Goddard*, 166–67.

12. *American Archives*, 4th series, 6:1460–61.

13. Hudak, *Early American Women Printers*, 325, 329.

14. Wheeler, *The Maryland Press, 1760–90*, 2.

15. Miner, *William Goddard*, 193–94.

16. Hazard to Gates, (New York, December 23, 1789. Emmet Collection at the New York Public Library) in Wheeler, *The Maryland Press*, 14.

17. Lawrence C. Wroth, *History of Printing in Colonial Maryland: 1686–1776* (Baltimore: Typolhetae, 122), 144–5. Cf. Miner, 194.

## 3. ANNE NEWPORT ROYALL

1. Bessie Rowland James. *Anne Royall's U.S.A.* (New Brunswick, N.J.: Rutgers University Press, 1972), vii. *See also* John Hersey, "Interview with Harry S. Truman," *New Yorker*, April 7, 1951, 55–56.

2. Ibid. *See also* Helen Beal Woodward, *The Bold Women* (New York: Farrar, Strauss, and Young, 1953), 14.

3. Frank Luther Mott, *American Journalism, A History: 1690 –1960* (New York: The MacMillan Co., 1962), 312.

4. James, *Anne Royall's U.S.A.*, viii.

5. Ibid.

6. Ibid., 262.

7. Ibid., 11. *See also* Richardson L. Wright, *Forgotten Ladies* (Philadelphia: J. B. Lippincott, 1928), 157f.

8. James, *Anne Royall's U.S.A.*, 49–55.

9. Ibid., 68–70.

10. Anne Royall, *Letters from Alabama, 1817–1822* (Mobile: University of Alabama Press, 1969.), 82–93. (Washington, D.C.: Private Printing, 1830.)

11. Ibid., 118–20.

12. Ibid., 138–40, 146.

13. Anne Royall, *Sketches of History, Life, and Manners in the United States* (New York: Johnson Reprint Corporation, 1970), 166, 169.

14. James, *Anne Royall's U.S.A.*, 158.

15. John Quincy Adams, *Memoirs of John Quincy Adams Comprising Portions of his Diary from 1795 to 1849*, ed. Charles Francis Adams (Philadelphia: J. B. Lippincott and Co., 1875), 6:-321.

16. James, *Anne Royall's U.S.A.*, 268.

## 4. SARAH JOSEPHA HALE

1. Frank Luther Mott, *History of American Magazines* (New York: D. Appleton and Company, 1930), 1:349–50, 583–92.

2. Ruth E. Finley, *The Lady of Godey's, Sarah Josepha Hale* (1931; reprint, New York: Arno Press, 1974), 266.

3. Ibid., 312–13.

4. Ibid., 195–204. Mott, *History of American Magazines*, 583–84.

5. Finley, *The Lady of Godey's*, 17–18.

6. Ibid., 70f.

7. Ibid., 38f.

8. Helen Beal Woodward, *The Bold Women* (New York: Farrar, Strauss and Young, 1953), 189.

9. Finley, *The Lady of Godey's*, 266f. *See also* Olive Burt, *First Woman Editor* (New York: Julian Messner, Inc., 1960), 46–47.

10. Finley, *The Lady of Godey's*, 39.

11. Ibid.

12. Burt, *First Woman Editor*, 90–93. *See also* Sarah Josepha Hale, "The Editor's Table," *Godey's Lady's Book*, Jan. 1853, 80f.

13. Ibid., November 1840, 240.

14. Finley, *The Lady of Godey's*, 17–23.

15. Mott, *History of American Magazines*, 581.

16. Hale, "The Editor's Table," January, 1840, 42.

17. Finley, *The Lady of Godey's*, 99f.

18. Ibid., 205f.

19. Vernon Louis Parrington, *Main Currents of American Thought* (New York: Harcourt, Brace and Company, 1927), 2:187.

20. Woodward, *The Bold Women*, 183.
21. Mott, *History of American Magazines*, 584.

## 5. MARGARET FULLER

1. William Harlan Hale, *Horace Greeley: Voice of the People* (New York: Collier Books, 1950, 1961), 128.
2. Miriam Gurko, *The Ladies of Seneca Falls* (New York: Schocken Books, 1976), 74.
3. Mason Wade, *Margaret Fuller, Whetstone of Genius* (New York: The Viking Press, 1940), 28f.
4. Ibid., 41f.
5. Ibid., 43f.
6. Gurko, *Ladies of Seneca Falls*, 74.
7. Margaret Fuller, *Woman in the Nineteenth Century* in *The Writings of Margaret Fuller*, ed. Mason Wade (New York: The Viking Press, 1941), 124f.
8. Wade, *Margaret Fuller*, 125.
9. Gurko, *Ladies of Seneca Falls*, 76.
10. Wade, *Margaret Fuller*, 108–18.
11. Hale, *Horace Greeley*, 127.
12. Ibid., 125.
13. Wade, *Margaret Fuller*, 156–58.
14. Ibid.
15. Ibid., 144.
16. Ibid., 155.
17. Hale, *Horace Greeley*, 12.
18. Fuller, *Woman in the Nineteenth Century*, 128f.
19. Maurine Beasely and Sheila Gibbons, *Women in the Media: A Documentary Source Book* (Washington, D.C.: Women's Institute for Freedom of Press, 1977, second printing, 1979), 15.

## 6. CORNELIA WALTER

1. Joseph Edgar Chamberlin, *The Boston Transcript: A History of Its First Hundred Years* (Boston: Houghton, Mifflin Company, 1930). Chamberlin uses 1815 as her birthdate but her death certificate in the office of the Massachusettes Registrar of Vital Statistics lists 1814.

2. "Cornelia Walter Richards," *Boston Evening Transcript*, January 31, 1898.

3. Ibid.

4. Elizabeth F. Hoxie, "Cornelia Wells Walter," *Notable American Women 1607–1950: A Biographical Dictionary*, Edward T. James, ed. (Cambridge: The Belknap Press of Harvard University Press, 1971), 3:52 and *Transcript*, January 31, 1898.

5. *Transcript*, August 9, 1843.

6. *Transcript*, August 14, 1843.

7. *Transcript*, January 2, 1844.

8. Roland Wolseley, *The Black Press U. S. A.* (Ames: Iowa State University Press, 1971), 19.

9. "On Douglass: Prompted by Reading His Autobiography," *Transcript*, May 30, 1845.

10. "Cornelia Walter Richards," *Transcript*, January 31, 1898.

11. *Transcript*, July 30, 1842.

12. *Transcript*, August 22, 1842; July 13, 1843; February 24, 1843.

13. *Transcript*, March 21, 1843; July 1, 1843.

14. *Transcript*, September 6, 1842.

15. *Transcript*, May 28, 1845.

16. *Transcript*, January 20, 1844.

17. *Transcript*, July 17, 1843.

18. *Transcript*, May 31, 1844.

19. *Transcript*, January 17, 1844.

20. *Transcript*, October 28, 1846.

21. *Transcript*, August 2, 1942; July 10, 1843; July 6, 1843.

## 7. JANE GREY SWISSHELM

1. Jane Grey Swisshelm, *Half a Century* (Chicago: Published by the author, 1880), 4.

2. Ibid., 49.

3. Ibid., 74–75.

4. Lester B. Shippee, "Jane Grey Swisshelm: Agitator," *Mississippi Valley History Review*, 7 (December 1920), 212. (Mrs. Swisshelm, Shippee says, "insisted on the *e*" in Visiter.)

5. Alice Tyler, *Freedom's Ferment* (New York: Harper & Row, 1944), 439.

6. Swisshelm, *Half a Century*, 147.

7. Jane Grey Swisshelm, *Letters to Country Girls*, (New York: John C. Riker, 1853), 123.

8. Shippee, "Jane Grey Swisshelm," 215.

9. St. Cloud *Democrat*, December 21, 1865.

10. St. Cloud *Democrat*, September 20, 1860.

11. St. Cloud *Democrat*, November 13, 1862.

12. Swisshelm, *Half a Century*, pp. 208–9.

13. S. J. Fisher, "Reminiscences of Jane Grey Swisshelm," *Western Pennsylvania Historical Magazine* (July 1921), 4:172.

14. St. Cloud *Democrat*, April 27, 1865.

15. New York *Tribune*, May 13 and 18, 1863, and St. Cloud *Democrat*, June 18, 1863.

16. Swisshelm, *Half a Century*, 294.

17. Ibid., 157.

18. Margaret F. Thorp, *Female Persuasion: Six Strong-Minded Women* (New Haven: Yale University Press, 1949), ch 3.

19. *Pittsburgh Commercial Gazette*, July 23, 1884.

## 8. JANE CUNNINGHAM CROLY

1. John Cunningham, "A Brother's Memories," in Carolyn M. Morse, *Jane Cunningham Croly "Jennie June"* (New York and London: G. P. Putnam's Sons, Knickerbocker Press, 1904), 11.

2. Mrs. Croly's nom-de-plume is spelled "Jennie" and "Jenny" in various of her own and others' writings. For consistency, the former spelling is used throughout this chapter.

3. John Cunningham, "A Brother's Memories," 5.

4. S. A. Lattimore, "Tribute of Friends," in Morse, *Jane Cunningham Croly "Jennie June*," 201–3.

5. Ishbel Ross, *Ladies of the Press* (New York: Harper & Brothers, 1936), 39.

6. Frank Luther Mott, *A History of American Magazines* (London, New York: D. Appleton & Co., 1930), 1:683.

7. Jane C. Croly, "The Positivist Episode," in Morse, *Jane Cunningham Croly*, 71–72.

8. Letters to the Editor, *Demorest Monthly Magazine*, August 1877, 446. (Citation provided by Kathryn Urbaszewski.)

9. Charles Forcey, *Crossroads of Liberalism* (New York: Oxford University Press, 1961), 14.

10. Ibid., 9.

11. Elizabeth Bancroft Schlesinger, "The Nineteenth-Cen-

tury Women's Dilemma and Junnie June," *New York History*, 42, no. 4 (October 1961), 373.

12. *Demorest's Monthly Magazine*, March 1880, 128.

13. Jane C. Croly, *History of the Women's Club Movement in America* (New York: H. G. Allen & Co., 1898), 15.

14. Letter by Jane C. Croly, October 1900. Reprinted in Morse, *Jane Cunningham Croly*, facing p. 164.

15. Croly, *History of the Women's Club Movement in America*, 23.

16. *Demorest's Monthly Magazine*, January, 1869, 65.

17. Charles Forcey, *Crossroads of Liberalism*, p. 14.

18. Ross, *Ladies of the Press*, 44.

19. John Cunningham, in Morse, *Jane Cunningham Croly*, 9.

20. Ibid., p. 12. (Other sources give the daughter's name as Viola, but John Cunningham calls her Vida.)

21. *Harper's Bazaar*, March 3, 1900. (Citation provided by Kathryn Urbaszewski.)

22. "Address by the Rev. Phoebe A. Hanaford, Vice-President of the Women's Press Club of New York City," in Morse, *Jane Cunningham Croly*, 23–26.

## 9. Eliza Nicholson

1. *Picayune*, October 2, 1888, p. 12.

2. James Henry Harrison, *Pearl Rivers, Publisher of the Picayune* (New Orleans: Tulane University Press, 1932), 25.

3. Pearl Rivers, *Lyrics* (Philadelphia: J. B. Lippincott & Co., 1873).

4. Thomas Ewing Dabney, *One Hundred Great Years: The Story of the Times-Picayune from Its Founding to 1940* (Baton Rouge: Louisiana State University Press, 1944), 266.

5. Elsie Farr, *Pearl Rivers* (New Orleans: The Times-Picayune Publishing Company, 1951), 7.

6. Harrison, *Pearl Rivers, Publisher*, 22.

7. Ibid., 26.

8. *Picayune*, March 23, 1886, 4.

9. *Picayune*, August 3, 1879, 10.

10. "Everybody's Business Is Nobody's Business," *Picayune*, March 23, 1884, 4.

11. Dabney, *One Hundred Great Years*, 309.

12. Catherine Cole, "Sunday Talk", *Sunday Picayune,* November 15, 1884.

13. Dabney, *One Hundred Great Years,* 313.

14. Ibid., 316.


## 10. IDA MINERVA TARBELL

1. Ida M. Tarbell, *All In The Day's Work.* (New York: The MacMillan Company, 1939), 241f.

2. Ibid., 3.

3. Ibid., 6f.

4. Ibid., 31–36.

5. Ibid., 87f.

6. Ibid., 84–86.

7. Ibid., 119.

8. Ibid., 154.

9. Ibid., 174.

10. Ibid., 163.

11. Ibid., 238.

12. Ibid., 241f.

13. Ibid., 370f.

14. Ibid., 377–84.

15. Ibid., 326f.

16. *New York Times,* Jan. 7, 1944, 17.


## 11. ELIZABETH MERIWETHER GILMER (DOROTHY DIX)

1. Dorothy Dix, "Mother Confessor to Millions," New Orleans *Times-Picayune Magazine,* May 5, 1946.

2. Ibid., and Harnett T. Kane, *Dear Dorothy Dix: The Story of a Compassionate Woman* (Garden City: Doubleday and Co., 1952), 264.

3. Kane, *Dear Dorothy Dix,* 195f.

4. Ibid., 10, 12, 296.

5. Ibid., 28.

6. Ibid., 53f.

7. Dix, "Mother Confessor."

8. Kane., *Dear Dorothy Dix,* 93–97.

9. Ibid.

10. Ibid., 110f.

11. Ibid., 114.

12. Ibid., 9.

13. Dix, "Mother Confessor."

14. Ibid.

15. Ibid.

16. Kane, *Dear Dorothy Dix*, 9, 233f.

17. Dorothy Dix, *Dorothy Dix, Her Book: Everyday Help for Everyday People* (New York: Funk and Wagnalls Co., 1926), 45.

18. Dix, "Mother Confessor."

19. Dix, *Dorothy Dix, Her Book*, 45.


## 12. IDA B. WELLS-BARNETT

1. Norman B. Wood, *The White Side of a Black Subject* (Chicago: American Publishing House, 1897), 381–82.

2. Roland E. Wolseley, *The Black Press, U.S.A.* (Ames: Iowa State University Press, 1971), 28–29.

3. Ida B. Wells, *The Crusade for Justice: The Autobiography of Ida B. Wells*, ed. Alfreda M. Duster (Chicago and London: The University of Chicago Press, 1970), 242.

4. Ibid., 265.

5. Ibid., 18–19.

6. Ibid., xvii.

7. Ibid., xviii.

8. Ibid., 52.

9. Ibid., xxi.

10. Ibid., xxii.

11. Ibid.

12. Ibid., xxv.

13. Ibid.

14. Ibid.

15. Ibid., xxvi.

16. Edward James, ed., *Notable American Women, 1607–1950* (Cambridge: The Belknap Press of Harvard University Press, 1971), 3:565–67.

17. Wells, *Autobiography*, xxvii.

18. Ibid.

19. Ibid., xxix.

## 13. Elizabeth Cochrane Seaman (Nellie Bly)

1. Mignon Rittenhouse, *The Amazing Nellie Bly* (New York: E. P. Dutton and Company, Inc., 1956), 107.
2. Ibid., 24f.
3. Ibid., 33.
4. Ibid., 42f.
5. Ibid., 44f. *See also* Elizabeth Cochrane, *Six Months In Mexico* (New York: American, 1888).
6. Rittenhouse, *Amazing Nellie Bly*, 57f.
7. Ibid., 114–40.
8. Ibid., *See also* Maurine Beasley and Sheila Gibbons. *Women In Media* (Washington, D.C.: Women's Institute for Press and Freedom, 1977), 47f.
9. Rittenhouse, *Amazing Nellie Bly*, 136.
10. Ibid., 156.
11. Ibid., 161f. *See also* Elizabeth Cochrane, *Nellie Bly's Book: Around the World in 72 Days* (New York: Pictorial Weeklies, 1890).
12. Rittenhouse, *Amazing Nellie Bly*, 202.
13. Ibid., 215.
14. Ibid., 246.

## 14. Winifred Black Bonfils

1. "Winifred Black, 73, Journalist, Dead," *New York Times*, May 26, 1936, 26.
2. Walton Bean, "Winifred Sweet Black," *Notable American Women, 1607–1950. A Biographical Dictionary* (Cambridge: Harvard University Press).
3. Ishbel Ross, *Ladies of the Press* (New York: Harper, 1936).
4. John K. Winkler, *William Randolph Hearst: A New Appraisal* (New York: Hastings House, 1955), 49.
5. "Winifred Black," *New York Times*.
6. Ross, 61–62.
7. "Winifred Black," *New York Times*.
8. Mrs. Fremont (Cora Baggerly) Older, *William Randolph Hearst: American* (New York: Appleton-Century Company, 1936), 100–101.
9. Ibid., 99.
10. Bean, "Winifred Sweet Black," 155.

11. Winifred Sweet Black, *The Life and Personality of Phoebe Apperson Hearst,* (San Francisco: J. H. Nash, 1928). Cf. Ross, *Ladies of the Press,* p. 66, where the author says individual volumes cost $150.

12. "Winifred Black," *New York Times.*

13. Patricia Schofler, "A Glorious Adventure . . . ," *American History Illustrated* (February 1981).

14. Bean, "Winifred Sweet Black," 33–34.

15. Ross, 63.

16. Schofler, "A Glorious Adventure," 34.

17. Bean, "Winifred Sweet Black," 156.

18. Ibid.

## 15. Rheta Childe Dorr

1. Rheta Childe Dorr, *A Woman of Fifty* (New York: Funk and Wagnalls, 1924), 101.

2. Rheta embellished the spelling of her maiden name, as much out of rebellion as out of a sense of the dramatic and the romantic. *See* Edward T. James, ed., *Notable American Women, 1607–1950. A Bibliographical Dictionary* (Cambridge: Harvard University Press, 1971), 1:503.

3. Dorr, *Woman of Fifty,* 96.

4. Ibid., 115–17. Cf. Zena Meth McGlashan, "Club 'Ladies' and Working 'Girls': Rheta Childe Dorr and the New York *Evening Post,*" unpublished paper presented to the History Division, Association for Education in Journalism, East Lansing, August, 1981.

5. This allocation was more than Congress had ever yet spent on women or their concerns.

6. Dorr, *Woman of Fifty,* 98.

7. James, *Notable American Women,* 1:504.

8. Dorr, *Woman of Fifty,* 183.

9. Ishbel Ross, *Ladies of the Press* (New York: Harper and Brothers Publishers, 1936), 114. Cf. Dorr, *Woman of Fifty,* 296, and James, *Notable American Women,* 1:505.

10. Rheta Childe Dorr, *Inside the Russian Revolution,* (New York: MacMillan, 1917), 127.

11. James, *Notable American Women,* 1:504.

12. "Death of Rheta Childe Dorr," *New York Times,* August 9, 1948, 3.

## 16. DOROTHY THOMPSON

1. Cover Story, *Time*, June 12, 1939, 47–51.

2. Ibid., 47.

3. Ibid., 50.

4. Marion K. Sanders, *Dorothy Thompson: A Legend in Her Time* (Boston: Houghton Mifflin Co., 1973), 65.

5. Ibid., p. 168.

6. Dorothy Thompson, *Let the Record Speak* (Boston: Houghton Mifflin, Co., 1939), 2.

7. Ibid., 12.

8. Sanders, *Dorothy Thompson*, 341.

9. Edward T. James, ed, *Notable American Women, 1607–1950. A Biographical Dictionary* (Cambridge: Harvard University Press, 1971), 3:685.

## 17. MARGARET BOURKE-WHITE

1. Obituary, *Time*, September 7, 1971, 46.

2. "Hall of Fame," unpublished memorandum for *Life*, July 2, 1965.

3. "Margaret Bourke-White," *Life*, September 10, 1971, 34.

4. Arthur Goldsmith, "Photojournalism," *The Encyclopedia of Photography*, 1964, 15:2779.

5. Frances and Winifred Kirkland, *Girls Who Became Artists* (New York and London: Harper and Bros., 1934), 34–46.

6. Ibid.

7. Margaret Bourke-White, *Portrait of Myself* (New York: Simon and Schuster, 1963), 21.

8. Ibid., 20.

9. Ibid., 29.

10. Ibid., 30f.

11. Ibid.

12. Ibid.

13. Ibid., 40. *See also* T. Otto Nall, "The Camera is a Candid Machine," *Scholastic*, May 15, 1937, 18.

14. Bourke-White, *Portrait of Myself*, 48f.

15. "Introduction to the First Issue of *Life*," *Life*, November 23, 1936, 3.

16. "Caldwell and Bourke-White Look at the Cotton Country," *Life*, November 22, 1937, 48–55.

17. Margaret Bourke-White, *Shooting the Russian War* (New York: Simon and Schuster, 1942), 57.

18. Ibid., 105.

19. Bourke-White, *Portrait*, 197.

20. "*Life's* Bourke-White Goes Bombing," *Life*, March 1, 1943, pp. 17–23.

21. Sean Callahan, *The Photographs of Margaret Bourke-White*, (Boston: The New York Graphic Society, 1975) p. 221.

## 18. MARGUERITE HIGGINS

1. Marguerite Higgins, *War is a Singular Thing* (Garden City: Doubleday & Company, 1955), 56.

2. "Marguerite Higgins Dies at 45: Reporter Won '51 Pulitzer Prize," *The New York Times*, January 4, 1966, 27.

3. Higgins, *War*, 25.

4. *New York Times*, "Marguerite Higgins Dies," 27.

5. Marion Marzolf, "Higgins, Marguerite," *Notable American Women: The Modern Period—A Biographical Dictionary*, Barbara Sicherman et. al. (Cambridge: The Belknap Press of Harvard University Press, 1980), 340.

6. Higgins, *War*, 30.

7. Ibid., 59.

8. *New York Tribune*, April 25, 1945, 1.

9. Marguerite Higgins, "Now the Russians Are Fleeing Russia," *The Saturday Evening Post*, 221, no. 49 (June 4, 1949), p. 29.

10. "Maggie," *Newsweek*, January 17, 1968, 83.

11. Ibid.

12. From a *Herald Tribune* article by Marguerite Higgins, as quoted by Carl Mydans, "Girl War Correspondent," *Life*, 29, no. 14 (October 2, 1950), 53.

13. "Last World," *Time*, July 31, 1950, 53.

14. "Maggie," *Newsweek*, 82.

15. Higgins, *War*, 205.

16. Marguerite Higgins, "Marguerite Higgins Round the World Diary," *Woman's Home Companion* (February 1952), 6.

17. Ibid.

18. Marguerite Higgins, *Our Vietnam Nightmare* (New York: Harper & Row, 1965), 125.

19. Ibid., 201.

20. Higgins, *War*, 249.

# BIBLIOGRAPHY

## General

*Books*

Beasley, Maurine, and Sheila Gibbons. *Women in Media: A Documentary Source Book.* Washington, D.C.: Women's Institute for Freedom of the Press, 1977. Second printing, 1979.

Bradford, Gamaliel. *Portraits of American Women.* Boston: Houghton, Mifflin, 1919.

Drewry, John, ed. *Post Biographies of Famous Journalists.* Athens: University of Georgia Press, 1936.

Hale, William Harlan. *Horace Greeley: Voice of the People.* N.Y.: Collier Books, 1950, 1961.

Hudak, Leona. *Early American Women Printers and Publishers, 1638–1820.* Metuchen, N.J.: Scarecrow Press, 1978.

James, Edward T., ed. *Notable American Women, 1607–1950. A Bibliographical Dictionary.* 3 vols. Cambridge, Mass.: The Belknap Press of Harvard University Press, 1971.

Kobre, Sidney. *The Development of the Colonial Newspaper.* Pittsburg: Colonial Press, 1944.

Marzolf, Marion. *Up From the Footnote: A History of Women Journalists.* New York: Hastings House Publishers, 1977.

Ross, Ishbel. *Ladies of the Press: The Story of Women in Journalism by an Insider.* New York: Harper & Bros., 1936.

———. *Sons of Adam, Daughters of Eve.* New York: Harper and Row, 1969.

## Winifred Black Bonfils

*Books*

Black, Winifred Sweet. *Dope: The Story of the Living Dead.* New York: Star Company, 1928.

———. *The Life and Personality of Phoebe Apperson Hearst.* San Francisco: J. H. Nash, 1928.

CARLSON, OLIVER, and ERNEST SUTHERLAND BATES. *Lord of San Simeon.* New York: The Viking Press, 1936.

GREEN, WARD, ed. *Star Reporters and 34 of Their Stories.* New York: Random House, 1948.

OLDER, MRS. FREMONT (CORA BAGGERLY). *William Randolph Hearst: American.* New York: Appleton-Century Company, 1936.

TEBBEL, JOHN. *The Life and Good Times of William Randolph Hearst.* New York: E. P. Dutton and Co., Inc., 1952.

WINKLER, JOHN K. *W. R. Hearst, An American Phenomenon.* New York: Simon & Schuster, 1928.

――――. *William Randolph Hearst: A New Appraisal.* New York: Hastings House, 1955.

## MARGARET BOURKE-WHITE

*Books*

BOURKE-WHITE, MARGARET. *Dear Fatherland, Rest Quietly.* New York: Simon and Schuster, 1946.

――――. *Eyes on Russia.* New York: Simon and Schuster, 1931.

――――. *Halfway to Freedom.* New York: Simon and Schuster, 1949.

――――. *Portrait of Myself.* New York: Simon and Schuster, 1963.

――――. *Shooting the Russian War.* New York: Simon and Schuster, 2d printing, 1942.

――――. *They Called It Purple Heart Valley.* New York: Simon and Schuster, 1944.

CALDWELL, ERSKINE, and MARGARET BOURKE-WHITE. *North of the Danube.* New York: Viking Press, 1939.

――――. *Say, Is This the U.S.A.?* New York: Duell, Sloan and Pearce, Inc., 1941.

――――. *You Have Seen Their Faces.* New York: Modern Age Books, Inc., 1937.

CALLAHAN, SEAN. *The Photographs of Margaret Bourke-White.* Boston: The New York Graphic Society, 1972.

GOLDSMITH, ARTHUR. "Photojournalism," *The Encyclopedia of Photography,* vol. 15. Edited by Willard E. Morgan. New York: Greystone Press, 1964.

KIRKLAND, FRANCES and WINIFRED KIRKLAND. "Margaret Bourke-White, Photographer of Steel," in *Girls Who Became Artists.* New York and London: Harper and Bros., 1934.

POLLACK, PETER. *The Picture History of Photography.* New York: R. N. Abrams, Inc. Rev. and enl. ed., 1969.

*Periodicals*

BOURKE-WHITE, MARGARET. Issues of *Life* 1936–52.

COUSINS, NORMAN. "Peggy." *Saturday Review,* September 11, 1971, 28–29.

"Margaret Bourke-White Dead," *The New York Times,* August 28, 1971, 1.

NALL, T. OTTO. "The Camera Is a Candid Machine." *Scholastic,* May 15, 1937, 18–19, 23.

PARTON, MARGARET. "The Lady of the Lens." *New York Herald-Tribune,* June 30, 1963, 3.


ELIZABETH COCHRANE (Seaman)

*Books*

COCHRANE, ELIZABETH. *Nellie Bly's Book: Around the World in 72 Days.* New York: Pictorial Weeklies, 1890.

_____. *Six Months in Mexico.* New York: American, 1888.

_____. *Ten Days in a Mad-House.* New York: Munro, 1887.

RITTENHOUSE, MIGNON. *The Amazing Nellie Bly.* New York: E. P. Dutton and Company, Inc., 1956.

WILLARD, FRANCES E., and MARY A. LIVERMORE. *A Woman of the Century.* Buffalo: Moulton, 1893.


*Periodicals*

Articles in New York *World,* 1887–1895.


JANE CUNNINGHAM CROLY

*Books*

CROLY, JANE C. *History of the Women's Club Movement in America.* New York: H. G. Allen & Co., 1898.

_____. Jennie Juneiana: *Talks on Women's Topics.* Boston: Lee and Shepard, 1864.

FORCEY, CHARLES. *Crossroads of Liberalism.* New York: Oxford University Press, 1961.

MORSE, CAROLINE M., ed. *Memories of Jane Cunningham Croly*

"*Jennie June.*" New York and London: G. P. Putnam's Sons, The Knickerbocker Press, 1904.

ROSS, ISHBEL. *Crusades and Crinolines: The Life and Times of Ellen Curtis Demorest and William Jennings Demorest.* New York: Harper & Row, 1963.

### Periodicals

SCHLESINGER, ELIZABETH (BANCROFT). "The Nineteenth-Century Woman's Dilemma and Jennie June," New York State Historical Assn., 1961. Reprinted from *N.Y. History* 42 (October 1961).

SMITH, HENRY LADD. "The Beauteous Jennie June: Pioneer Woman Journalist," *Journalism Quarterly*, 40 (Spring 1962), 170.

### Thesis

BOLQUERIN, M. JAMES. "An Investigation of the Contributions of David, Jane, and Herbert Croly to American Life." Master's thesis, University of Missouri, 1948.

## DOROTHY DIX (Elizabeth Gilmer)

### Books

DIX, DOROTHY. *Dorothy Dix, Her Book: Everyday Help for Everyday People.* New York and London: Funk and Wagnalls Company, 1926.

KANE, HARNETT T., with ELLA BENTLEY ARTHUR. *Dear Dorothy Dix: The Story of a Compassionate Woman.* Garden City: Doubleday and Co., 1952.

### Periodicals

DIX, DOROTHY, "Mother Confessor to Millions," New Orleans *Times-Picayune Magazine,* (May 5, 1946), 6–7.

MOREHEAD, ALBERT, "Meet the Confidante." New Orleans *Times-Picayune Magazine,* (Dec. 24, 1944), p. 5. (Released by the Bell Syndicate; Copied from *Redbook Magazine.*)

Obituary, New Orleans *Times-Picayune,* Dec. 17, 1951.

Obituary, *New York Times,* Dec. 17, 1951.

PITTS, STELLA. "She was Read by Millions." New Orleans *Times-Picayune,* (March 21, 1976).

## Rheta Childe Dorr

*Books*

Dorr, Rheta Childe. *A Soldier's Mother in France.* Indianapolis: Bobbs-Merril Co., 1918.

_____. *A Woman of Fifty.* New York: Funk and Wagnalls, 1924.

_____. *Drink: Coercion or Control?* New York: Frederick A. Stokes Co., 1929.

_____. *Inside the Russian Revolution.* New York: MacMillan, 1917.

_____. *Susan B. Anthony—The Woman Who Changed the Mind of a Nation.* New York: Frederick A. Stokes Co., 1928.

_____. *What Eight Million Women Want.* Boston: Small, Maynard & Co., 1910.

Filler, Louis. *Crusades for American Liberalism.* New York: Harcourt Brace, 1939.

Pankhurst, Emmeline. *My Own Story.* New York: Source Book Press, 1970.

Viroubova, Anna. *My Memories of the Russian Court.* New York: MacMillan, 1923.

VonVoorst, Bessie, and Marie Von Voorst. *The Woman Who Toils: Being the Experiences of Two Ladies as Factory Girls.* New York: Doubleday, Page and Co., 1903.

## Margaret Fuller

*Books*

Anthony, Katherine. *Margaret Fuller, A Psychological Biography.* New York: Harcourt, Brace and Howe, 1920.

Bell, Margaret. *Margaret Fuller* (with an introduction by Mrs. F. D. Roosevelt). New York: C. Boni, 1930.

Chevigny, Bell Gale. *The Woman and the Myth: Margaret Fuller's Life and Writings.* Old Westbury, N.Y.: The Feminist Press, 1977.

Deiss, Joseph Jay. *The Roman Years of Margaret Fuller.* New York: Thomas Y. Crowell, 1969.

*Eckermann's Conversations with Goethe.* Trans. Margaret Fuller. Boston: Hilliard, Gray, 1839.

Emerson, R. W., W. H. Channing, and J. F. Clarke. *Memoirs of Margaret Fuller.* Boston: Phillips, Sampson, 1852.

Fuller, Margaret. *At Home and Abroad.* Ed. by A. B. Fuller. Boston: Crosby, Nichols, 1856.

————, trans. *Gunderode*. Boston: E. P. Peabody, 1842.

————. *Life Without and Life Within*. Boston: Brown, Taggard, and Chase, 1859.

————. *Love-letters of Margaret Fuller, 1845–46* (with an introduction by Julia Ward Howe). New York: D. Appleton, 1903.

————. *Papers on Literature and Art*. 2 vols. New York: Wiley and Putnam, 1846. (Reprinted as 1 vol., 1848).

————. *Summer on the Lakes, in 1843*. Boston: C. C. Little and James Brown, 1844.

————. *Woman of the Nineteenth Century*. New York: Tribune Press, 1845.

————. *The Writings of Margaret Fuller*. Edited by Mason Wade. New York: The Viking Press, 1941.

GURKO, MIRIAM. *The Ladies of Seneca Falls*. New York: Schocken Books, 1976.

HEALEY, CAROLINE W. (DALL). *Margaret and Her Friends*. Boston: Roberts Brothers, 1895.

HIGGINSON, THOMAS WENTWORTH. *Margaret Fuller Ossoli*. Boston: Houghton, Mifflin, 1884.

HOWE, JULIA WARD. *Margaret Fuller (Marchesa Ossoli)*. Boston: Roberts Brothers, 1883.

MACPHAIL, ANDREW. "Margaret Fuller," from *Essays of Puritanism*. Boston: Houghton, Mifflin, 1905.

STERN, MADELINE B. *The Life of Margaret Fuller*. New York: Dutton, 1942.

WADE, MASON. *Margaret Fuller, Whetstone of Genius*. New York: The Viking Press, 1940.

## MARY KATHERINE GODDARD

*Books*

EARLE, ALICE M. *Colonial Dames and Goodwives*. Boston: Houghton, Mifflin Co., 1895.

MINER, WARD L. *William Goddard, Newspaperman*. Durham, N.C.: Duke University Press, 1962.

WHEELER, JOSEPH T. *The Maryland Press, 1770–90*. Baltimore: Waverly Press, 1938.

WOODY, THOMAS. *A History of Women's Education in the United States*. 2 vols. New York: The Science Press, 1929.

WROTH, LAWRENCE C. *The Colonial Printer*. Charlottesville, Va.: Dominion Books, 1964. Reprinted from an earlier edition, 1931, Grolier Club of the City of New York.

————. *History of Printing in Colonial Maryland: 1686–1776.* Baltimore: Typolhetae, 1922.

*Periodicals*

CHUDACOFF, NANCY FISHER. "Woman in the News 1762–1770—Sarah Updike Goddard." *Rhode Island History,* 32, no. 4, (November 1973), 99–105.

HENRY, SUSAN. "Sarah Goddard, Gentlewoman Printer," *Journalism Quarterly* 57, no. 1 (Spring 1980).


SARAH JOSEPHA HALE

*Books*

BURT, OLIVE. *First Woman Editor.* New York: Julian Messner Inc., 1960.

FINLEY, RUTH E. *The Lady of Godey's.* Philadelphia: Lippincott, 1931.

FORD, HENRY. *The Story of Mary and Her Little Lamb.* Dearborne, Mich.: Henry Ford, 1928.

GILMAN, ARTHUR. *The Story of Boston.* New York: G. P. Putnam's Sons, 1894.

HALE, SARAH, JOSEPHA BUELL. *Flora's Interpreter.* Boston: B. B. Musey, 1852.

————. *Genius of Oblivion and Other Poems.* Concord, Mass.: Jacob B. Moore, 1823.

————. *Ladies' Wreath.* Boston: Marsh, Capen & Lyon, 1837.

————. *Liberia.* New York: Harper's, 1853.

————. *Northwood.* Boston: Bowles and Dearborn, 1827. New York and London: Johnson Reprint Corp., 1970.

————. *Poems for Our Children.* Boston: Marsh, Capen & Lyon, 1850.

————. *Woman's Record.* New York: Harper & Bros., 1874.

————, ed. *The Lady's Book.* Philadelphia: Louis A. Godey, January 1837 to December 1877.

————. *Ladies' Magazine.* Boston: Putnam & Hunt, 1828–37.

MOTT, FRANK LUTHER. *History of American Magazines.* Vol 1. New York: D. Appleton, 1930.

PARRINGTON, VERNON LOUIS. *Main Currents of American Thought.* New York: Harcourt, Brace & Co., 1927.

WOODWARD, HELEN BEAL. *The Bold Women.* New York: Farrar, Strauss, and Young, 1953.

WRIGHT, RICHARDSON. *Forgotten Ladies*. Philadelphia: J. P. Lippincott Co., 1928.


## MARGUERITE HIGGINS

*Books*

HIGGINS, MARGUERITE. *News is a Singular Thing*. Garden City, N.J.: Doubleday & Co., 1955.
———. *Our Vietnam Nightmare*. New York: Harper and Row, 1965.
———. *War in Korea*. Garden City, N.J.: Doubleday & Co., 1951.

*Periodicals*

HIGGINS, MARGUERITE. "Marguerite Higgins' Round the World Diary." *Woman's Home Companion*, November 1951, 32–33, 126–28.
———. "Marguerite Higgins' Round the World Diary." *Woman's Home Companion*, December, 1951, 26–27, 56–57.
———. "Marguerite Higgins' Round the World Diary." *Woman's Home Companion*, January, 1952, 3, 6, 8.
———. "Marguerite Higgins' Round the World Diary." *Woman's Home Companion*, February, 1952, 4, 6, 9.
"Lady at War." *Time*, January 14, 1955, 61.
"Last Word." *Time*, July 31, 1950, 53.
"Maggie." *Newsweek*, January 17, 1968, 83.
"Maggie vs the Boors." *Time*, September 24, 1951, 75–76.
"Marguerite Higgins Dies at 45: Reporter Won '51 Pulitzer Price." *The New York Times*, January 4, 1966, 27.
MYDANS, CARL. "Girl War Correspondent." *Life*, 29, no. 14, October 2, 1950, 51–60.
RODGERS, JOHN G. "Marguerite Higgins; Won Fame as War Correspondent For Tribune." *The New York Herald Tribune*, January 4, 1966, 28.


## ELIZA NICHOLSON

*Books*

DABNEY, THOMAS EWING. *One Hundred Great Years, The Story of the Times-Picayune From Its Founding to 1940*. Baton Rouge: Louisiana State University Press, 1944.
FARR, ELSIE S. *Pearl Rivers*. New Orleans: The Times-Picayune Publishing Co., 1951.

HANAFORD, PHOEBE A. *Daughters of America.* Augusta, Maine: True and Company, 1883.

HARRISON, JAMES HENRY. *Pearl Rivers, Publishers of the Picayune.* New Orleans: Tulane University Press, 1932.

*Periodicals*

BRIDGES, LAMAR W. "Eliza Jane Nicholson of the *Picayune.*" *Journalism History*, 2, no. 4 (Winter 1975–76), 110–15.

"Death of A. M. Holbrook," *Daily Picayune*, January 6, 1876, 1.

"Death of Mrs. E. J. Nicholson," *Daily Picayune*, February 16, 1896, 1.

"Letter from Pearl Rivers." *Daily Picayune*, February 19, 1871, 1–2.

"Mrs. E. J. Nicholson ('Pearl Rivers')." Frank Leslie's *Illustrated Newspaper*, January 7, 1888, 375.

"A Week with 'Pearl Rivers.'" *Daily Picayune*, September 12, 1869, 2.

## ANNE ROYALL

*Books*

JACKSON, GEORGE STUYVESANT. *Uncommon Scold.* Boston: Bruce Humphries Co., 1937.

JAMES, BESSIE ROWLAND. *Anne Royall's U.S.A.* New Brunswick, N.J.: Rutgers University Press, 1972.

PORTER, SARAH H. *The Life and Times of Anne Royall.* Cedar Rapids, Ia.: Torch Press, 1909.

ROYALL, ANNE. *The Black Book; or, A Continuation of Travels in the United States.* 3 Vols. Washington, D.C.: Private Printing, 1828, 1829.

_____. *Pennsylvania or Travels Continued in the United States.* 2 Vols. Washington, D.C.: Private Printing, 1829.

_____. *Letters from Alabama 1817–1822.* Mobile, Ala.: University of Alabama Press, 1969. Washington, D.C.: Private Printing, 1830.

_____. *Southern Tour, or Second Series of the Black Book.* 3 Vols. Washington, D.C.: Private Printing, 1831.

_____. *Sketches of History, Life, and Manners in the United States.* New York: Johnson Reprint Corporation, 1970. New Haven: (Private Printing, 1826.)

WOODWARD, HELEN BEAL. *The Bold Women.* New York: Farrar, Strauss, and Young, 1953.

## JANE SWISSHELM

*Books*

LARSEN, ARTHUR J., ed. *Crusader and Feminist*. St. Paul: Minnesota Historical Society, 1934.

SWISSHELM, JANE GREY. *Half a Century*. Chicago: Jansen, McClurg and Company, 1880.

———. *Letters to Country Girls* New York: John C. Riker, 1853.

TYLER, ALICE. *Freedom's Ferment*. New York: Harper & Row, 1944.

*Periodicals*

BEASLEY, MAURINE. "Jane G. Swisshelm; Pioneer Washington Journalist." *Matrix* 60, no. 3 (Spring 1975), 4–5, 14.

———. "Pens and Petticoats: Early Women Washington Correspondents." *Journalism History* 1, no. 4, (Winter 1974–75), 112–15, 136.

ENDRES, KATHLEEN. "Jane Grey Swisshelm, 19th Century Journalist and Feminist." *Journalism History* 2 no. 4, (Winter 1975–76), 128–32.

FISHER, S. J. "Reminiscences of Jane Grey Swisshelm." *Western Pennsylvania History Magazine* 4 (July 1921), 165–74.

MARZOLF, MARION. "The Woman Journalist: Colonial Printer to City Desk." *Journalism History* 1, no. 4, (Winter 1974–75), 100–107, 146.

SHIPPEE, LESTER B. "Jane Grey Swisshelm: Agitator." *Mississippi Valley History Review* 7, (December 1920), 206–27.

"A Stanch Foe of Slavery: Death of Jane Grey Swisshelm, the Philanthropist." *The New York Times*, July 23, 1884, 5.

STEARNS, BERTHA-MONICA. "Reform Periodicals and Female Reformers: 1830–1860." *American Historical Review* 37 (July 1932), 678–99.

## IDA TARBELL

*Books*

CHALMERS, DAVID MARK. *The Social and Political Ideas of the Muckrakers*. (New York: Citadel Press, 1964).

MOTT, FRANK LUTHER. *A History of American Magazines*. vols. 3 and 4 (Cambridge, Mass.: Harvard University Press, 1938–1957).

PETERSON, THEODORE. *Magazines in the Twentieth Century.* (Urbana, Ill.: University of Illinois Press, 1956).

TARBELL, IDA M. *All in the Day's Work.* (New York: MacMillan Company, 1939).

_____. *The Business of Being a Woman.* (New York: MacMillan Company, 1912).

_____. *The History of the Standard Oil Company.* (New York: McClure's Phillips, 1904, and MacMillan Company, 1933).

_____. *The Life of Abraham Lincoln.* (New York: Doubleday & McClure Co., 1900). Two volumes.

_____. *The Life of Elbert H. Gary.* (New York and London: D. Appleton and Company, 1925).

_____. *A Life of Napoleon Bonaparte.* (New York: The Macmillan Company, 1901. Second Edition).

_____. *New Ideas in Business.* (New York: The Macmillan Company, 1916).

_____. *Owen D. Young.* (New York: The Macmillan Company, 1932).

_____. *The Ways of Woman.* (New York: The Macmillan Company, 1915).

WEINBERG, ARTHUR and LILA, eds. *The Muckrakers.* (New York: Simon & Schuster, 1961).

WILSON, HAROLD S. *McClure's Magazine and the Muckrakers.* (Princeton, N.J.: Princeton University Press, 1970).

## DOROTHY THOMPSON

*Books*

SANDERS, MARION K. *Dorothy Thompson: A Legend in Her Time.* Boston: Houghton Mifflin Co., 1973.

SHEEAN, VINCENT. *Dorothy and Red.* Boston: Houghton Mifflin Co., 1963.

THOMPSON, DOROTHY. *Courage to be Happy.* Boston: Houghton Mifflin Co., 1957.

_____. *Dorothy Thompson's Political Guide; A Study of American Liberalism and its Relationship to Modern Totalitarian States.* New York: Stockpole Sons, 1938.

_____. *I Saw Hitler!* New York: Farrar, Strauss and Cudahy, Inc., 1932.

_____. *Let the Record Speak.* Boston: Houghton Mifflin Co., 1939.

———. *Listen, Hans.* Boston: Houghton Mifflin Co., 1942.
———. *Once on Christmas.* New York: Oxford University Press, 1938.
———. *Refugees, Anarchy or Organization?* New York Random House, Inc., 1938.
———. *The New Russia.* New York: H. Holt and Co., 1928.
———. "Collected papers", Syracuse University Library, Syracuse, N.Y.

*Periodicals*

HARRIMAN, MARGARET CASE, "The It Girl," *The New Yorker Magazine:* April 20 and April 27, 1940. (Two parts.)
Cover story, *TIME,* June 12, 1939.

## ELIZABETH TIMOTHY

*Books*

COHEN, HENNIG. *South Carolina Gazette.* Columbia, S.C.: University of South Carolina Press, 1953.
DEXTER, ELIZABETH. *Colonial Women of Affairs: Women in Business and the Professions in America Before 1776.* 2d ed. Boston: Houghton-Mifflin, 1931.
HUDAK, LEONA M. *Early American Women Printers and Publishers 1639–1820* Metuchen, N.J.: Scarecrow Press, 1978.
KING, WILLIAM L. *The Newspaper Press of Charleston, S.C.: A Chronological and Biographical History, Embracing a Period of One Hundred and Forty Years.* Charleston, S.C.: Edward Perry Book Press, 1872 Reprint New York: Arno Press, 1970.
MCMURTIE, DOUGLAS C. *Middle and South Atlantic States. A History of Printing in the United States: The Story of the Introduction of the Press and of Its History and Influence During the Pioneer Period in Each State of the Union.* New York: Burt Franklin, 1969.
SPRUILL, JULIA C. *Women's Life and Work in the Southern Colonies.* Chapel Hill: University of North Carolina Press, 1938.
THOMAS, ISAIAH. *The History of Printing in America, with a Biography of Printers.* 2 vols. New York: Burt Franklin, 1964. (First published in 1810.)

*Periodicals*

KING, MARION REYNOLDS. "One Link in the First Newspaper Chain, The South Carolina Gazette," *Journalism Quarterly*, 60 no. 3, September, 1932, 257–68.

*Thesis*

BAKER, IRA LEE. "Elizabeth Timothy: America's First Woman Editor." Unpublished M.S. thesis, University of Illinois, Urbana, Ill., 1963.


CORNELIA WALTER


*Books*

CHAMBERLIN, JOSEPH EDGAR. *The Boston Transcript: A History of Its First Hundred Years.* Boston: Houghton Mifflin Company, 1930.


IDA B. WELLS-BARNETT


*Books*

BONTEMPS, ARNA, and JACK CONROY. *Anyplace but Here.* New York: Hill and Wang, 1966. (First published as *They Seek a City* in 1945.)

PENN, I. GARLAND. *The Afro-American Press and Its Editors.* New York: Arno Press and the New York Times, 1969.

WELLS, IDA B. *Crusade for Justice: The Autobiography of Ida B. Wells.* Alfreda M. Duster, ed. Chicago and London: The University of Chicago Press, 2d printing, 1972.

WOLSELEY, ROLAND E. *The Black Press, U.S.A.* Ames, Iowa: Iowa State University Press, 1971.

WOOD, NORMAN B. *The White Side of a Black Subject.* Chicago: American Publishing House, 1897.

*Dissertation*

PRIDE, ARMISTEAD SCOTT. "A Register and History of Negro Newspapers in The United States, 1827–1950." Unpublished Ph.D. dissertation, Northwestern University, 1950.

*Periodicals*

WOLSELEY, ROLAND E. "Ida B. Wells-Barnett, Princess of the Black Press." *Encore American & Worldwide News.* April 5, 1976.

# INDEX

Madelon Golden Schilpp has received degrees with honors from Northwestern University and Southern Illinois University. For many years she was a practicing journalist, associated with such newspapers as the Chicago *Sun-Times*, Chicago *Tribune*, and St. Louis *Post-Dispatch*. At present she is a member of the journalism faculty at Southern Illinois University, Carbondale.

Sharon M. Murphy, Director of Journalism Graduate Studies at Southern Illinois University, has been a newspaper reporter, public relations director, and magazine editor. In the course of her twenty-four-year career in teaching she has authored or coauthored six other books and numerous articles on mass communications and education. Her courses frequently focus on the roles and images of women and minorities in the mass media.